CENTURY OF INSIGHT

CENTURY OF INSIGHT

The Twentieth Century Enlightenment of the Mind

Derry Macdiarmid

Edited by Sue Macdiarmid

KARNAC

First published in 2013 by
Karnac Books Ltd
118 Finchley Road, London NW3 5HT

British Library Cataloguing in Publication Data

A C.I.P. for this book is available from the British Library

  ISBN 978 1 78049 075 5

Edited, designed and produced by The Studio Publishing Services Ltd
www.publishingservicesuk.co.uk
e-mail: studio@publishingservicesuk.co.uk

Printed in Great Britain

www.karnacbooks.com

CONTENTS

Dedicated to my family, past, present, and future

ACKNOWLEDGEMENTS

Derry Macdiarmid completed the manuscript of *Century of Insight* in September 2006, but without an opportunity for revision. The book is both remarkable and inspirational for our time, so I can only hope that my subsequent edit accurately reflects the intention he had in writing it, and the message he wished to pass on.

I wish to express my gratitude to all who have given support and practical help to enable its publication. I particularly wish to thank those friends who have generously offered their time and ideas over recent years. Also, Alice Bing for designing a book cover that makes use of a water-colour painting by the author. Finally, my sons, Calum, Dugal, and Fionn, for their constant encouragement. It has been a rewarding journey.

I am grateful to the following for permitting text to be reprinted in *Century of Insight*:

Karen Horney: Pioneer of Feminine Psychology, by S. T. Hitchcock, © 2004 Infobase Publishing. Reprinted by permission of the publisher.

"The touchstone for family life is still the legendary 'and so they were married and lived happily ever after.' It is no wonder that so many families fall short of this ideal." Reprinted by permission of the publisher from *Families and Family Therapy*, by Salvador Minuchin, p. 47, Cambridge, MA: Harvard University Press, © 1974 by the President and Fellows of Harvard College.

"There is no love without aggression." Reprinted by permission of the publisher from *On Aggression*, by Konrad Lorenz, p. 208 (2002), London: Routledge.

I am grateful to Birlinn Publications, Edinburgh, for making available the photo of a poetry reading in Edinburgh, around 1962, author second from left.

Sue Macdiarmid
September 2012

Born a son of the manse in Scotland in 1928, his early interest in Jung led him into analysis, then medical training before becoming an NHS psychiatrist and finally consultant psychotherapist at Guys Hospital, London. Married with three sons, he lived in Clapham where he also practised privately as a Jungian analyst for over twenty-five years. *Century of Insight* was based on his teaching of psychotherapy throughout his career. He died in 2006.

Derry Macdiarmid
1928–2006

FOREWORD

My husband began writing this book as a result of lectures he had been giving to junior psychiatrists at Guys Hospital in London from 1994 onwards, as part of their training programme.

As the content evolved over the years, so the purpose of the book moved beyond his original intention of merely writing a postgraduate training course, towards addressing a wider readership with a message that is relevant to all of us: who we are, how we are, and why we do things the way we do.

The book enthuses and encourages about this experience called life. It is poignant, and at times moving in its generosity of understanding human frailty: our capacity to get things so staggeringly wrong, and then the dogged persistent drive of the human spirit to put things right. It asks us to take risks with our own thinking, our assumptions about ourselves, and others, and to be willing to re-examine ideas that we thought we had understood. It is also funny, very funny at times, and by the closing chapter, there is a real sense for the reader that they will have come to know something of the author himself: his weaknesses, honesty, and humanity.

Derry Macdiarmid was not given to big statements, so when he said that he thought of it as a world book, I saw this for the truth that it is. *Century of Insight* could have a place in the reading programmes for psychology students from Islamabad to Idaho; it could be background reading for UN negotiators as well as family therapists, responsible heads of governments, and citizens the world over.

In the Introduction, he explains ideas about the discovery of the unconscious mind that have been formulated throughout the twentieth century. The principal ideas come from Freud, Jung, and Adler, but they are followed by major and important contributions from other theorists. Each set of ideas has been seen as separate within itself, often in contrast to what has gone before. Macdiarmid argues that this is a mistake. Instead, he describes these successive ideas as layers of understanding in a developing story. Contrary to Freud, Jung, and others, Macdiarmid sees the purpose of understanding the unconscious as *to enable us to find our capacity to love*. As he says, when we love well, we live well. This is the meaning of the twentieth century Enlightenment of the Mind, as he called this period in our history, and it is the purpose behind this book.

As a foundation, we are taken on a historical journey through the origins of psychoanalytic thought, from pre-Freud (including some anthropology, just to set the scene), then the great man himself, and then his followers, who eventually became his rivals: Jung, Adler, and others, all with their different theories.

The strength of these chapters lies in looking at how the childhood of each of these great originators was shaped by their personalities, so it was understandable for them to come up with the ideas that they did, and how, because of their different personal histories, they could not share each other's point of view!

This is unique in understanding the development of psychodynamic thought throughout the twentieth century, as it analyses the ideas of these men and women as a consequence of who they were. Biographies abound of Freud, Jung, and others, but here the author understands their ideas in the light of their own psychology, why they thought what they did, and how it affected their dealings with each other.

Freud, Jung, and Adler were all giants in their contributions to the Enlightenment of the Mind, but important too was the work of other, less well known practitioners throughout the twentieth century. For example, John Layard, whose anthropological adventures and experiences in Malekule in the 1930s gave him unique insights about how best to use our instincts, or Minuchin in the USA, who understood about conflict avoidance and how important it is to help some patients just to stay and fight it out in their families. Derry Macdiarmid argues that there is no truth more important than the one discovered by each of us for ourselves, and it does not matter where the original source of help lies, but, rather, that it is there at all.

In the later chapters, we leave behind the historical perspectives of the therapist's consulting room, and return to our own internal world, where we explore our emotions, and what this Enlightenment of the Mind can do for us. We explore personality, and why it can be so fragmented, how anxiety and depression can imprison us, and the essential value of hate. Why are some driven to starving themselves, and others to murder? We discover aspects of ourselves that have lain camouflaged or dormant beneath our roles within families or other relationships. It has truths for each of us, or others whom we know.

The book moves on to the final great tool of uncovering the unconscious: dreams. Human dreaming is explained first through biology and neurology, before moving on to the psychological process of unconscious storytelling. Dream themes are described through individual case histories, including the author's own.

Derry Macdiarmid was committed to giving us all the means to raise our awareness as individuals or family members, spouses or friends, work colleagues or members of communities, whether local, national, or international, about how we relate to each other. If we get it right we treat each other better, we are happier individually and as a community and society, and we become personally and collectively richer.

The most challenging chapter, and the author asks the reader to be prepared to be challenged, is the final one, where he offers a series of insights about how we are living now, and what we can do to create a better environment for personal growth. It is through these insights that we perceive the true value of this journey of discovery throughout the book: Derry Macdiarmid has sought to join the strands along the entire length, from anthropology, and from Freud and all others, and to make them part of the same purpose. These ideas all contribute to the Enlightenment of the Mind, the ultimate goal of which is the discovery of our capacity to love, and, in so doing, the meaning of life.

Sue Macdiarmid

Introduction

Dynamic psychotherapy is a psychobabble term used by psychiatrists and therapists to mean the process of revealing the unconscious mind, with the idea that buried memories and desires can be brought to the surface, and understood by the conscious self.

If that isn't a beginning designed to put you off reading more, I do not know what is. However, I hope to entice you on a journey of discovery into the unconscious that will include the ideas of Freud, Jung, and Adler, and others from the 1890s through to the end of the twentieth century. I think it is an extraordinary story, in which the men and women who developed our understanding of the unconscious mind did so in the manner of the great explorers. We will follow their journey, but we will also travel further, using their combined knowledge and genius to help us on our way.

Each of these masters of the mind brought something new and original that built upon the work of their predecessors. True, Freud, Jung, and Adler all managed to fall out spectacularly with each other, as we shall see. (Therapists over the past hundred years have managed this easier than most other professions.) Since each of them formed their ideas from within their own culture, and from strikingly different personalities, perhaps it was no wonder that they failed to agree. Imagine how difficult it would have been for Freud, living in an anti-Semitic environment, to accept Jung's Christian superiority, or for Jung, an adventurous risk-taker, to submit to the over-control of a paternalistic Freud. We shall see how their personalities and backgrounds shaped their ideas, in the same way that we are all influenced by our history and environment.

What began with Freud in *fin de siècle* 1890s bourgeois Vienna, defining the unconscious only in terms of repressed wishes and the sexual instinct, has gradually, over the past century, progressed to a new Enlightenment of the Mind. We have brought a new reason and a new morality to our understanding of human behaviour, and culture, art, and literature throughout the twentieth century have all reflected this like a mirror. Strictly speaking, given the definition in the first paragraph above, and because I am both a psychiatrist and a Jungian analyst, it should have the more accurate title of the Psychodynamic Enlightenment, but that seems a mouthful. Let's just call it the Enlightenment of the Mind, which seems to have evolved out of ideas from the twentieth century.

Mental health is a growth sector within the NHS, and we doctors working with mental illness have been using the "shrink's bible", or *Diagnostic and Statistical Manual of Mental Disorders* (*DSM*) since 1952 to define our trade. First published in the USA, it is used worldwide, and claims to label and define every known mental disorder. Beyond definitions of illness, our Enlightenment has encouraged a growth of various therapies that seek to ameliorate all the discontents of the modern world.

I suggest that in this new millennium, despite all the social and other progress made by the liberal democracies, we have failed to understand the real meaning of this Enlightenment of the Mind. It seems to me to have had no further purpose so far than to reveal the unconscious, so that it can be known and integrated by the Self. Well, yes. But that tells only part of the story, and I want to tell the rest of it in this book; it is that all unconscious human behaviour is motivated, prompted, and driven by a simple, essential need: to love.

Freud did not know this, ever, because he spent his energies annihilating the work of his successors, Jung and Adler, as though his life depended on it. Even at the end of his life in 1939, he did not see it, as he watched his country being trodden under the heel of Nazism. Jung did not spot it either because he was so preoccupied with his relationship with God and perhaps his own reputation.

Despite them both, they would become forefathers in this Enlightenment, and their contributions, along with all others described here, are the building blocks in the progress of humans to seek love, and to find it, despite sometimes dire circumstances. This is the meaning of the Enlightenment of the Mind, and it is the journey that I wish to share with you.

We will explore the ideas of these forefathers, and include more than a glance at the contributions of Kierkegaard and Neitzsche, and the lasting effect of the liberation they offered for the unconscious well over a century ago. Then we will look at how psychoanalysis gradually became humanised by the ideas of many others throughout the twentieth century, including family therapists whose practice is in use today.

Then we move out of the consulting room and into the world that we all inhabit. We shall revisit the stages of babyhood that bind us all, but divide us, too, when the needs of some of us are badly frustrated. What happens when things go so wrong that we turn to delinquency or murder as a way of having our needs met? We look at how hate and aggression are vital for our ability to truly love, and how we can learn to manage both. We explore the internal world of those who are afflicted by psychiatric disorders such as multi-personality and anorexia, because of the shafts of light that they throw upon ourselves in normal life. Finally, we become dreamers, and begin to unravel dreams and messages that our unconscious minds bring us each night, free of all charge, with an invitation to dare to look beyond our waking lives to our inner world of emotion and imagination.

I shall describe my experiences over thirty-four years as a psychiatrist within the NHS and as a Jungian analyst in private practice, with explanatory case material. All were happy for their story to be told, but, in as much as I may have misunderstood them, the error will always be mine. Not all have survived, but to those who have, I give my hearty good wishes and my gratitude for all that they have taught me.

I will begin by setting the scene with a short prelude from one of our predecessors from anthropology, and a master of psychotherapy in action, Ihembi.

PART I
PREDECESSORS

CHAPTER ONE

Ihembi and anthropology

"A layman will no doubt find it hard to understand how pathological disorders . . . can be eliminated by 'mere' words. He will
feel that he is being asked to believe in magic"

(Freud, 1890a)

Medicine among preliterate and tribal societies often has psychodynamic elements but is remarkably various, so I have chosen just one example to show how effective tribal medicine could be. In 1957, the Glaswegian anthropologist Victor Turner travelled to central Africa with his wife to study the Ndembu tribe. There, he met Ihembi, a doctor of the Ndembu people. Turner described Ihembi as a charismatic white-haired man with "a smile of singular sweetness" (Turner, 1967, p. 370). The original paper, "Schism and continuity in an African society: a study of Ndembu village life" is quite astonishing and because of it, I have always regarded Ihembi not only as a colleague, but also a master.

Ihembi had a patient called Kamahasanyi, who was complaining of tiredness, heart palpitation, and severe bodily pain. He felt that people were speaking against him, and would withdraw to his hut for long spells.

Ihembi's treatment methods, though described in the mid twenti-eth century, were probably ancient. His system of psychopathology was a theory of witchcraft, which, essentially, involved uncovering secret hostilities between people. (In the Highland village where I grew up you would hear an old lady, if some accident befell her, saying darkly, "It's baad wishes!") In fact, there was a great deal of social conflict amongst the Ndembu tribe, especially marital woes. But, apart from the black magic they secretly employed to hurt others, there was another possible cause of the pains. In local culture, it was believed that the eyeteeth of hunters were where their power resided. These precious fragments were carefully kept after death, but they also had the magical ability to get inside the body of a living man and hurt him; this act was a sign that the ancestors were not happy with his behaviour. It was believed that Kamahasanyi was afflicted with the incisor of his own father as punishment for evading his social respon-sibilities by quarrelling with his family.

Ihembi and his helpers settled in the village and learnt all there was to be known about Kamahasanyi and everybody else there, too. The doctor examined the source of the witchcraft that was being directed towards Kamahasanyi and decided that the most likely witches, in this case, were Kamahasanyi's fourth wife, Maria, and her mother. Maria was a dominant personality (as was Kamahasanyi's father) who was showily unfaithful, and her mother, perhaps, wanted a different son-in-law. But Ihembi never accused or confronted them. With the aid of rites, he reflected his way through his differential diag-nosis and treatment alternatives and finally developed his plan: to perform rites "to make 'the livers of the Nswanamundong'u people white towards one another,' to remove the state of mutual ill-feeling" (Turner, 1967, p. 387) in the village.

If you have lived in a village you will appreciate the audacity of Ihembi's plan, in addition to its warm humanity, to remove mutual ill-feeling in the village. Goodness! But he had at his disposal powerful forces lost to us, in the form of magico–religious rites and perfor-mances.

The rites included drumming and singing, in which all the villagers took part. Then Ihembi made small incisions in Kama-hasanyi's skin and fixed some antelope horns over them with the intention of drawing out the tooth. Ihembi would check the horns regularly and if they were empty he would give what we might now call a case history of the patient, his life story and a description of his affliction, but he would declare it to all the village, so that they would know and share the information. He would ask them to contribute by confessing any bad feelings, especially secret ones, towards the patient. (These days we would call this family, or group, therapy.) Ihembi created his own formula for the treatment, one which the community understood: he whipped up excitement with drumming and singing, louder and louder, with declarations of prayers and confessions, until, after many hours, all felt sympathy for Kamahasanyi, and were longing for the tooth to be removed from his body.

Turner also reported that Ihembi gave tasks to family members to involve them. For example, the unfaithful Maria had to collect certain leaves and chew them and spit the juice on parts of her husband's body, and tap him with a small hand-rattle to give him strength. Turner said that these acts reaffirmed "her wifely duties and her goodwill—the reverse of witchery" (Turner, 1967, p. 389). Many others had to join in with similar tasks.

Kamahasanyi, too, spoke out. He complained that no one had raised a finger to help him in his illness, and he had to go to a diviner himself, but that he was glad at last that he had been able to air his grievance. Finally, at the crisis of the last long, complex, and emotional rite, Ihembi managed to get the punishing tooth out of his patient's body, ran outside the village with it, and called to the elders and Turner to come and see.

Some time later, Turner reported that villagers who had not been on speaking terms with each other became friendly, and the village more relaxed and at ease.

Turner attempted to get the Ndembu doctor to admit that the tooth removal was a trick, but the doctor denied it. Indeed, using deception to cure a patient is often the source of many a heated debate. More than a year later, Turner revisited the village and found Kamahasanyi flourishing: Maria was with him and they seemed to be getting on well.

We can see why anthropologists do not like the word "primitive" to be applied to these tribal rituals. Ihembi's therapy apparently enabled Maria to resolve her feelings and become less hostile towards her husband. Surely this method is more enlightening than primitive. Indeed, in seventeenth-century England, Maria and her mother would have been burnt alive for witchcraft.

Ihembi used pharmacology, individual, marital, and especially group psychotherapy, religious ritual, a theory of witchcraft, common sense, drama, hypnosis (in producing dissociation in Kamahasanyi during part of the rites), personal charisma, all the force of traditional culture, and outright conjuring trickery, in an apparently irresistible attack on his patient's illness.

However, Turner reported that by the 1950s the influence of missionaries on the village chiefs had already led to fines being imposed on Ihembi for deceiving the people. Thus, European culture was seeping in with a deeper devilry than Ihembi could cure. Over the twentieth century in Europe and America, we laboriously recovered some of Ihembi's techniques. But we have had to dive deeper than he to get to the source of the real devilry.

CHAPTER TWO

Moral treatment and hypnosis

"[T]he deeper the emotions lie, the greater is the importance of discovering them"

(Carter, 1853)

For much of the nineteenth century, way before Freud, there was a kind of psychotherapy called "moral treatment". Moral treatment grew out of the need to treat disturbed or "insane" individuals with more care and understanding. Prior to this new wave of thought, the insane were regarded with contempt by society and treated like animals. Moral treatment was seen as a more humane way of dealing with these sufferers.

Dr Robert Brudenell Carter, an ophthalmologist and GP in Leytonstone, was another master therapist and, like Ihembi, was a warm, humane man. He used moral treatment during therapy when dealing with patients suffering from hysteria, and, in 1853, published a book titled *On the Pathology and Treatment of Hysteria*.

A century later, the diagnosis of "hysteria" would be denounced as a snare and a delusion and, for a time, would vanish completely from the diagnostic manuals. But in the nineteenth century, during

Carter's time, it meant hysterical "fits" (collapsing in violent tears and laughter, etc.) and a great variety of symptoms presented as physical diseases but with no physical cause. The subject of "hysteria" is important to this history, as the way it was treated led to the discovery of dynamic psychotherapy at the end of the nineteenth century.

Almost no modern psychiatrist has ever heard of Carter, but his account of the illness and its cure was excellent apart from one missing observation, which would later be further explored by Freud.

Carter began his book by describing the effects of emotion on the body; for example, how emotion is discharged through muscular action, including the facial muscles, through the cardiovascular system (palpitations, heart missing a beat, blushing, turning pale etc.), the alimentary system (loss of appetite, nausea, bowels or bladder losing control, etc.—he could have added bulimia and anorexia), the lungs (sighing, gasping, sobbing, laughing, breath-holding, rapid breathing (hyperventilation)), the secretory glands (mouth dry, sweating), and so on. Carter was impressed by how powerfully emotions affected the body.

He assumed that animals could express their emotions without control, but when it came to our own emotions, he believed that society at the time would not allow for the release of these feelings, instead demanding that people control and sometimes suppress them. If suppressed, the emotions might come out in hysterical fits and, in the longer term, manifest into other hysterical symptoms. Carter gave examples from life to illustrate his point: a maidservant berated by her mistress for unfinished work falls into a hysterical fit. It later turns out that, earlier that day, the maid had told her lover that she was pregnant and received no offer of help. Carter also cites the case of Miss A, whose engagement had gone on for years with no sign of marriage, and comes home to find her sister in the drawing room with *her* new fiancé, to whom marriage is already arranged. Rather subdued, Miss A says little, but on her way to the door collapses into a hysterical fit.

Carter believed that it was a matter of common observation that "hysterical" symptoms were caused by suppressed emotion, occurring more frequently in women than men, as women were more often required by society to suppress their emotional reactions. Feelings women especially had to conceal were primarily sexual, followed by anger, hostility, then grief and care.

So, seventy-seven years before Freud wrote *Civilisation and its Discontents*, Carter had already stated that social norms were the cause of neurosis. He called hysteria "one of the misfortunes entailed upon the civilised female by the conditions of her existence" (Carter, 1853, p.93). In fact, Carter pointed to the effects of suppressed sexuality three years before Freud was even born.

The fit or other symptom obtains *sympathy*, which Carter believed was a deep and universal need of mankind. The day after the fit, the friends visit to sympathise with the sufferer, who is reminded of the emotions that caused the fit the first time, so she has another, and so it is with the other symptoms. As the sympathy never reaches the true sore place, because we only get sympathy for the symptom and not for the secret hurt, the need, never assuaged, can become an addiction.

Carter believed his patients were malingering, cheating. Sometimes, they did it in a certain indirect way. He observed that when we want to assume a facial expression suitable to an occasion, a funeral or a wedding, say, we do not do it by deliberately moving the muscles of the face (there are at least thirty) like raising a hand, but by thinking of something, or at least thinking up a mood or attitude, that will produce the desired expression. For example, some actors used to claim that they would think of corpses to stop a fit of giggles on stage. Similarly, one of Carter's patients could make herself vomit by thinking of a putrid dead cat made into a pudding.

Although Carter thought his patients were just cheating, morally culpable, and in desperate need of moral treatment, he treated them with quite remarkable respect and sympathy. He believed that they lacked the moral education their families should have provided in how to digest and deal with disappointments and unfairness. However, Carter never revealed his suspicions about his patients' dishonesty to their families or friends (although he sometimes threatened to). He saw his patients as sympathy starved rather than attention seeking.

Carter also saw that hysterical symptoms were sometimes caused by negative feelings towards the person making them angry—an observation of great importance, to be heard of again, often! He believed that frustration was not to blame, but the inability to talk about the problem and get sympathy for it. Besides, there were other things to be frustrated about apart from sexual fulfilment, such as the difficulty of getting revenge on our nearest and dearest, etc.

Carter took his patients to live in his own home, where they were treated with firm kindness by his wife and daughters, and the servants were trained to ignore the symptoms, which, thus, ceased to be a source of sympathy. But by talking to everybody who was close to the patient as well as to the patient (a bit like Ihembi), Carter tried to find out the original source of the upset.

Then he set up a one-to-one confrontation, in which he patiently and *au fond* kindly uncovered the deception. This provoked some very stormy scenes, and his accounts were the first recorded descriptions of what I call the Battle with the Patient (an important and recurring theme in psychotherapy):

> The patient needs to hear the truth, and have her conduct put before her, in a light which no ingenuity of hers can possibly pervert into the interesting or romantic; while at the same time, all this must be done with a degree of self-possession and good temper on the part of the operator. (Carter, 1853, p. 114)

In other words, if the doctor is on the verge of losing his temper, he must make an excuse to stop the interview and take it up again later.

Carter would stick to his guns until the patient admitted he had got it right. Evidently, after uncovering the original emotional wound, he offered sympathy and understanding *for that instead of for the symptoms.*

Thus, if in your family you cannot show your hurt and get sympathy for it ("Come and have a cuddle, love!"), if you cannot reproach whoever has hurt you and get an apology ("Oh, I'm *sorry*! Come and have a cuddle!"), and if you cannot resolve a fight by plain speaking ("Yes, all right, I see what you mean, I'm sorry, give me a cuddle!"), then an alternative is symptoms that get sympathy or revenge so indirectly that they do not satisfy.

Carter believed his patients were only pretending, and that worsening of the symptoms only meant further moral decline. However, he did record that when certain patients told him they were *not* pretending, that the symptoms were just there, and they really did not know why, he somehow knew that, actually, they were telling the truth. The explanation of that was to come forty years later at the Salpêtrière Hospital in Paris.

Jean-Martin Charcot was a neurologist and chief physician at the women's Salpêtriere Hospital in the later nineteenth century. The Salpêtrière had essentially been an asylum for the impoverished women of Paris who suffered from "nervous diseases". Charcot believed there was a neurological basis for insanity and set out to prove that it was possible to successfully treat the "incurable". He was interested in hysteria and in hypnosis, the latter of which he was prestigious enough to make medically respectable. Charcot was as famous for his pupils as his theories, and taught Freud, Babinski, Janet, and Bouchard, among others.

He believed that hysteria was a neurological disorder and used hypnosis to demonstrate what he thought of as the typical hysterical fit, which was very similar to an epileptic one. He carried out these experiments often using his favourite patient, "Blanche", otherwise known as the "Queen of Hysterics". Blanche was young, pretty, and a bit of a star who was inclined to bully the other patients. When Freud went home after his months at the Salpêtrière, he took with him a print of a painting by André Brouillet, which portrayed Charcot and Blanche demonstrating to a crowd of doctors, students, and distinguished visitors. Blanche looks dressed for the occasion, and is so curved back in the opisthotonic arc of her hysterical fit that her décolleté seems just about to spill its charming contents.

Thus, Charcot carried on his exploration into hypnosis with fascinating results. Even Freud once said that it was impossible to overestimate the importance of hypnosis for psychoanalysis. Hypnosis is a collaboration between two people in which one person (the subject) willingly and temporarily delegates conscious control of his mind to the other (the hypnotist), allowing his own usual consciousness to be left aside as though in sleep. This enables a verbal dialogue between the hypnotist's conscious mind and the subject's unconscious mind, the latter being dramatically open to suggestion, even down to a hypothalamic or brainstem level of functioning. This is still a bit uncanny to those not familiar with it, and generally accepted models of the mind are not adequate to describe it.

It is weird that *words* from the hypnotist can so affect the subject's body by a route bypassing consciousness, and if only we knew the neuronal pathways of it, then we would really know something about the brain. It can alarm people, ethically, and the way stage hypnotists use it for entertainment does not encourage us to take it seriously. However, it remains now more than ever a wastefully neglected method of treatment. All psychiatrists, doctors, and dentists should be able to use hypnosis because it is so cheap and sometimes so effective, in too many ways to describe here, and all trainees in psychotherapy should have some experience, however limited, of this procedure on which psychoanalysis is based, even if they never develop its therapeutic use. Indeed, it might be that psychoanalysis is only a form of slow hypnosis.

However, back at the Salpêtrière, Blanche was about to demonstrate something remarkable, quite by accident. On one occasion, Charcot hypnotised Blanche to show his audience whether an individual could be hypnotised to commit a crime. The hypnotised Blanche proceeded to stab Babinski to death with a rubber dagger, and shot at him, etc. Afterwards, Charcot and the distinguished audience left, accidentally leaving Blanche under hypnosis. One of the medical students (all male back then), taking advantage of her hypnotised state, suggested to Blanche that she should take off her clothes, and have a bath. Blanche did no such thing, but went into a classic fit, and then came to and left. Thus, Charcot had, unknowingly, discovered a very important part of hypnosis: when it came to Blanche doing something she really did not want to do, hypnosis could not make her do it.

Later research in the twentieth century would show that a "hidden observer" was present in the background of the mind when a person was hypnotised, an entity that knows what is going on. During a trance, whenever the mind receives an unwelcome suggestion, the individual is prompted to return to full alertness, just as a mother who is able to sleep through excessive noise will wake at the smallest whimper from her baby.

Because of this hidden observer, we can promise people, when teaching them self-hypnosis, that if anything urgent occurs during their trance they will be able to come out of it straight away. However, during "post-hypnotic suggestion", it is possible to programme the hidden observer not to tell what he has heard:

Hypnotist: "When you wake *you will not remember me saying this* but if I cough you will ask for a glass of water."

The subject comes out of the trance and the hypnotist coughs. The subject immediately asks for a glass of water.

Hypnotist: "Why are you asking me for a glass of water?"

Subject: "Well, I'm so thirsty, it's so hot in here."

Hypnotist: "Now remember the real reason why you are asking."

And then the veil hiding the unconscious instruction is lifted, and the subject remembers what he was previously told to forget. Post-hypnotic suggestion is clear proof of how we can be unconsciously controlled by something in the unconscious, and think we *know* why we are acting so, *and be wrong*, and also of how the hidden motivation can be restored to consciousness.

It is remarkable that the usually submerged part of the self, which appears and takes over under hypnosis, and is in such good rapport with, and so obedient to, the suggestions of the hypnotist, has access to a still deeper unconscious depth of the mind that is denied to the usual conscious self. It can get into the brain's total memory store, and directly access the autonomic nervous system with its wealth of bodily effects, even to the extent, it is claimed, of producing an actual blister in response to the suggestion of being burned. This is the part of the psyche which can create, usually behind the back of the conscious mind, which knows nothing of what is going on, really convincing hysterical conversion symptoms with actual bodily changes. It can produce local anaesthesia, so that you can stick a needle through someone's flesh without their feeling it.

I knew of a case where a hypnotist forgot to remove the anaesthesia from the hand of a woman after a demonstration and she came back with a burnt hand as she had put it on the stove without feeling it. This is very, very strange, because normally a spinal reflex would whip the hand away before informing the brain that it has done so. Using hypnosis to dissociate pain, say, from cancer or during operations, is a treatment option still under-used in medicine and dentistry, especially with children. We are most easily hypnotised between the ages of five and fifteen, then the graph of hypnotisability falls away to a plateau, falling still further in old age. It makes sense that we should be most suggestible at the age in life when we are hungrily drinking in the attitudes and mindsets of the adults, and become less so in adolescence, when we are more concerned to differentiate ourselves from them.

Through the suggestible and co-operative and usually unconscious part-self reached in hypnosis, the hypnotiser can help the subject recover lost memories, or alter or expunge them, or even create them. They can enable the subject to regress in age and become a child again. For example, if you were to tell someone under hypnosis that they are aged, say, fifteen years old, then seven, then five, and ask them to write something, then their handwriting will be childlike, reflecting how they wrote at those ages, until they go so far back they will no longer know how to write. This phenomenon of age regression was to become enormously important in psychoanalysis, as we shall see later on.

Through hypnosis we can remove or create in the body all the very various symptoms of what was formerly called hysteria. As Charcot's team found, we cannot simply cure a hysterical paralysis by sugges-tion under hypnosis, or move it from one arm to the other, but we can also give a healthy person such a paralysis. The hypnotiser can do all this, of course, *only* if the hidden observer (or the usual self, or poten-tial waker-upper, who has agreed to be dissociated) is somehow enjoying himself enough, or at peace enough in his quiet limbo, not to interrupt the game.

During hypnosis, the normally responsible conscious self relin-quishes control and responsibility for a little while, and seems to enjoy the holiday, as in sleep, except that it is conscious and clearly aware of what is going on. It certainly enjoys any freedom from pain. Indeed, occasionally, it refuses to obey the suggestion to come back. ("You may stay in trance longer if you really want to," a colleague says. "I shall charge you for the extra time," he adds, reassuringly.)

Here was the explanation as to why some of Carter's patients were telling the truth when they said that they did not know where their symptoms came from. Maybe, in fact, *most* of his patients did not know, although he thought they did, and maybe his confrontation of their "deception" was having the same effect as when a subject under the influence of post-hypnotic suggestion is reminded of, and then does remember, the suggestion that had been made to him under hypnosis. In the Salpêtrière, the first assumption was that the patients were, indeed, helplessly suffering from the effects of an illness, a hysteria, over which they had no control—the opposite of Carter's assumption.

What have all of these ideas back in the nineteenth century to do with our Enlightenment of the Mind, you ask? Here's my reply: it is about learning to talk to people and understand that while they are being truly honest and sincere, they might also say things that are not actually true, because of what has been banished to their unconscious mind. A young woman says to me that she has a live-in lover, but is going to get rid of him because she wants to live alone for the rest of her life. I then think, well, maybe such a life really would do for her, but it would certainly not do for me, so I do just wonder if she has some desires that are dissociated and present only in her unconscious mind. Has something, completely forgotten by her, scared her off her own potentialities? I know she is telling the truth as far as she knows it, but *does* she know what she wants?

There is a story about Tolstoy's aunt: her husband recorded one of her angry tirades on the new-fangled phonograph and then played it back to her. When confronted with it, she exclaimed, "I never said that!" She was quite probably telling the truth. The "I" listening to the recording had never said that. It had been said by another side of her personality in a temper.

To sympathetically listen to someone who is being completely honest, and understand that they then tell you something that is not actually so because their emotional survival has depended on losing some truth, has, alas, *not* diffused into our common culture. It is a mystery to me why it should remain a professional skill used only by psychotherapists.

At the Salpêtrière, using hypnosis, the doctors were experimenting with different sorts of dissociation of one part of the self from another. Such styles of dissociation are so important for this history that I have devoted the following chapter to ordinary, emergency, and pathological dissociation.

CHAPTER THREE

State of mind

"Not until we are lost do we begin to understand ourselves"

(Attributed to Henry Thoreau, Thoreau & MacIver, 2006)

I n the Salpêtrière, several major discoveries about dissociation
were made by Charcot's successor, the philosopher and psychiatrist, Pierre Janet. The following types of dissociation shade into
each other, and essentially describe what will be familiar to us as the
way our mind can distance us from trauma in order to protect us. We
are able to recognise three main types of dissociation as a result of
Janet's findings at the Salpêtrière.

1.   Ordinary dissociation
Whenever we concentrate on anything, we are dissociating other
input. If you will kindly now turn your attention to your bottom, you
will become aware of the sensory input from the chair, which you
were dissociating until this moment because you were so absorbed in
this book! All the time, we are unconsciously dissociating input both
from the outside and inside just to get on with what we are doing.
People who are easily hypnotised are often those who can get so lost

in a television drama that they are completely incapable of hearing a loved one calling their name—they are that good at dissociating, that is, concentrating. However, dissociation in schizophrenia is quite different: the individual is unable to maintain the normal dissociative filters and barriers against mental input from the inside.

It can be very handy to dissociate complex actions, such as driving a car, as though, by setting up an unconscious autopilot, we can drive while thinking about something else. Then we suddenly wake to find we have arrived at our destination (or, occasionally, somewhere else). The capacity to do this might be linked to intelligence. I was once mortified to find that a very intelligent secretary at the Maudsley Hospital had no awareness at all of the witty, perceptive, and most interesting content of my letters, which she typed on my behalf; she took them down in shorthand, and typed them out in a state of dissociation, her conscious mind clearly occupied with more important things, like what she would give her children for supper.

2.   Emergency dissociation.

In an emergency, we can dissociate awareness of physical pain or emotional reaction until the crisis has past. The broken collarbone hurts only after the match; grief only begins after the funeral, etc. This is normal and useful. Well known examples include the incident where David Livingstone was mauled by a lion but felt no pain during the experience, or Mrs Thatcher not weeping after the Brighton bomb until the following Sunday, in church. Most people have had some such experience of deferring emotional reactions, for example, dealing with a car crash efficiently at the time but starting to shake later on at home. A bank manager who was tied to a chair for several hours while robbers tried to get into the safe told the news reporters that, from early on, he felt he was watching a play that had nothing to do with him.

While the conscious mind cannot dissociate by will (just try *not* to think of something), there is a kind of trick that we can learn or discover that allows it to happen, so we can deliberately bring on the dissociation. When the psychiatrist R. D. Laing, as a boy, was being beaten by his father, he located his mind outside his head so as not to feel the pain. I knew a boy who was also able to dissociate on those occasion when himself, his mother, father, and mother's mother were in the car together—usually a recipe for pure hell. From the moment he got into the car until the moment he got out, he dissociated and would not have been able to tell you a thing that had been said. What is dissociated might never return.

A neuropsychiatrist colleague of mine discovered that victims of violence often go into a dissociated state during the violence, as do the perpetrators. I once read about a woman who denied the murder of her husband's girlfriend, and told the court that when she pulled the trigger "I was somewhere else in my head". I believe her. This brings us towards the pathological.

3.   Pathological dissociation
In pathological dissociation, the parts of the self, for whatever reason, are separated: (a) cannot come together again, and (b) are of substantial and not negligible size, and might even live as separate sub-personalities.

Pierre Janet thought that in pathological dissociation, the split-off part of the mind is dominated by an *idée fixe* (Vanderlinden & Vandereycken, 1997, p. 124), a fixed idea (like Kamahasanyi's grudge or Miss A's hurt at her sister's engagement). He believed this *idée fixe* was the essential phenomenon of hysteria. Janet subdivided pathological dissociation into three degrees of increasing severity: somnambulism or sleepwalking, fugue states, and lastly, multiple personality.

Somnambulism or sleepwalking

Sleepwalking is so common, especially in children, that it is really like a normal outlet for anxiety or even just preoccupation. A girl at school was so anxious about her new duty of ringing the chapel bell on time that she woke in the night to find herself pulling on the curtain.

When people talk in their sleep, you can get into a conversation with them, like talking to a hypnotised person. They can talk out of their dream. A colleague of mine woke to find his father in his room, looking in the wardrobe, the chest of drawers, and under the bed.

"Father, what are you doing?"

"I'm looking for the meaning of life."

Typically, Father remembered nothing of it in the morning.

Very occasionally, someone wakes in a dangerous situation—on a high ledge, for example. People have been known to kill in their sleep, and courts have been known to accept their innocence. A veteran fighting off a murderous Japanese soldier might wake to find himself fighting his wife.

Janet collected striking cases, like his patient, Irene, who went into dreamy altered mental states and re-enacted the agonising details of her mother's death, but in her apparently normal state had no memory of the event. Thus, she wondered, if it was true what they told her, that her mother was dead (and they had shown her the grave), why had she no sense of loss or grief? She said she felt as though her mother was just away somewhere and would come back. The unbearable memory of her mother's death was her *idée fixe*, dissociated from normal consciousness but returning to take over as though to demand attention, but never succeeding; she was dissociated from her grief because it was unbearable. (Perhaps we could apply Carter's theory here: that the pain was unbearable because Irene had lost her only source of sympathy when her mother died.) When Irene began to remember and think of her mother's death at will, her symptoms ceased.

Fugue

In hysterical (as distinct from epileptic) fugue, typically, a person vanishes from their environment and turns up in Accident and Emergency, complaining of loss of memory, not knowing who they are; or they start a new life in a new place with a new name as a person with no past. Often, they have taken themselves away from a bad situation that is part of what they have dissociated. In the cases I have known, I found it curious that they never had any ID on them, as though at some point something in them had made sure they would not be able to identify themselves, however much they consciously wanted to. But still, there is no doubting their honesty when they claim they have lost their memory and identity. Movingly, a woman wept as she told me what it was like to resume family life with her husband, who had suffered from memory loss but had been identified and brought home. Yet, he still did not really know her. The man had been told that she was his wife and believed it, and thought she was great, but she felt as if she was like a new acquaintance to him, and even in intimacy she knew he still did not really know her.

Dissociated matter is not necessarily something dreadful, but can be something much desired, which we dare not usually hope for, or that does not seem to fit in with the life to which we are committed. This is a possibility that must be considered in all neurosis: that the trouble might be that the person dares not even think of some quite valid desires that lie deep in his heart.

Janet took a cultural step of enormous significance in understanding that it is not only psychiatric patients who are at the mercy of forces within themselves over which they have no control. We *all* are. The amazing power of *stories* over us, and where they come from, has been another discovery of the Enlightenment of the Mind that will unfold as we go on. The story of Oedipus was only the tip of the iceberg.

Multiple personality

The *Diagnostic and Statistical Manual III*, published by the American Psychiatric Association in 1980, gives the following diagnostic criteria:

A.   The existence within the person of two or more personalities or personality states (each with its own relatively enduring pattern of perceiving, relating to, and thinking about the environment and self)

B.   At least two of these personalities or personality states recurrently take full control of the person's behaviour.

Multiple personality was known at the Salpêtrière during Freud's time there, and, in *Studies in Hysteria* (1895d) he wrote that the dissociation found in "the well-known cases" (Freud, 1895d, p. 229) of multiple personality was the basic pathology in all hysteria. Janet believed the idea dominating the split-off part was the important thing, whereas Freud thought it was the dissociating itself. However, Freud did not seem to have many cases of multiple personality disorder and, perhaps, lacked direct experience of it. Later, he came up with a curious suggestion that it was caused by having a series of love objects. Well, his idea was not completely daft; I knew a squaddie in the Army who formed a new personality every time he adapted to someone new, but then he could not be anyone else with that person. The personality he adopted was so tailored as to be liked by whomever it was he was getting to know. The helpful person who hid an AWOL comrade clashed with the obliging side of him, who revealed to his sergeant the whereabouts of the concealed man.

Multiple personality disorder is an extreme of dissociation, but we are all living with the unknown at the back of our minds and it is normal to, sometimes, feel more like a committee than one person. We blame and praise ourselves, or debate inwardly on what to do. "There is another man within me, that's angry with me", wrote Sir Thomas Browne, the seventeenth century English doctor (Browne, 2006, p. 55).

Sometimes, we do have a clear sensation of something or someone more powerful than us down there inside ourselves who is really in charge. Indeed, there are people who do not suffer from multiple personality disorder but, sometimes, behave as if they do: when a high-profile politician with a successful career, marriage, and children is caught kerb-crawling for prostitutes, who or what exactly is running him? As Freud later put it, sometimes the rider has to go where the horse wants.

PART II
FOREFATHERS

CHAPTER FOUR

Freud: the early years

"If a man has been his mother's undisputed darling he retains throughout life the triumphant feeling, the confidence in success, which not seldom brings actual success along with it"

(Freud, 1917b)

Sigmund Freud was the eldest of eight children (his only brother, Julius, died as a little boy). His father was a Jewish wool merchant in Vienna and struggled to support such a large family on his meagre income. However, from an early age, Freud showed great intellect and his parents sacrificed a great deal in order to provide him with a good education. His mother, especially, doted on him and favoured him above the other children; indeed, her fondness of him was a great influence on him later in life. His closest companion as a child was his half-nephew, John. He wrote,

... my warm friendships as well as my enmities ... go back to my childish relations to my nephew, who was a year older than I ... we lived together, were inseparable, and loved one another, but at times ... we used to squabble and accuse one another.

An intimate friend and a hated enemy have always been indispensable to my emotional life; I have always been able to create them anew,
and not infrequently my childish ideal has been so closely approached
that friend and enemy have coincided in the same person . . . (Freud,
1900a, p. 424)

We shall see how his early relationships contributed to fragmenting
the early years of the Enlightenment of the Mind.

In 1885, Freud, as a young doctor, went to study under Charcot in
Paris at the Salpêtrière. There, he witnessed the presence and power
of the unconscious mind as demonstrated by hypnosis. The following
year, Freud left the Salpêtrière to set up his budding practice as a
neurologist, where he used his newly learnt hypnotic skills.

One of his patients was a young woman who complained that she
was unable to feed her baby; every attempt made would result in
gastrointestinal trouble. Freud cured her by hypnosis, but thought his
patient and her husband a little stinting in gratitude. He found out
why a year later when she returned to him again to cure her of the
same trouble with the latest baby. Apparently, she was upset that a
stranger was able to make her feed the baby, when she, with all her
willpower, had failed. Freud was struck by the power of what he
called a "counter-will" (Freud, 1892–1893, p. 122) in her unconscious
mind, which controlled her behaviour like a post-hypnotic suggestion,
and over which, despite her best efforts, she had no control.

At that point, Freud knew what Carter did not know, that the
patient was not malingering but dissociating. However, Freud had not
yet begun to employ Carter's technique of searching for the hurt feelings underlying the symptoms. The great clue about how to do that,
how to cure hysterical conversion symptoms by using hypnosis to dig
up the painful emotions underlying them, had actually come to him
before he went to the Salpêtrière, and it is strange that Charcot did not
see the significance of the story about Breuer's patient, Anna O, which
supplied that clue. Breuer was a psychiatrist, and friend of Freud, and
Anna O was the most famous of his patients. She had a lot of symptoms, including going into an altered mental state for an hour or so
each evening in which, utterly unlike her well-brought-up self, she
acted like a naughty child, tearing buttons off her clothes, throwing
cushions, and was totally impossible. Then, when she came to herself
again, she complained of a time gap in her memory. If she had given

herself another name during her *condition seconde*, she would have been a case of multiple personality disorder.

Anna O recovered from her symptoms when she told Breuer, under hypnosis, what had been going on when the symptoms started. For example, she recovered from a paralysis when she told Breuer how scared she had been one night when, half-asleep, she thought she saw a snake going for her father but could not move to help. Similarly, her inability to eat or drink was cured when she revealed her horror about witnessing a disgusting little dog, owned by a lady companion, up on the table drinking from someone's bedtime cup. Whenever Anna O recalled painful events and expressed the emotion she had not expressed at the time, she recovered from her symptoms. Abreaction (expressing previously suppressed emotions) under hypnosis worked better and required less effort than Carter's confrontational style.

At first, Breuer and Freud included a need for revenge among the repressed emotions: for example, sometimes the problem was that the patient had taken no action to resolve the clash with the other person—in Anna O's case, she never confronted the lady companion about her unruly dog. Both Breuer and Freud believed that a memory normally fades (does not become an *idée fixe*) if "there has been an energetic reaction to the event that provokes an affect" (Freud, 1893a, p. 8) ("affect" means "emotion").

> By 'reaction' we here understand the whole class of voluntary and involuntary reflexes – from tears to acts of revenge . . . An injury that has been repaid, even if only in words, is recollected quite differently from one that has had to be accepted. . . . The injured person's reaction to the trauma only exercises a completely 'cathartic' effect if it is an *adequate* reaction – as, for instance, revenge. (Freud, 1893a, p. 8)

Freud's scientific tendency caused him to say "event that provokes an affect" rather than "person who hurt you", which had the virtue of a more broadly applicable generalisation, but it rather lost the idea that the patient might be better off sorting things out with the person who had upset him. Since "language serves as a substitute for action" (Freud, 1893a, p. 8), Freud thought that the patient could be cured by pouring out the emotion to the *doctor* instead. It was only later in the century, during family and marital therapy, that the offender and the offended resolved the resentments between them, and only near the end of the century that the therapist was actually able to help the patient to *get* revenge, or at least justice, through the legal system, by going to court to speak up for them (like Monica Lewinski's therapist, Dr Irene Kassorla, in the case against President Clinton).

"Hysterics are suffering from reminiscences" (Freud, 1895d, p. 108), Freud and Breuer said, and used the word "trauma", wound, rather than *idée fixe* to refer to those reminiscences. At first, Freud had used hypnosis to access the unconscious mind to tell it what to think, to alter memories, for example, and other rather bossy procedures, but now he moved on to hypnotising patients, asking them what had been going on in their lives to provoke such symptoms. He was embarrassed when hypnosis sometimes (or often) did not work. When this happened, he began to use a trick he had learned from a French hypnotist; he would put a hand on the patient's head and say something like, "When I take my hand away something will come into your mind, and that will be what we are looking for." Freud was a great believer in this trick, but he soon found an even better method.

On one occasion, one of his patients asked Freud if he would just let her remember things in her own time, and that she was sure if he allowed her to do this that they would both come across the memories he was looking for. Thus was born the famous analytical technique of *free association*. The patient lay on the couch as though to be hypnotised, while Freud sat sideways at the head end, avoiding the patient's gaze but still able to keep an eye on the patient's facial expressions (which he apparently became expert at reading upside down), with his dog under his chair, and the picture of Charcot and Blanche on the wall above the couch, and listened, and listened, and listened. Psychotherapy is not really the talking cure; it is the listening cure. In psychotherapy, you are listened to as never before in your life.

As Carter would have predicted, Freud heard a lot of unhappy love and sexual stories. The most delightful case history originated from a holiday in the Alps, when the unhappy-looking niece of his landlady took him by surprise on the top of a mountain to ask for his help with regard to her anxiety attacks. Freud called her "Katerina":

> I was interested to find that neuroses could flourish in this way at a height of over 6,000 feet . . . I could not venture to transplant hypnosis to these altitudes . . . I should have to try a lucky guess. I had found often enough that in girls anxiety was a consequence of the horror by

which a virginal mind is overcome when it is faced for the first time with the world of sexuality. (Freud, 1895d, p. 127)

His guess enabled the girl to remember and share with him her memories of two series of sexual attempts on her by her uncle. "At the end of these two sets of memories she came to a stop. She was like someone transformed. The sulky, unhappy face had grown lively, her eyes were bright, she was lightened and exalted" (Freud, 1895d, p. 131).

That is a good clinical description of effects of *abreaction*: pouring out emotion that has otherwise been unexpressed or even dissociated, and releasing suppressed reactions, getting things off your chest you hardly knew were there. Abreaction remains a treatment by itself to this day. With or without the aid of drugs or hypnosis, it is used, for example, to treat post traumatic stress disorder, where it is also sometimes referred to as "psychological debriefing".

Years later, Freud added in a footnote to the case study something he had not dared to publish at the time; it was actually Katerina's father, not her uncle, who had tried to seduce her. Freud heard the same story from his patients so often that he thought the problem must be universal. From May 1893 to September 1897, Freud believed the root of all hysteria was sexual seduction by the father, often of a perverse kind. Indeed, he interpreted a sexual dream he had about his niece as a disguise for unconscious sexual wishes towards his own daughter.

But Freud was impressed by the method of free association, how it uncovered the unknown inside us. And it is amazing how much you can find in yourself if you can talk and talk and know the person to whom you are telling it all will never use it against you, unlike friends and family. So, in 1897, at the age of forty-one, ten months after the death of his father, having already analysed some of his own dreams, he tried free association on himself in earnest, sitting down and writing whatever came into his mind. Amazingly, he believed in his theory so much that he fully expected to uncover hidden memories of his father sexually abusing him.

Freud might have expected that, by uncovering his own memories of abuse, his neurasthenia would be cured (headaches, moodiness, digestion problems, fits of lack of energy and depression). But, true to the value of the technique, what he discovered was not what he expected. Instead, he uncovered childhood memories where he some-times hated his father (whom he thought he had only loved), and sexually desired his mother.

Freud recognised, alive in himself, the ancient myth of Oedipus, who was fated to kill his father and marry his mother. One particular memory was sharing a sleeping compartment on a train with his mother as a little boy, where he assumed he must have seen her naked, and desired her. At the time of this free association, Freud was forty years old and could not exactly remember his actual feelings at the age of seven, and if he had even felt desire towards his mother, but Fliess, another friend and part of the psychoanalytic circle at that time, had told him how his little boy had had an erection on seeing his mother naked and Freud presumed he must have felt the same.

But, Freud thought, if *he* had sexual desires so early on in life, what about his patients? Could they *all* have been sexually interfered with by their fathers? Or could they have imagined it because they *wanted* it? Shock. Freud now saw that his earlier conviction that hysteria was caused by premature sex might not be right.

And, at this point, going by what he had discovered in himself during his self-analysis, and listening to his patients with sharper ears, Freud *turned his previous theory exactly upside down*. It was not just a case of "pre-sexual sexual shock" (Friedman, 2001, p. 168), that is, where the virginal young mind was shocked and traumatised by encountering adult sex, but of us as adults being so shocked and traumatised by memories of our own childhood sexuality that we forget all about them. We dissociate our memories of our infantile and childhood erotic and aggressive desires towards our parents because we are so shocked by them, and blind ourselves, just as Oedipus literally did with a pin when he found out what he had done. Indeed, the night after his father's funeral, Freud had a dream that he was in a place with a sign: "You are requested to close the eyes" (Freud, 1900a, p. 317).

This, then, he thought, had to be the essential, universal, uncon-scious, emotional conflict, between the instinctual self and the moral self. The nearly unacceptable new discovery was just *what* the instinc-tual self in all of us specifically wants in childhood—sex with one par-ent and the death of the other. This was at the heart of Freud's first really significant publication, *The Interpretation of Dreams*, published in 1900.

The revelation of the book was that dreams are the fulfilment of wishes. He gave harmless examples, such as the dreams his little daughter had of eating strawberries when she had been denied them the previous day, progressing to more challenging dreams about the deaths of loved ones, in which he described the Oedipus complex. He wrote,

> If the dream is a wish-fulfilment, then painful feelings should have no place in it. It should always produce pleasure. The question is pleasure to whom? Naturally, to him who has the wish. We know, however, that the dreamer has a very peculiar relation to his wishes. He rejects them, he censors them, in short he does not like them. The dreamer, therefore, in relation to his dream wishes, can only be likened to the fusion of two separate persons who have something in common: instinctual man and moral man. The wish-fulfilment of the one can naturally lead to the displeasure of the other, if the two are at loggerheads. (Boss, 1958, p. 38)

"Two separate persons"—remember how he and Breuer thought that the pathology of hysteria was essentially that of multiple personality. Janet thought that minds *fell* apart, through weakness, because they did not have the strength to hold themselves together, but Freud said no—minds are *pushed* apart, when one part rejects another and will have nothing to do with it, will not even know it exists.

So, the word *repress* replaced the word *dissociate*. The pushing away itself is unconsciously done, and the conscious mind feels only perhaps that it is a little happier and freer. But what is pushed away does not die; it stays there hidden but unchanged, and returns from the unconscious in the form of neurotic symptoms and in dreams, when the instinctual self returns to challenge the moral self once more.

It was not fair, by the way, to accuse Freud of *suppressing* the truth about actual child sexual abuse when he moved on to the new theory (as some believed, later in the century); he was the hound who had scented the fox and forgot about rabbits, that was all.

With his new theory, Freud realised he was on to something big. The discovery of his childhood longing for sex with his mother, and that he had sometimes hated his father as well as loved him, meant that he understood himself more deeply than he could have ever imagined possible. He continued with the self-analysis and proclaimed, in 1899, that it had done him good and he was more normal for it. However, later on, he said that any children's nurse could tell all about infantile sexuality, and joked that it was his fate to discover what everyone knew already.

It was a big thing for anyone to take seriously: that a little girl actually *wanted* sex with her father, and the boy with his mother, and each had murderous jealousy towards the other parent. It would imply that Katerina was disturbed because her instinctual self had *wanted* the sex with her father, while something else in her did not. Freud was a very straight person and would not dismiss sex with a knowing nudge and wink, as many bourgeois Viennese men would have at that time, living as they did in a society with a vividly active, irresponsible, brothel-centred underworld. Neither did he react to the subject of sex and children with the conventional righteousness that got his fellow Viennese, Egon Schiele, the painter, jailed in 1912 for his erotic drawings. What he found, he took seriously, with humane gravity and scientific objectivity.

Part of Freud's ambitiousness was that he needed to be a prophet. This early ambition would one day lead him to announce to his followers, "We possess the truth" (Jones, 1957, vol. 3, p. 215). The fundamental importance of sex was a truth for him to preach.

The more he thought about it, the more it seemed to him that sex explained just about *everything.* In *Three Essays on the Theory of Sexuality,* published in 1905 and its six editions in his lifetime, he explained how sexual desire (which he called "libido") is the foundation of all we want and do. It is opposed only by the instinct for self-protection (for example, out of fear of father castrating us if we do not renounce the sexual desire for mother).

Freud believed that everything could be explained by sex and the self-protecting reactions to it. The baby's sucking at the breast is sexual, wherever there is contact with mucous membranes there is sex, the baby's pleasure in urinating and defecating, in the many forms of sensuality, cruel and loving, thumb-sucking, sexual play of all kinds. "Polymorphous perverse" (Freud, 1905d, p. 28) he called it, the evolving genital sexuality, the instinct for knowledge, muscular activity, intellectual work, even higher spiritual functions, such as art, through a special mutation of sex through *sublimation,* which

> enables excessively strong excitations arising from particular sources of sexuality to find an outlet and use in other fields . . . The multifariously perverse sexual disposition of our childhood can accordingly be regarded as the source of a number of our virtues . . . (Freud, 1905c, p. 238)

Real people are unbelievably different from each other. Some infants seem to continue from breastfeeding, eventually to sensuality through sensual enjoyment of parts of their own and others' bodies, and on into full sexual sensuality, without missing a beat. Others have it nipped in the bud: a woman in Guy's paediatric outpatients, when asked why she had stopped breastfeeding her baby so soon, replied, "I *had* to, doctor, he was getting *knowing*, he was beginning to *enjoy* it!"

Freud saw that the wonderful "multifarious" sexual sensuality of the baby and small child, if given a fair chance, grows naturally, stage by stage, into full adult love. But if the environment scares the child into dissociating the sexual feelings, and they become repressed, then they do not develop, but remain infantile in form. The fully committed adult pervert, he said, never *became* a pervert; he just *remained* what he was at the beginning instead of developing his sexuality like everyone else.

He believed that neurotics were usually disturbed not by repressed normal sexuality, but by repressed infantile forms: neurosis is the negative of perversion, he said, it is normal infantile "perversion" negated and suppressed.

Freud was more prudish than we are nowadays. Homosexuality was "the perversion which is most repellent to us" (Freud, 1907a, p. 50). Yet, in spite of his prudish fastidiousness, Freud became the champion and culture-hero of the sensual, erotic end of love, on behalf of which he had to fight a long-established cultural prejudice too exclusively favouring the spiritual, altruistic side.

"Love suffers long . . ." wrote St Paul to the Corinthians; "Love . . . makes things wet" (Freud, 1907a, p. 72), said Freud to his young patient, Dora, who did not need to be told but only coaxed to admit to herself what she already knew.

So, according to Freud, there were two ways in which natural development could go wrong:

1. We get stuck—"fixated"—in the infantile form of sexuality, if it is repressed or otherwise split off from the growing personality. Then it restricts our behaviour from the unconscious mind, so that we never properly grow up.
2. We grow up to a point, but then retreat—"regresse"—back to the family romance and infantile sexuality, out of timidity, perhaps, when challenged by meeting someone we could love, but for

some reason lose our nerve and back off. This is the approach Dora had initially taken.

Note on the meaning of "complex"

At the beginning of the century, "complex" meant a collection of memories, wishes, imaginings, etc., on a theme: remember again Janet's *idée fixe*, and the autopilots we can set up in ourselves, and the powerful stories that govern our actions. The complex says, "I want . . ." something or other. The Oedipus complex is "I want to kill Father and have Mother".

"Complex" is another horrid example of psychobabble, but it is, unfortunately, very useful, when thinking about the actions people take that are hard to explain. The ghosts of Kamahasanyi's ancestors tormenting him were complexes, guilt feelings in himself (unless they really *were* spirits). An anthropologist acquaintance of mine, with feminist leanings, attended a ceremony of spirit possession in Nepal and was pleased to hear a woman possessed by the spirit speaking spiritedly against her husband and the unfair lot of women. But when she congratulated the woman the next day on so boldly speaking out, the woman said she had never said those things at all, it was the spirit speaking. Her protest-complex remained well dissociated from her conscious attitude.

Autonomous complexes (complexes so independent that they are a law unto themselves) or, in other words, unconscious wishes, cause otherwise unexplainable disasters. The analyst William Fairbairn used the term "internal saboteur" (Pereira & Scharff, 2002, p. 15). Imagine a young woman deeply fed up with her life, but who puts aside her recurrent impulse to kill herself and forgets about it. She finds a new man to love and it vanishes from her mind. But it has not really gone away, and can still influence events from the unconscious. One night she has been partying with friends, they are all a bit under the influence, and she drives home without fastening her seat belt. Who would be so prissy when life is so exciting! The accident that follows allows the unconscious autonomous complex to get what it wanted. It would be interesting to research whether people who have attempted suicide and failed remain more accident prone than normal.

I knew two women, good women, who survived suicide attempts by overdose and were later horrified at how they could have ever done such a thing to their small children. The autonomous complex, in their case, the dissociated suicidal wish, or the internal saboteur, whatever you want to call it, had come up and taken over. Similarly, we can speculate how far unconscious suicidal drives influenced great disasters, for example, say, the historically doomed aggressions of Germany and Japan in the middle of the twentieth century. Actual suicides followed defeat. Similarly, I wonder how much unconscious suicide complexes contribute to deaths on the roads, or cause physical illness.

The power of the *unconscious wish*, operating like a hidden sub-personality in the background, was the first great revelation of the Enlightenment of the Mind. Indeed, unconscious desires play havoc in families, nations, and the world. Persons closely scrutinised, such as parents by their children, or the leaders of nations by the public, often look hypocritical when they are not hypocrites at all, but just unintegrated personalities (as most of us are), so that their right hand *really does not know* what their left hand is doing—even after we've told them.

CHAPTER FIVE

Freud and the beautiful mind

"The poets and philosophers before me discovered the unconscious. What I discovered was the scientific method by which
the unconscious can be studied"

(Attributed to Sigmund Freud)

In *Studies in Hysteria* (1895d) Freud wrote that *transference* was the
worst obstacle to treatment - when the patient became emotionally
involved with the doctor. However, his discovery of the Oedipus
complex a few years later gave transference a new interest.

Freud found that young women whom he believed really wanted
sex with their fathers would transfer their affections to him instead.
This would not have been too difficult for many of his female patients,
as Dr Freud, in his thirties, was very handsome—lovely eyes. In fact,
in *Studies in Hysteria*, Freud describes how a young woman reveals
during free association that she wants him to kiss her. However, she
then remembers how once before she had wanted a young man to
kiss her, but was so excessively well brought up that she had banished
the thought and forgotten it—until she had re-enacted it with
Freud.

From this, Freud deduced that the patient had a kind of choice: *either* to remember something *or* act it out and repeat it by *transferring* it to the doctor.

Falling in love with the analyst became a cliché of psychoanalysis. Transferring the early love for the father on to Dr Freud in this way was a neat way of avoiding the deeper disgraceful fact. It was a *defence*, which could be interpreted: "You really want sex with your father."

Freud's encounter with an extraordinary patient whom he named "The Rat Man" (thought to be a twenty-nine-year-old lawyer called Ernst Lanzer) caused him to turn his first idea of transference upside down. Soon, he came to realise that transference was not an obstacle, but the main instrument of cure.

In *Notes on a Case of Obsessional Neurosis* (1909d), Freud described the case of his patient: Lanzer's life had been brought to a halt by his own obsessional thoughts and behaviours. He felt compelled to carry out endless, complex rituals to prevent something bad happening to his father or woman friend. The case was even more intriguing as Lanzer's father had actually been dead for a number of years.

Freud began the treatment by making his patient promise to submit to "the one and only condition of treatment – namely, to say everything that came into his head" (Freud, 1909d, p. 159), however unpleasant, unimportant, irrelevant, or senseless it seemed. Freud was, of course, interested in hearing about Lanzer's childhood fantasises that he was sure would emerge from the rich hoard of memories produced by free association.

It was not too long before Lanzer's *resistance* halted his flow of memories. He broke off, got up from the sofa, and begged Freud to spare him the recital of what was in his mind. But Freud was no softie when it came to the Battle with the Patient:

> . . . naturally I could not grant him something which was beyond my power. He might just as well ask me to give him the moon. The overcoming of resistances was a law of the treatment and on no consideration could it be dispensed with. (Freud, 1909d, p. 166)

With great difficulty, Lanzer described his fears to Freud. He was afraid that if he did not carry out his obsessive practices, then a horrible torture would befall his father and the young woman he loved.

This torture involved heating a pan full of rats, which would then be applied to the victim's anus, from where they would eat their way in.

By this time Freud was becoming an expert at reading the upside down expressions of his patients lying on the couch beside him. When Lanzer told Freud about the rat torture, "his face took on a very strange, composite expression. I could only interpret it as one of *horror at pleasure of his own of which he himself was unaware*" (Freud, 1909d, pp. 166–167).

As the treatment continued, Lanzer revealed to Freud that he had broken down into his illness when his wish to marry the poor girl he loved had clashed with his father's wish for him to marry a rich girl.

During his transference, Lanzer imagined the Freud family was rich, and that the young woman his father wanted him to marry was Freud's daughter. To his distress, the relentless law of free association obliged him to utter hostile and critical thoughts against Freud. On some occasions, Lanzer would get up or duck, as though Freud were about to hit him for his effrontery. His father might have, but not Freud.

By transferring his aggression against his own father to Freud, Lanzer was able to repeat or act out the original dilemma: Freud was now the father who wanted him to marry the rich young woman against his own desires, but this time, by the law of free association, he was forced to voice his hostility to Freud as he had not dared to his own father.

Freud spent a year treating Lanzer and was able to lead his patient by the way Freud himself had come, by acknowledging that his fears were wishes, derived from the hatred of his father which had been kept hidden away in the unconscious.

Quite early in the treatment, Freud explained the theory of psychoanalysis as it then stood (about 1905) to his patient. He explained how dissociated and repressed wishes do not die when they are disowned by the conscious mind but live on in the unconscious mind and cause inexplicable trouble from there. He told him that "the unconscious must be the precise contrary of the conscious" (Freud, 1909d, p.180), and that it was his love for his father that had banished his hate to the unconscious.

In the same way, Freud expected to find repressed sexual desire for a parent in every case of hysteria; in obsessive–compulsive disorder he expected to discover a clash between love and hate, resulting in repressed hate which would produce symptoms from the unconscious: the unconscious wish to harm, causing an obsessive terror of harming.

However, it was not easy for Freud to convince his patient that his conscious fearfulness and guilt were reactions to an unconscious wish to hurt his beloved father, or, indeed, that he felt anything but love for him. In fact, he only became convinced by Freud's theories through the transference as the analysis unfolded.

Freud liked Lanzer and treated him kindly: he fed him when he arrived hungry one day, spent time explaining psychoanalysis to him, and repeatedly assured his patient of his respect for him. Following a year of therapy, Lanzer became well enough to go off and get engaged. Freud never had the chance to follow up on the case—the Rat Man was killed in the First World War.

The case of the Rat Man reinforced Freud's theories about the unconscious mind: when the unconscious (repressed) desires become conscious, one can then do something with them, whether it is only to consciously reject them again or to cultivate them so they can be directed to some good aim. A positive outcome of nurturing conscious desires would be to convert unacknowledged hostility to honest open assertiveness: if that cannot be done then the energy might be somehow diverted or *sublimated* into some creative activity, such as art.

Freud's uncovering of his own Oedipus complex as the cause of his neurosis led to one of the great insights of the century: that understanding people's childhood development explains how they are, and offers a way to cure their suffering. Early wounds can be recovered by expressing the repressed emotions, and unsatisfactory early deals with others—grown into deals made with the whole world—can be renegotiated.

Through his discovery of the Oedipus complex, Freud believed that the next generation's chance of happiness could be improved by better child rearing. This insight really did filter into the common culture in the later part of the twentieth century, and there has been enormous work put into the study of human emotional development and good child rearing.

Although what Freud wrote is marvellously lucid and consistent, the messages that came across to the public, who read little of what he actually wrote, were more mixed. For example, some people picked up on the idea that the unconscious mind was a snakepit of sex and aggression, full of destructive dangerous drives.

In Germany at the time, this was not a million miles from the truth. Brutal violence simmered beneath the surface of many Germans, and every time Freud walked the street he could have been passing individuals who would become Hitler's willing helpers, some who would eventually kill his sisters and friends. However, Freud saw a different side to the tension around him, viewing it as a clash between civilisation and instincts, and he sympathised with the instincts. He believed that fear of our instincts makes us ill. Whereas society thought that lust and hate were simply sins that had to be punished, he saw them as a normal part of growing up. He believed that it was healthier if civilisation embraced and accepted these perceived "sexual perversions" rather than repressing them.

As time went on, Freud's great message, sex is good, began to be taken more seriously by the English middle classes. The novels of Aldous Huxley in the earlier half of the century involved female characters struggling with their sexuality: for example, the young girl who is terribly hurt when her budding sexuality is jarringly rejected by a boy; or the girl who has sex because the new ideas say it is good for you, only to find that she has become emotionally involved with the young man she has slept with. These novels illustrated the influence of Freud in society and encouraged sexual acceptance and experimentation.

In 1915, Freud published a paper about depression that he titled "Mourning and melancholia". This time he did not cite the case of any particular patient, but wrote as though he had in his mind some married woman discontented with her husband. He described that her disappointment in her husband was as if she had experienced a loss, or bereavement. She expressed unhappiness like one bereaved, but with one strange difference: she was loud in self-blame, a common behaviour with clinical depression, but not one that normally occurs during the mourning process.

Freud believed that the blame she experienced was actually the way she felt towards her husband, but she turned it on herself. Blaming herself was a way of avoiding confrontation, yet she still punished her husband indirectly by being so miserable to live with. (This observation is linked with the psychoanalytical proposition that no one who commits suicide has not first wanted to commit murder.)

Identifying with the blameworthy other person as a way of taking the other person into oneself—*introjection*—is an idea that would later appear in object relations theory. Here, Freud had just begun looking at the problems of how we get into other people emotionally, and how they get into us.

But modestly nestling in one paragraph of this paper is a culture-bomb:

> We see how in [the depressed person] one part of the ego sets itself over against the other, judges it critically, and, as it were, takes it as its object. What we are here becoming acquainted with is the agency commonly called '*conscience*'; we shall count it . . . among the major institutions of the ego, and we shall come upon evidence to show that *it can become diseased on its own account*. (Freud, 1917e, p. 247, my italics)

Back in 1896, in *Studies in Hysteria*, Freud had used the word *trauma* to describe things that caused upset, such as one's father dying, as in the case of Anna O. Freud then applied the condition of trauma to physical symptoms that arose from perceived guilty desires, such as sex or revenge. For example, Anna O developed a cough, which derived from her guilt about wanting to dance to music when she was supposed to be concerned only with her dying father. Another patient, Dora, also got a cough when she had to deal with sexual fantasies about her father.

Thus, Freud described how, in hysterical conversion, a painful or disgraceful memory or wish is *somehow* banished from the conscious mind and converted into a physical symptom. He thought that this was an act of moral cowardice, in so far as it represented a refusal to own these feelings of lust or hate, and instead dissociate them off into one's unconscious where they can manifest as physical symptoms.

In "Mourning and melancholia", the sickness of conscience consisted in the woman blaming herself for her husband's faults. Partly, this was an unconscious, indirect way of punishing him, but it was also a way of avoiding confrontation, as when one apologises to the person who has trodden on one's toes, or gets on with everyone by placating them. She might have blamed herself for not being a good wife, but to Freud her real "sin", or moral failure, was not acknowledging to herself the rage she felt towards her husband and finding a use for it, such as getting him to behave better.

I do not think Freud wrote of "moral cowardice" or "moral courage" as a factor in mental health ever again after the 1890s. The idea of moral cowardice and courage clashed with Freud's personal need to win intellectual freedom by rejecting conventional moral accountability: free will, religion, etc., and replacing them with a sceptical scientific rationalism, psychological determinism, and active atheism. He wrote in *Studies in Hysteria* that he worked "as a teacher, as the representative of a freer or superior view of the world" (Freud, 1895d, pp. 282–283)—a superior view that could save people from their hang-ups of sexual guilt. Freud was against Judaism and Christianity for sure, but perhaps, beneath his prudery, he had an earthy Jewish warmth that he shared with Jesus of Nazareth, who also saved some from being punished for sex.

Later on, it became an axiom of dynamic therapy that the therapist must on no account give any moral advice; the patient must develop his own authentic conscience for himself.

Freud thought the essential cause of hysteria was the same dissociation as found in multiple personality disorder. But, at some point, he began to see divisions into sub-personalities as universal, not only in all kinds of neurosis, and in all human beings, normal and abnormal alike.

The first sub-division Freud made was into *two*, the conscious and unconscious mind. But that was superseded. By 1923, the *three* sub-personalities Freud had observed in action in the Rat Man, others, and himself, had crystallised out in his mind as three "institutions" of the self, which he called *Es, Ich, UberIch*, translated as *id, ego*, and *superego*. By renaming the conscience as "superego", Freud could get an objective scientific grip on it, dissect it out of the messy human being, and raise it in mental tweezers away from any contaminating ideas of "right" and "wrong".

The superego is simply ego's internal boss: self-control. The word "unconscious" changed its use at this point, too: it became a descriptive adjective, describing one end of the ego, one end of the superego, and all of the id, rather than just the part of the mind that held repressed desires, etc.

Freud derived this term id, or "It" from the German physician, Georg Groddeck (1866–1934). What Groddek wrote in 1923 is so central I put it here in emphasis:

> *... man is animated by the Unknown, ... there is within him an 'Es', an 'It', some wondrous force which directs what he himself does, and what happens to him. The affirmation 'I live' ... expresses only a small and super-ficial part of the fundamental principle, 'Man is lived by the It'.* (Groddeck, 1923, p. 199)

When Freud took over the word "It" from Groddeck, he narrowed its meaning. But he did agree with Groddeck that the unconscious mind was not just a rubbish bin for repressed wishes, but also the source of the mighty instincts within our lives. The mind is the home of the "wondrous force", the "It" that lives us, the source of the instincts, desires, and their symbols (such as the Oedipus drama) that live them-selves out in us. Other writers gave 'It' other names, such as "life force", "*élan vital*", etc.

So, Freud renamed conscience as "superego", which he believed was "the heir of the Oedipus Complex" (Eysenck, 2004, p. 581). The superego begins in a boy when he restrains himself from desiring his mother because he fears his father will castrate him for it. The too-severe, sick superego can cause the hysteric, the obsessive compulsive, and the depressive to become ill. The hysteric has to repress her naughty desires, the compulsive to repress his natural and, perhaps, well-justified hostility, and the depressive to deal with her reactive hostility and critical capacity by indulging in self-blame. Misguided guilt makes neurotics of them all, and they need Freud's more liber-ated and superior view to free them.

Thus, Freud saw the hysteric as one who has dissociated unman-ageable emotion, the obsessive as one who has mixed feelings as a result of keeping the love conscious and dissociating the hatred, and the depressive as a self-suppressed rebel. However, Alfred Adler, at first an intimate friend and one of Freud's closest supporters, had such different ideas about the conscience, and other areas, that Adler was to become one of Freud's most hated enemies.

CHAPTER SIX

Adler: a complex man

"To be a human being means to feel oneself inferior"

(Adler, 1939)

K aren Horney's plea—why can't we think differently but still be friends?—would never be answered, because defects in Freud's character had been faithfully taken on by his disciples, through several generations, just as the lisp of a Spanish prince centuries ago changed the pronunciation of Spanish for ever.

For Freud, there was no question of maintaining a friendship with anyone who started to think differently from him. He would cut such a person in the street, old friend or not. The funniest example was an incident that took place at a conference: while ignoring the out-stretched hand of a once trusted friend and colleague, the Swiss physician, Alphonse Maeder, Freud managed to get his pocket caught on a door-handle and had to be released by the man he was trying to shun.

In 1911, Freud set up a meeting of his Psychoanalytical Society to debate the views of Alfred Adler, which resulted in Adler (president of the society, at the time) and six others leaving the group. By this time the Psychoanalytic Movement, as Freud called it (although I wonder why a society that focused on medical treatment was called a *Movement*, for goodness' sake, like the Nazi Movement or the Student Christian Movement), was becoming fundamentalist, and Adler and his supporters had no hope of being listened to by Freud. Freud's definition of a group was where people accepted the superego of its leader; the idea of a happy, pluralistic democracy was as alien to his way of thinking as to his Emperor, Franz Josef.

Freud took against Adler, claiming that his writings showed "an antisexual trend" (Adler, 1956, p. 70)—blasphemy! Freud went on, "The core of a neurosis is the anxiety of the ego confronted by libido and Adler's presentation has only reinforced this interpretation . . ." (Adler, 1956, p. 71).

This was a nasty crack, hinting that Adler had only demonstrated his own fear of sex. Adler had dared to think that neurosis was really about how we relate to others in *all* ways, not just sexually.

The contrasting childhoods of Freud and Adler had put them on a collision course before they even met. Jung once commented that psychological theories were autobiographies, confessions, and Adler and Freud, simply, had different biographies.

Adler was fourteen years younger than Freud. Although both men had fathers who were Jewish merchants in Vienna, and came from poor families, Freud still emerged as the more up-market of the two. Adler was slightly scruffy, some said a bit common, street-wise, and had *menschenkenntnis* (good knowledge of others); Freud wasn't anything like this. While Freud's meetings comprised of a carefully chosen few who had been invited to his nice flat, Adler welcomed everybody, including patients, and held his gatherings in various different cafés. Freud was not street-wise. Paranoid, maybe; streetwise, no. Indeed, it beggars belief that Freud could have been so naïve about the intentions of the Nazis—two of his sisters ended up perishing in the Holocaust and he had a narrow escape, himself.

Adler was the second son in a family of two girls and four boys, who played and, no doubt, fought with the other local street urchins. His mother was far from the pampering type, Adler believed she did not love him, and he preferred to live in the streets—happiest in a crowd. Adler was a friendly and lively child, popular with the other boys and girls in that neighbourhood, where many of them were poor. It was said that even the pigeons came down to greet him when he came home from school. He was a favourite with his eccentric and kind father, who encouraged him and taught him some things he never forgot, such as "Never believe what anyone *tells you*" (Bottome, 1957, p. 34). When Adler was an infant, he developed rickets, which delayed him from walking until he was four years of age. His earliest memory was sitting with his bandaged legs looking up at his elder brother, Sigmund, who was big and strong and healthy.

So while Freud's attractive, young mother doted on him, and was the source of his Oedipus complex, Adler had to combat and defeat an *inferiority complex* which arose from his childhood illness, and his feelings that his mother was not that fond of him. Like Freud, his contribution to dynamic psychotherapy, to the world really, was down to his understanding his own complex, but it was a different sort of complex.

Unlike many children who feel inferior and defeated, Adler seized chances to build his confidence, such as the time when no one in his class could answer a maths problem but little Adler, who found the courage to go out and put his solution on the blackboard. The answer was correct and he never forgot the praise and encouragement he received. Yes, he had rickets and thought his mother did not like him, but he was a fighter.

Adler decided to become a doctor because of an incident that took place when he was five years old. He contracted pneumonia and the doctor told his father not to bother with the young Adler as he was going to die anyway. There and then, the little boy made up his mind to become a doctor himself and make a better fist of it. Another story says it was because he woke one morning to find one of his brothers dead in the bed beside him: "I decided at an early age to come into close contact with all difficult problems, in order that I might be in a better position to solve them" (Bottome, 1957, p. 33).

Adler married a Russian girl, Raissa Epstein, independent-minded and an ardent socialist, who was at university in Vienna; they had children, but the marriage broke up. Perhaps it failed because, although Adler strongly urged the liberation of women, Raissa really *was* liberated and maybe she was too radical. Later in life when he was ill, she came to join him in New York (where he had a flat over Times Square and loved going to the cinema, especially to see Charlie Chaplin and Marx Brothers films) and they were reconciled. But then their eldest daughter disappeared in Russia while visiting relatives and Adler did not live long after that. A colleague of mine at Guy's was once shown by her father the very spot in Union Street, Aberdeen where Adler had died from a heart attack, aged sixty-seven. When Freud heard of his death, he said, "For a Jew boy out of a Viennese suburb a death in Aberdeen is an unheard-of career in itself and a proof of how far he had got on" (Jones, 1957, p. 208).

Adler overcame his own inferiority complex by attacking life in every possible positive, one could almost say jubilant, way. Adler, at first, thought that organ inferiority, like his own childhood rickets, caused a reactive urge towards superiority and power. Later, he saw that initial feelings of inadequacy would give way to an urge to rise upwards, and blossom and flourish, and that this is innate in all of us. The crucial thing is whether we have the courage to follow these growth impulses whole-heartedly and bravely, or whether we lose courage and settle for the cheap substitutes of superiority and power.

He believed that parents who neglect to teach children courage and co-operation lead them to a timid avoidance of the wonderful possibilities of life, out of fear of failure. This shrinking back is compensated by an urge to be one up on other people, a search for glory that is never really attainable. While such a goal might compensate for feelings of inferiority or helplessness, it misses out on the real satisfactions of life that are found in *social feeling*: contribution and co-operation with others, which provide true self-esteem. Adler wrote the following, in reference to an unconfident child, "His goal will lie beyond the boundaries of the attainable, but far behind the fighting front of life" (Adler, 1927, p. 25).

Thus, independence and co-operation are the twin strengths that should be brought out in a child.

Once, as a young doctor, he escorted home a mental patient who had persuaded the doctors to discharge him. The man told him, triumphantly, "You see, I always win!" Adler was amazed; in every aspect of life the man was a loser, but he had convinced himself he was a winner. Adler saw crime, neurosis, and psychosis as alike when it came to giving in to an urge for slick superiority. Psychosis is easiest—a person can just claim he is Christ or Einstein, or whatever.

So, whereas Freud had a superego, or ego ideal, Adler's life and deeds were motored by the joys and satisfactions of social feeling, an emotion that did not enthuse Freud. Adler thought that it was, normally, the good parent, and first the mother, who brought out the innate capacity for social feeling in their children, but he also thought that psychotherapy could bring it out in patients. It is this, he thought, that makes possible unhampered *growth* of a person.

Adler was not as clever as Freud and did not write as well. (Few do.) Unfortunately, he or his translator used the word "superiority" for two opposite aims: empty neurotic superiority *vs.* the true superiority of fulfilment of our potentialities in a context of social feeling.

Adler saw the symptoms of the hysteric, or the obsessional, or the depressive as timid and devious attempts, *not done deliberately, but unconsciously arranged by their timidity*, to assert themselves against others and not be inferior. This includes the need for revenge noted by Carter, and by Freud in his early days. Adler believed there were endless subtleties to the tricks in achieving superiority: "A child will make use of anxiety in order to arrive at its goal of superiority—of control over the mother" (Mairet, 1999, p. 29).

> One way of attaining superior-feelings is by the irritation of others. Parents or teachers, husbands or wives, as the case may be, will be more or less subtly exasperated until they burst into a rage, and begin to attack or punish. To many children this proof of their power over others is a great satisfaction . . . (Mairet, 1999, p. 31)

Adler's account of depression shows how the depressed person needs to *really, genuinely* suffer, to win the covert battle against the loved one. This was a radical insight for doctors and therapists, who assumed that everyone wanted to escape their suffering. The doctor should routinely find out who it is that the neurotic person is directing his suffering *at*. The importance of this insight can hardly be overestimated, because a situation where the patient has to make the doctor feel he has failed in relieving the suffering can create what the psychoanalyst, Tom Main, called revenge disguised as treatment. Making the doctor (or the family) fail might be absolutely necessary to the patient's self esteem and sense of self. A person might be willing to pay a high price.

I remember a patient who had been reluctantly discharged by a registrar returning to the hospital, pouring petrol over himself in the grounds, and setting himself alight. It was a spite suicide against the registrar who had discharged him. It was worth it to him because his life was unrewarding and well worth sacrificing to get revenge on the registrar, who, by the way, was an unusually good and conscientious doctor, but was, indeed, censured by the coroner, and so the patient won in the end.

Neurosis is the weapon of the coward, and the weapon most used by the weak. We cannot ignore the heavily veiled aggressive or vindictive element in most neuroses. In the investigation of a neurotic style of life we must always suspect an opponent, and note who suffers most because of the patient's condition. Usually, this is a member of the family, and sometimes a person of the other sex, though there are cases in which an illness is an attack on society as a whole. There is always this element of concealed accusation in neurosis, the patient feeling as though he were deprived of his right—that is, of the centre of attention—and wanting to fix the responsibility and blame upon someone. By such hidden vengeance and accusation, the problem child and the neurotic find some relief from their dissatisfaction (Mairet, 1999, p. 80).

Neurosis is about fear and hate, when someone feels that they are not being acknowledged or when they are too timid to fight openly, fight fair, and fight friendly. Understanding it as witchcraft, Ihembi had it nearly spot on, but among the Ndembu the hatred was more secret than unconscious, as it is with us civilised folks. Our fear of each other is the fear of our desires that will make trouble between us. Adler concentrated more on our fear of each other, the outer, social thing, while Freud concentrated on the resultant fear of our own desires, the inner thing. Freud believed that the main threat came from our sexual desires, and ignored our need for respect from others, but Adler understood this, and it was what he was referring to when he talked about "superiority". The demands of the need for respect, when made unconscious by fear, became one of the most important things discovered by the Enlightenment of the Mind—*hatred that is genuinely unconscious*.

Adler thought that hate could show itself in various ways: high intensity episodes such as temper tantrums, milder forms such as nagging and maliciousness, or by a general critical attitude. Of course, hate can also be disguised as kindness and all sorts of opposite things—again not consciously, but unconsciously converted in appearance.

But, however clearly Adler saw his clients' hidden hate, timidity, and unconscious self-deceit, like Carter he treated them with patience, tact, and respect. In the Battle with the Patient, Adler's version was to coax him into a receptive frame of mind with friendly encouragement and tolerance, before the eventual moment of "unmasking", and explaining how he was living a life through illness.

Freud helped his patients become conscious of their unconscious, incestuous, sexual, and murderous wishes. He accepted these as natural developmental things, and made his patients' consciences less severe against their natural sexuality, so that their self-esteem did not depend on pretending they had no sexual desires and needs. Adler wanted his patients to be aware of their unconscious *life goal*, as he called it, so that they could disengage their self-esteem from the useless aim of always being one-up through empty superiority and power, and attach it to being useful. An inferior life goal forms one's *life style* as a habitual dysfunctional emotional dance with the other person (Adler's term for the other person in the dance was *gegen-spieler*, the game opponent), where healthy self-esteem has been replaced by sick conscience.

Adler saw the life style of a patient as a power game in action the moment he walked through the door of his consulting room. If the patient trips on the carpet, is he pitching for sympathy? One female patient told him:

'I have seen so many doctors that you are my last hope in life.' 'No,' I answered, 'not the last hope. There may be others who can help you too'. Her words were a challenge to me; she was *daring* me not to cure her . . . This is the type of patient who wishes to shift responsibility upon others. (Mairet, 1999, p. 8)

For Freud, the cause of neurosis lay in the past, but for Adler, it lay in the future. Thus, Adler held that it was our future that was making us ill, the timid self-preserving *goal* that has been planned for us by our dissociated desires and fears. He had a little trick where he would ask a patient what he would be doing if he were not ill. Whatever the patient said would be taken as evidence of what he was actually *avoid-ing*, out of fear of defeat. The illness allowed him to avoid it.

Adler believed that whatever theory was used in psychotherapy, the cure comes about always because the patient has been *encouraged* by the therapist. Most of the patients described so far in this book might not seem as much winning superiority and power as making a weak and futile attempt to assert themselves against people and situations stronger than they are.

Freud thought the conflict between civilisation and instinct was inevitable, and he reacted to that with humorous resignation. Adler, by contrast, talked as though he believed that the id wants the brotherhood of man, not just sex and murder. At the end of *Studies in Hysteria*, Freud said that successful treatment could only replace hysterical misery with common unhappiness, against which, however, the mind was better armed after treatment. Conversely, Adler simply wanted people to be happy. In books such as *What Life Should Mean to You* (1931), Adler pioneered the use of dynamic psychotherapy beyond the treatment of diseases, to think that self-fulfilment and happiness were desirable aims for everybody.

All three of the fathers of dynamic psychotherapy became prophets: Freud for his views of sex and naturalness against convention and religion, Adler for social humanity, while Jung spoke of something so appalling that no one takes any notice of it.

As tensions mounted in the Vienna Society before the 1911 debate, the Vice President, Stekel, tried to soften the rebellion by flattering Freud, but Adler did not bother. With typical wry humour, Freud summed up the course of events by stating that it appeared as if Stekel was willing to accord him a first-class funeral while the President (Adler) was merely planning a routine one. During the great debate itself, some tried to show that Freud's and Adler's views were reconcilable, but Freud was unyielding, pointing out that, unfortunately, there were two present who did not agree: himself and Adler.

And so it remained, until Jung presented a paper with typical aggressive behaviour at the 1913 Psychoanalytic Conference in Munich, a paper that ended up showing that Freud and Adler were *both right*. He did this by introducing an observation that was not new to psychiatry, but new to the Movement. In the next chapter, we shall see how he applied this theory to Freud and Adler.

CHAPTER SEVEN

War of nerves

"We cannot tear out a single page of our life, but we can throw the whole book in the fire"

(George Sand, 1837)

A t first, Jung was mainly a supporter of Freud. But in 1913, a meeting of the Psychoanalytical Society took place in Munich. By this time, relations between Freud and Jung were hostile and this was the last time they would meet. In his presentation, Jung explained how both Adler's and Freud's views, contrary to what Adler and Freud thought, were actually reconcilable.

He did this by referring to an observation of psychiatry at that time, that schizophrenics were too little emotionally involved with others, whereas hysterics tended to be overly emotionally involved. Jung believed that we all oscillate between looking outwards to others, and inwards into our own hearts. He thought this normal, like systole and diastole. But he also saw that some of us do more of one than the other; in other words, that we lead with our best card, and mostly use the one that works best for us. So, as a result, some of us are more extroverted, while some are more introverted.

Jung's theory was that whatever behaviour we lead with, the other behaviour is in us, too, but less developed, waiting in a more immature form in the background, in the unconscious. (In some of us, of course, both our introversion *and* extraversion can be immature . . .)

In the population, there is a normal distribution of introversion and extraversion; most of us are well mixed, but it is easier to talk about it by using the half-fictional terms "introvert" and "extrovert".

Jung illustrated his point by describing two young men out for a walk, one introverted and the other extroverted. The introvert sees a castle, and, being an introvert, wonders what is inside. The extrovert, being an extrovert, gets them inside. The introvert finds old books and becomes absorbed in them—that is, his inferior, self-centred, extraversion takes over, and he ends up ignoring his friend. This means that the extrovert is thrown back on his own thoughts and, with his inferior introversion, begins to resent his friend. The harmonious symbiosis they had at the beginning is gone, because the less developed and less socialised side of each has taken over.

It is a common mistake to think that the well-developed introvert is less adapted socially because he is less gregarious. In some ways, he is better adapted: for example, he is usually more reliable than the extrovert. It is just that the introvert reaches inside himself for his gifts to the other, while the extrovert responds, givingly, to the stimulus of the other.

In hindsight (and overlooking Jung's vacillation about whether Freud was extrovert or introvert, *and* his remark on one occasion that Adler was an introvert!), we can offer a useful oversimplification. Freud was more introverted in that he studied what went on inside people, while Adler was more extroverted in that he concentrated on the relationships between people. Freud was an introvert who dug up his unconscious inferior extraversion in the form of his Oedipus complex. Thus, he could understand the games of infantile, poorly socialised, extraversion, such as:

1. clinging without admitting it (the clingy Oedipus complex kept repressed);
2. keeping dissociated and unconscious—unconscious, not just secret—anything in the individual that would spoil their manipulation of the other if it showed;
3. using manipulation of the other to avoid the risks of love.

Conversely, Adler was an extrovert who could understand the temptations of inferior, poorly socialised, introversion, which were:

1.   withdrawal and avoidance;
2.   devalue the other person;
3.   shun emotions (which are the links to the other person);
4.   use distance to keep power, avoiding the risks of love.

Jung claimed that any actual case of neurosis revealed both Freud's and Adler's observations, large as life. Too-long-continued entanglement in the emotional politics of the family of origin (Freud) and lack of courage compensated for by power and superiority (Adler) are two sides of the same coin. Later, Jung said more loosely that a man might have a Freudian psychology until he married and an Adlerian one afterwards. He could have added, and a Jungian psychology when his children are grown up. In an exhilarated little ego-trip during a seminar in Zurich in 1938, Jung said,

> Voluptuousness, the lust principle, is Freud; passion for power is Adler; and selfishness—that is myself, perfectly simple. You see my idea really is the individuation process and that is just rank selfishness ... First came Freud, then Adler ... and mine is the last ... (Jung, 1988, p. 145)

We can hardly dare think what was going on in Freud's mind as he sat in Munich in 1913 and listened to Jung so helpfully *explaining* him. But it was probably a fleabite compared to the really big conflict going on at the time, and in the next chapter we shall find out more about why Freud should feel Jung wanted to kill him.

CHAPTER EIGHT

Jung: the crown prince

"To you all hearts are open"

(Freud, 1961, Letter to C. G. Jung, 2 September 1907)

U nlike his contemporaries, Carl Gustav Jung was a total charmer, and a lot more fun. He had a great belly-laugh, told coarse jokes, and was known for setting his farts alight while camping with his children.

He was a huge, powerful, erect Swiss with a barrel chest, bullet head, and small, sharp eyes; an impulsive, passionately emotional man, at home with sex, aggression, and violence.

There was a nineteen-year age gap between Jung and Freud, which perhaps accounted for the differences between them. Freud was surrounded mostly by men, while Jung was surrounded mostly by women. Where Freud ran a very tight ship in his Movement, keeping everyone in order by complex hidden manipulation, Jung's Psychological Club in Zurich was a mess of conflicts, with Jung in the thick of the ugliest, rudest, and most dramatic of the rows and walkouts. Prudish Freud claimed he gave up sex at forty (there is evidence that that was not quite true), an act with which Jung wholly disagreed:

"The prerequisite for a good marriage, it seems to me is the license to be unfaithful" (MacGuire, 1974, p. 289).

Jung did exactly what he wanted in life and was known for his volcanic rages and sulks. At the age of twenty-three, he fell in love with a sixteen-year-old called Emma. The moment he saw her in pigtails on the stairs, he knew he wanted her for his wife. Not as convinced as he, Emma refused him a couple of times before eventually succumbing seven years later. She was also an heiress and her fortune became his by Swiss law. He was lucky to get her. In contrast to Jung, she was quiet, calm, self-possessed, nurturing of friends and family, and had a firmer grasp of reality than her husband. She was often admired for how she handled him. The more one hears of her, the more one admires her.

Jung's most significant extramarital affair was with Toni Wolff, a patient of his, thirteen years his junior, and who would later become a Jungian psychoanalyst. It was a relationship that lasted over ten years. In a way, Emma befriended her husband's mistress, at first, grateful to Toni for giving her husband the intellectual stimulation that she herself could not. However, as Jung openly flaunted the relationship, Emma's tolerance began to wane. Three times she made the decision to divorce him, but each time changed her mind because he was ill or otherwise needed her.

The son of a country clergyman (me, too, so I know where he was coming from), his childhood was immersed in spirituality and animality. Sex did not come as news to him in the way it did to town-bred Freud, and neither did he regard any aspect of it as taboo. Incest was something people did sometimes, not something to be feared.

Sex feels different in communities where being able to feed one's family depends on the lecherousness of one's stallions, bulls, rams, ganders, cocks, etc. Children see mightier matings in the fields and farmyards than they overhear from their parents' bedroom. They help with lambing and calving, watch the pigs being slaughtered, and also have the educational advantage of animal sex play. When fourteen-year-old Arabella cuddles her pony's head as he is being shod and he gets an awesome erection, she has learnt something.

The country child feels the rooks' delight in surfing the updraught at the cliff, sees the tears frozen on the faces of the cows the morning after their calves are taken away. He sees the bull licking the genitals of the cow as she urinates before sex, the bull calves in the sun playing at mounting each other and trying it on with their mums and aunts too, goats having homosexual unions, red deer masturbating by drawing their penises delicately through the heather, and dogs trying it on with humans.

He discovers the thrill of killing, and perhaps compunction as well; awe at the beauty of the fish or bird or animal he has killed. He has the feel of how creation works, and, somewhere in him, he knows that he is part of a world driven by animal instincts that might have God as the creator.

My mother accidentally clued me up about that as a boy by the special tenderness on her voice when she quoted Francis Thompson's poem about God making the snowflake "to lust of His mind" (Boardman, 2001, p. 192).

Thus, Jung was surprised that Freud made so much of sex. To him, as a country boy, it was everywhere. He was one of those who was not turned on by other people's sex, but rather put off.

He was not a great hunter–killer either, but he thoroughly beat up schoolfellows in fights. A photograph of him as a student, when he used to carry a revolver to go home through the woods at night, shows a young man triumphantly aggressive. He could not bear ever to lose an argument and did not do so. When he became a psychiatrist, no madman ever attacked him, as if sensing what would happen if he did. On one occasion, a woman accustomed to slapping her doctors threatened to hit Jung. "Ladies first," he said to her, but also warned her that if she was to strike him, he would hit her right back. At once, she subsided.

Jung and his family had an uncanny side—telepathy and paranormal occurrences. Once a week, his grandfather would talk with his first, dead wife, who he claimed would come and sit in a chair that was reserved for her weekly visits. Apparently, this all took place without his current, living wife objecting. His mother was deeply into séances, as was Jung as a child. He occasionally showed uncanny telepathic awarenesses, and once or twice poltergeist-like phenomena occurred in his vicinity (the doorbell that rang of its own accord, the blanket that was snatched twice off his daughter's bed, etc.).

Jung and Freud began to communicate in 1906, when Jung sent Freud some of his work. When they met in 1907, Freud began to idealise Jung, and Jung let him. Freud loved Jung's Aryan respectability, joking that he had saved psychoanalysis from becoming "a Jewish national affair" (Bair, 2004, p. 115). At the 1910 Conference in Nuremberg, Freud established the first International Psychoanalytic Association (IPA), announcing Jung as President for life, ignoring protestations from his peers.

Jung was expert at talking to people in their own language and editing himself down to fit into what he thought they could take. He certainly made no exceptions for his role model, Freud. One comic archive of the Movement is the group photograph of the Psycho-analytic Society in 1911 at Weimar, which shows Freud (5'7") standing raised on a concealed box and Jung diminishing his six-foot frame by crouching over his wife's chair. So it is a picture of Freud narcissisti-cally posing in the middle of the crowd with Jung apparently know-ing his place.

Sigmund Freud and Carl Jung at Clark University, Massachusetts, USA, 1909.

Poetry reading, Edinburgh, 1962. Author standing, second from left.

Freud twice fainted at Jung's speeches as he expounded his own theories and it was not long before the cracks began to emerge in their relationship. In 1912, Jung published *Transformations and Symbolisms of the Libido*. In it, he described the incest theme as a religious symbol, a theory completely at odds with that of his idol. Freud recoiled from the betrayal. After their final quarrel, Freud never spoke the name of Jung again (well, hardly ever), while Jung would complain of Freud at length whenever he got the chance.

It is impossible for us fully to appreciate the achievements of those early fathers of twentieth century insight because, educated by them, we cannot really empathise with the blind ignorance of where they started.

Jung's life began with experiences he could not comprehend, and influences that would stay with him all his life. With a father and eight uncles in the clergy, it was little wonder that Jung's early thoughts were steeped in religion.

At age three or four, Jung had his most momentous dream, "a dream which was to preoccupy me all my life" (Jung, 1965, p. 11). He dreamt of an erect pillar of flesh enthroned in an underground chapel. He then heard his mother's voice call out that this pillar was "the man-eater!" Thus, he got the impression from his mother that the Devil ate children, but Jesus would eat them first to prevent the Devil getting them. Terrified, he was afraid to go to sleep for a while after that in case he had another frightening dream.

Much, much later, Jung interpreted the pillar of flesh as a ritual phallus, a God under the ground, with echoes of cannibalism underlying the symbolism of the Catholic Mass. He told no one of that dream until he was sixty-five. Reserve, secrecy, and keeping his real thoughts to himself was a necessity for him to survive through the first half of his life—no one near him could have suspected what was going on inside him.

However, his early confusion with religion did not stop there. At the age of twelve, Jung came out of school in Basel, looked at the cathedral, admired it, thought of God sitting in the beautiful blue sky above, and this aroused feelings in him that he knew to be wrong. For days, he wrestled in agony, using all he had been taught at home, in church, and at school, to try to manage these dangerous thoughts.

In his anguished reflections, he thought about how God had set up Adam and Eve to sin; drawing the conclusion that it must have been what He intended all along. In the end, he concluded that it could only be God who wanted him to think the unthinkable, so he let himself think what he wanted and felt an enormous good feeling that he called "grace".

The thought he had been so desperately trying to quell was one of God shitting from heaven on the cathedral. This perception was so at odds with his upbringing and his family life that it caused Jung to question the God that his father and uncles spoke of in their sermons.

It was a long time before Jung could even begin to understand, and then tell, what he knew from the age of three. He made a beginning in 1911 with the book that he knew as he wrote it would lose him Freud's friendship. But it was only a few years before he died that he finally started writing the astonishing simple truth of his lifelong dealings with God, his mother and father and his childhood; stories at the root of his life's work. In an attempt to keep his personal life private,

Jung's secretary Aniela Jaffe and daughter Marianne bowdlerised the book even as he was writing it. As a result, *Memories, Dreams, Reflections* was published only about two years after his death, by which time the battle to publish what Jung actually wrote was, for the most part, largely won. (Editor's note: written before the publication of *The Red Book*, by C. G. Jung, published by Norton in 2009.)

To give Jung his due, as early as 1909 he did try, but in vain, to tell Freud what was really going on in his mind. Once, on the ship going to America, he recounted to Freud a dream that had hinted to him how the unconscious mind extends into really, but *really*, unknown territory. He described a dream where he had been in a house in which each storey was older than the one above it. He went down and down into successive cellars; the lowest dated from Roman times, but still below it there were steps down into a cave cut into the rock, where he found two disintegrating ancient skulls.

Freud interpreted the dream as being about death wishes, and Jung dishonestly pretended to accept his idol's theory. Privately, Jung thought that really the dream signified the existence of the primitive psyche, "bordering on the life of the animal soul" (Jung, 1965, p. 160). This was a revelatory experience for Jung and served as a catalyst for the book that would end his friendship with Freud.

Jung formulated the theory of a *collective unconscious*, a term he used in books and lectures, but in informal conversation was just as likely to refer to it using the word God. As he said, we just do not know how far the unconscious extends, any more than we know how far the universe extends.

To put it another way, Jung recognised something in the turbulent chaos going on below consciousness, something that Freud called primary process thinking. He saw that the basic themes of religion, wishes, and passions come from somewhere deeper than ourselves.

As a young psychiatrist, Jung had been fascinated by the mad utterances from some of his psychotic patients. Often, they would refer to mythological motifs and archaic symbols. This led Jung to believe these thoughts emanated from ancient images buried deep in the unconscious.

The book that caused the rift with Freud, *Transformations and Symbolisms of the Libido* (1912), was about a young woman called Frank Miller, whom Jung thought suffered from schizophrenia. This woman retreated into fantasies that were full of mythology that she had never been taught, but which came out of her own unconscious mind. At first, she regressed to fantasies of the parent as a love-object, but then moved on to images such as God, sun, fire, snake, etc. Jung drew from this that the libido was not wholly related to sexual energy (as Freud had claimed) but also sprang from psychic energy.

Thus, Jung distinguished between two types of imagination. The first is when we play with fantasies that are under our control, using metaphors and mythological symbols that are part of our language and culture, taken from *other people's minds* through art and literature, or religious studies in school, or wherever.

The second is the kind of imagination that intrudes from the unconscious, the raw unprocessed original symbols which push themselves unasked into our minds from behind or below or above or anywhere, appearing in dreams, hallucinations, or other spontaneous imaginings. Jung believed that when we hear from the inner depths, we are hearing the voices of our real masters, our own living instincts, the It that is living in us. The schizophrenic talking to his voices is talking to real forces in him that control him and are trying to live his life for him, and can—though rarely—force him to kill and maim in reality.

During the second half of the century, I had many patients who had suffered secondarily from the effects of the Second World War. Many of these came from families where father had gone to war and never returned, or had come home but was crippled in body, soul, and mind.

One of my patients taught me a lot about schizophrenia. Fate had dealt him a hard hand of cards. His father had been killed in the war when he was a baby, and he had grown up fatherless and with no brothers. I first met him when he was coming out of a psychotic episode. His Voice had told him that he was the Messiah, his father, God, and Gerard Manley Hopkins, the Holy Spirit. He believed it. Then the Voice told him it was blasphemous to believe it and that he should plunge his hands in boiling water as punishment, and so he did.

His Voice took part in our conversation. He told me his first wife had done nothing for him, but then his Voice butted in and contradicted what he had just said, saying that his first wife had actually been a very good friend to him and still was.

I realised that his Voice was what I would call thoughts popping up from the back of his mind. During one session, he asked if I would read his writings, and in my compulsive placatory way, I was about to agree, but *my* Voice quickly put in, "Don't! You'll resent the time it takes." I quickly did a deal with my Voice and said to my patient, "Yes, of course—I'll charge you for the time." He laughed and agreed.

What I noticed was that when he was in a psychotic state he could not reconcile those clashing impulses in the same way I could. Also, he could not treat an intruding symbol merely as an informative metaphor, instead taking it literally, concretely. When my patient was ill, there was no cleared space in his mind, no debating chamber or boxing ring where impulses could be discussed before action. There was no room for interpretation of symbols and no function where conflicts could be worked out.

One recovering schizophrenic described the blissful feeling of the cleared space in her mind as being on an island with a dry beach where thoughts could wash up only when wanted, so that they could be dealt with one at a time.

From my experiences with schizophrenia, I found that a big difference between my mind and those of my patients was the inability of their conscious mind to handle the messages from their unconscious. A lot of us receive the same messages occasionally, voices that tell us, "I am pretty marvellous—godlike even", or negative voices that tell us we are "evil". But we only believe them a little. However, my patient's Voice just walked all over him; this gave me a feeling for the weakness of the conscious mind in schizophrenia. In his recovering state, he saw how his belief system came from within, telling me with a wry smile, "We [schizophrenics] all have our own homespun religion!"

The 1912 version of Jung's controversial book is full of obscurities and hard going to read. Jung had a mind like an ammunition dump on fire, so it is difficult to make a system out of Jung's super-prolific sayings and writings. His style was the opposite of Freud's pedantic, patient, persistent, systematic thought, one that ticked along steadily like an elegant ormolu clock. But the book made two things clear: that Jung believed human desire to be not only related to sex, and that fantasies of incest were not literal (as Freud understood), but were part of religious mythology.

Freud was outraged that his "dear son and successor" (McGuire, 1974, p. 343) had moved away from his theories, and saw Jung's differing opinions as a treacherous stab in the back. Over the next few months they gradually stopped communicating.

Losing Freud in 1913 was a huge blow to Jung. Freud had been his best friend, the older man, the courageous leader and father, and a genius who had explained the psyche to him in the early days. Freud had loved Jung in his touchy controlling way, and for Jung to lose his master and idol hit him hard.

His son Franz described how Jung threw himself into childhood play, at first with his children and their cousins on holiday. They played a wild game of Indians and English; each side had a horse and they burned down each other's wooden tepees. This was in stark contrast to the way Freud spent his family holidays, preferring to pick flowers and look for mushrooms.

Jung became disorientated for at time, and his dreams and visions during this period (outlined in *Memories, Dreams, Reflections*) were weird and sometimes terrible, and took him over the edge of madness for a while, or something very like it. He had conversations with inner figures with which he sort of hallucinated, similar to having a waking dream. One was a wise old man called Philemon (reminiscent of his childhood's No. 2 personality), whom he painted beautifully as an old man with wings, and who said to him things he would never have thought of for himself. Another was an unknown woman whom he came to call the Anima, the soul, who also had a life, will, and ideas of her own and had to be dealt with accordingly.

Jung's genius was that he was quite extraordinarily open to input from the inner world (or the collective unconscious, or It, or whatever one calls it). He could access his deepest thoughts without falling prey to them. He had an extraordinarily strong sense of self with which to digest whatever came at him. Like my patient, he, too, for moments felt like a God, but to Jung it was just an experience and not a literal truth.

This was a weird adventure of Jung's: on the border of normality, if not right over it. For him, it was a new beginning in his great love affair with the unconscious. In his childhood, God had intruded on him uninvited, scaring and disturbing him. In those early days, God had assaulted him, but now Jung had totally seized the attacking role for himself; the hunt was up for what he could find in the unconscious, and his hopes and expectations were high.

He and Freud had opposite expectations from the unconscious. Freud found an evil, sensual, and murderous child in himself, whereas Jung believed the unconscious to be a neutral entity, only a problem when the attitude of the conscious mind is unhealthy.

Jung's weird experience had several outcomes. He believed that the unconscious mind of the patient had a "back door" which could access both basic instincts and the sources of old and new culture. It was able to provide impulses and understandings superior to anything already present in the conscious mind of both the therapist and the patient.

Jung wanted patients to have an experience like his, to hallucinate their own instincts or archetypes and have conversations with them. However, not many of his patients ever experienced this and, in my career, I have never met anyone that could tap into their unconscious the same way Jung could.

One or two of his patients had visions, but mostly he used what he called "active imagination", encouraging his patients to sit down and paint or draw whatever came into their heads.

But dreams came strongly into his treatment, which he called "analytical psychology" to distinguish it from Freud's "psychoanalysis". Sometimes, he made no bones about it being a search for religious experience: "All science is merely a tool and not an end in itself" (Jung, 1972, p. 377). And again, "Analytical psychology only helps us to find the way to the religious experience that makes us whole" (Bishop, 2002, p. 23).

True, there was a limitation in wanting the same for his patients as he had himself. Just as Freud's trainees and patients were encouraged to uncover an Oedipus complex, Jung's followers and patients had to have a direct experience of the awesome archetypes.

Jung also adopted the term *Persona* for the "mask" we put on for everyday life, the outward image we portray to others while concealing our true selves. He called the hidden part of our personality "the Shadow". For example, the Shadow of a criminal, or of a policeman in a police state, might contain soft impulses of sympathy or kindness that he has had to repress for fear his life would be endangered. In fact, the feeling of pity became generally dissociated and repressed within the Third Reich.

I had a patient who had been educated at Borstal, where he had been taught to be hard and ruthless. However, years after his harsh education, he could neither bear to see children suffering nor stand the feelings of sympathy or pity that came up into his conscious mind. Jung thought that people who prided themselves on being gentle, good, and peaceable were more likely to be haunted by a violent criminal "shadow". Similarly, someone whose ego ideal is being coolly rational might have an irrational moody self.

Jung believed that dreams tried to compensate for one-sidedness in the conscious attitudes. The "shadow" appears in dreams to compensate for our conscious bias, and is, therefore, to be respected, mastered, and befriended. He liked it when people's Shadows showed and delighted in provoking people to lose their cool and show their nasty side.

Jung claimed that dealing with the Shadow was his apprentice work, while dealing with the Anima and Animus was his masterwork. He believed that every man has an *Anima*, an unconscious feminine side, and every woman has an *Animus*, an unconscious masculine side.

We can choose to live out the opposite sex side of ourselves, or we can project them elsewhere; they can be in a good or bad state inside us, and they can be dead dangerous. Sometimes we project Anima and Animus on to others, whom we then see as magically attractive, or evil, or whatever.

While exploring his own anima, Jung came across several mythological archetypes in his own fantasies and was especially impressed by the way squares and circles appeared in his dreams. For a while, he drew or painted a mandala (Sanskrit word for circle) himself every day that would turn out to have a special form relevant to that day of his life. He saw the mandala as a symbol of perfection, wholeness, and completeness. Jung described this process of becoming whole as *individuation*. By joining the unconscious with the conscious and harmonising different parts of the Self, Jung believed we could all achieve individuation.

He also believed that people had differing personality types and fell into the categories of being introvert or extrovert. Jung regarded himself as an introvert and, thus, expected truth and energy to come from inside him rather than from others. His writings were all about the inner world, and one can get a wrong impression that individuation was *all* introversion. But, actually, Jung thought it natural to start looking inward to the collective unconscious, or God, only after we have properly grown up and become rooted in the *outer* world, in the community, through work, marriage, social standing, etc.

Toni Wolff, his own wife, children, and profession kept him grounded during his crisis. I do not know what he would have made of the

1960s fashion of dropping out to "find oneself". Although, he had taken Freud's rejection of him badly, it had also provoked a growth spurt in Jung, not only in finding his own inner depths, but also improving his ability to relate to others more authentically.

Not only was Jung operating twenty years later in European history than Freud, but he thought and conversed and argued in a Swiss culture that had gone through different developments from Freud's: the fourth century conversion to Christianity, the Reformation, and the political upheavals connected with it. Freud had been influenced by these, too, but less directly, and was scalded by Jung's "Aryan religiosity". Freud retreated, pulling his Jewishness, his Jewish disciples and interlocutors, closer around him. Freud's mind was structured differently from Jung's: it was like the Austro-Hungarian Empire with a superego for emperor and a dream censor for secret police. In contrast, Jung's mind operated more like Swiss democracy, with constant referendums, listening to the will of the people.

Jung's weird experience, borderline pathological though it was, was the logical next step for world culture. Great men in the past founded religions by sourcing for themselves through a "creative illness", and these great individuals passed on what they could to their followers. But Jung saw that latching on to a great religious genius instead of finding one's own source can kill one's own experience of God.

Jung found an even more radically subversive precedent for his analytical psychology in alchemy. He discovered that alchemical books were full of the same archetypal images as those that appeared in the dreams of himself, his patients, and his students. Jung saw the substances found in alchemy as metaphors for the personality and the way it operates in life. Whether the alchemists themselves realised they were playing with the heat of their emotions of love and hate and projecting them into their chemicals and furnaces is not clear.

At the time, alchemy led to chemistry, and science was seen as hostile to religion. Jung claimed to have resolved the clash between religion and science by making a boundary: science can study religion by recognising that its images can appear spontaneously in the psyche of man and always have, but science cannot tell whether the images of God refer to a reality beyond themselves. That is the boundary. Neither Marx nor Freud saw it or respected it, and, as a result, could only approach religion dogmatically rather than scientifically.

Jung's near-psychotic experience was an acute example of the latest advance in evolution: our new-found ability *as a separate individual* to face the roots of our energy in their form of inner sub-personalities—finding, meeting, taming, and cultivating them like hunters and farmers and colonisers of the inner world, while letting them live in us and become us after we have confronted them as others. We live in this shifting ambiguity and have to get used to it. We are not merely lived by the It but can turn and face it, know it, and do deals with it.

Thus, we have to acknowledge the terrible power of the archetypes–instincts even when they appear in consciousness in the flimsy forms of imagination. They are comparatively safe as art, but in living minds they are projected between people and can release powerful human interactions. Remember what happened when a neurotic and his community got possessed by it and got it wrong in Germany in the 1930s and 1940s.

Freud's exposure of the destructiveness of the too-powerful super-ego is more than confirmed. If aspiration is what turns you on, then stop aspiring to perfection. The Self wants you to live out all of yourself, not just the facile, esteem-seeking good bits. So *wholeness* should replace perfection as your ideal—if you need one.

Salvation, cure, rebirth all start with irresponsibility, with play. Play must be taken dead seriously; seriousness and work must be subordinated to, and serve, play. Shakespeare's plays are published as his Works, but they had to start as play and, some say, so must psychotherapy. Play is living imagination, and, at its highest value, it is God.

For Freud, God was a wish-fulfilling illusion, the imagined ideal parent giving perfect care and love, a neurosis, an idea used by top dogs to manipulate underdogs. For Jung, God was someone he met and had dealings with in his dreams and fantasies, which came at him in different forms.

It has to be remembered about Jung, too, though, that in spite of all his wide cosmic thought, he once said that his great aim was to become an ordinary human being. Later in his life, he half-joked that all he really wanted was to pass the time drinking in taverns, if only his liver could stand it.

CHAPTER NINE

Jung and God

"I am distressed for you, my brother . . ."

(2 Samuel 1:26)

The above epigraph, from the Second Book of Samuel, introduces Jung's book *Answer to Job*, published in 1952 when he was seventy-seven. The awful thing he claimed in the book was that God was partly evil. No one seems to talk about this. In my long training as a Jungian analyst, no one ever asked me how I was getting on with God being partly evil.

Jung's genius lay in the unusual access between his conscious and unconscious minds. For him, he had access to the other world, the face of God. "The difference between most people and myself is that for me the 'dividing walls' are transparent. That is my peculiarity" (Jung, 1965, p. 355).

He thought his perception of the stream of life might have been triggered by his early dreams. But his most profound experience came in the form of a heart attack, which he had at the age of sixty-nine. This was essentially what we would call a "near death experience" (NDE) (Jung, 1965, p. 309), and had a great impact on Jung, himself, and his writings.

Whereas most people who have an NDE float above their bed for a bit, go through a tunnel to a bright light, and have an adventure in the next world for maybe some minutes, Jung floated a thousand miles up above the world and had nightly visions for three weeks. (Typical! we exclaim enviously.) As NDEs are said to do, it changed him. Each day he returned to the boring drab world of reality, and it depressed him, then at night everything changed.

> I felt as though I was floating in space, as though I were safe in the womb of the universe—in a tremendous void, but filled with the highest possible feeling of happiness . . . (Jung, 1965, p. 293)

> It is impossible to convey the beauty and intensity of emotion during those visions; They were the most tremendous things I ever experienced . . . I would never have imagined that such experience was possible. It was not a product of imagination. The visions and experiences were utterly real; there was nothing subjective about them; they all had a quality of absolute objectivity. (Jung, 1965, p. 295)

When his heart illness began, he felt a bit to blame, as though there must have been something wrong with his attitude for him to get ill. But then he thought that his illness had instead given him an opportunity to affirm his own destiny to endure, even when disasters occur. When such incomprehensible things happen, it is the ego's chance to turn defeat into victory.

It was after this experience that he wrote his deepest works, like *Aion* (1951), *Answer to Job* (1958), and *Mysterium Coniunctionis* (1956). *Aion* begins grandly, but is all about fish, *Mysterium Coniunctionis* is too deep for me, but *Job* is something else.

Jung had heard voices of God from the collective unconscious in his own dreams, fantasies, and hallucinations, and had seen how, in schizophrenia, the same voices spoke in delusions and hallucinations and were taken literally and not understood. In *Answer to Job*, he wrote about voices of God in the fantasies, dreams, and visions of the men who wrote the Jewish–Christian Bible. The God of the Old Testament is clearly not good—no need here to go into details of his behaviour.

When Jung spoke about God, he talked about his experiences, rather than his beliefs. So, in 1959, when John Freeman of the BBC asked him if he now believed in God, he replied, "Now? . . . Difficult to answer. I *know*. I don't need to believe. I know" (Freeman, 1959). But then Freeman went further and asked for a clarification of Jung's interpretation of God, for example, did Jung mean by "God" something that forces us to do wrong? Or were they talking about completely different beings? As if, on one hand, a God who is good whom we never meet and who might not exist, and, on the other, a God who is partly evil and is constantly getting at us from the unconscious, and sometimes pushing us to do bad things.

Jung's solitary development had put him two steps away from the rest of us, not just one: first, he did not believe in what people usually interpreted as "God", and, second, he did not "believe in" what he meant by God either. He had interactions with and knew a real living agent. Thus, how could he possibly get across what he was talking about?

> It is the problem I so often had to deal with in treating the neuroses of intelligent patients. It can be expressed in a more scientific, psychological language; for instance, instead of using the term God you say "unconscious", instead of Christ "Self", instead of incarnation "integration of the unconscious", instead of salvation or redemption "individuation", instead of crucifixion or sacrifice on the Cross "realisation of the four functions or of wholeness". I think it is no disadvantage to religious tradition if we can see how far it coincides with psychological experience. (Jung, 1977, p. 736).

This did not always work. One intelligent modern man was not taken in. After a conversation with Jung, H. G. Wells said, "Sounds suspiciously like God to me—never knew why he side-stepped the word so often" (Hayman, 2002, p. 293).

From early childhood, Jung set against the Christian insistence that God is good, a belief held by his father and everyone around him, since his own experience of God within him had *not* been good. From the time of his terrifying first dream involving the underground God onwards, Jung was very cautious about the promptings from within. It took days of anguished thinking, at the age of twelve, before he could allow God to make him think of God Himself shitting on the Cathedral. Then, when Jung did this wrong thing that he thought God wanted of him, he thought he had God's reward by feeling very good indeed. But that did not make him casually ready to give in to the voices.

He was specially guarded against urges coming by way of the Anima, although with regard to his affair with Toni Wolff, his grandson, Dr Rudolf Niehus (himself an analyst), did not think he was guarded enough.

Jung had a different view of his affair with Toni. He had received a message from God that He wanted Jung to live out all aspects of his personality, not just the good bits. People followed him in this, and "Wholeness, not Perfection" became the goal of aspiration in Zurich. How sexually promiscuous this made him is not fully known. The Jungian analyst, Jolande Jacobi, once told John Layard that Jung tried to seduce her (he also threw her downstairs once when he was so angry with her), but she said he was so inelegant about it that she could not be bothered.

His relationship with Toni became utterly serious and, at first, it was hell for her, Jung, and Jung's wife, Emma. Once, while he was swimming, Jung had the momentary impulse to drown himself, but he just would not give up either woman. In the end, Toni learnt to put up with cold treatment, the tricks played on her by Jung's children, and others in the Club, and accepted that she would never be a wife and mother. Emma, meantime, made an astonishing adaptation to her husband's mistress, a testament to the depth and largeness of her personality, and, eventually, they formed a working partnership of three (albeit, a partnership still full of tensions). In Jung's terms, this relationship must have been what God wanted.

So, Jung believed that the real God that we actually experience is dangerous because He is partly evil. Jung once said that the words "lead us not into temptation" give the game away, and that if the early fathers of the Church had been more alert they would have censored them out of the Lord's Prayer.

In *Answer to Job*, Jung described how the God who spoke out of the collective unconscious to the writers of the Bible had evolved in time. (He once remarked in a letter that, for all we know, God may have evolved further in other inhabited planets than he has here on earth.) He described how God's nastiness (already well described in earlier books of the Bible) was so shown up in His disgraceful behaviour towards Job that when Job (in spite of how evilly he had been treated) appealed to Him, He, God, was provoked to try to do better, which he did by becoming man, a good man: Christ. But the bad side of God did not go away: the God of the collective unconscious is made up of opposites, and we still have to deal with the dark side of God, Satan, the opposite of Christ. God is in conflict with himself, and man as an incarnation of God "becomes a vessel filled by divine conflict" (Jung, 1958, p. 89). Talking to the historian and philosopher, Mircea Eliade, about *Answer to Job*, Jung said that Satan represents evil, and that the only possibility of integration is to raise the it to the level of consciousness; in other words, a similar process as individuation. If we took the trouble to observe the messages of dreams and waking dreams, they can bring solutions to psychological crises. The collective unconscious, he said, already has the solution, since every imaginable situation has already been foreseen.

"He was seduced by the Dark Side of the Force" (Lucas, 1977), said Alec Guinness so gravely as Obi Wan Kenobi in *Star Wars*, when explaining the evil Darth Vader to Luke Skywalker. Whether this observation that the Force has a Dark Side came from Jung by way of George Lucas's guru, Joseph Campbell, or whether it was Lucas's own discovery of the terrible truth, I do not know. He never replied to my letter asking him. The film came out twenty-three years after the English language publication of *Answer to Job* in 1954. *Answer to Job* maybe reached thousands; *Star Wars* reached millions, so the thought has been dropped into plenty of minds and hearts, and might have met there the same message coming from each individual's unconscious mind. But it is no good thinking it unless you think it with enough energy to realise what it means.

The traditional Christian dogma of God's omniscience is a bridge to acknowledging that God shares every evil pleasure that any man ever has, along with every other feeling that anyone ever has. So where was God at Auschwitz? He was hoisting people into the singing trees to die slowly overnight, where they screamed inhumanly through closed jaws perforated with the meat hooks they were hanging from. He was throwing living babies into the gas furnace with the best of them, and enjoying it, but also suffering the misery. That is what is meant by Jung's detached words about man being filled with God's conflict with himself. If we look into the inner world through dreams and fantasies and intuitions and believe we are seeing the Id, or the Collective Unconscious, or the Self, we are less likely to see eyes looking back at us than if we think we are seeing God or his agents.

Jung's uncovering of the psychological roots of religion could be the part of the Enlightenment of the Mind that will become politically useful in the twenty-first century, especially with regard to the increasing influence of religious fundamentalists.

The evidence of Creation is that God was not evil, but only stupid and blundering—imagine trying to reach love in a creation based on the mutual fierce devouring of all creatures. He has never been cleverer than his creation at any given stage of the wasteful sequences of trial and error in which evolution proceeded. About eight years after *Answer to Job*, when he was about eighty-five, a benign old Jung wrote at the end of *Memories, Dreams, Reflections* a deeply moving testament. It was almost like a deathbed repentance or prophecy. It is put with some clumsiness, as he seems to navigate his way through reflection and rationality into feeling. This, rather than *Job*, is better for the last word on Jung. He speaks about love, and how he has encountered love in work and life but never been able to explain it, and how we are merely the victims and instruments of love, of "cosmogonic"[1] love—and we are at its mercy, and we might as well call it God.

By now, it might seem that the three great founders of the twentieth century Enlightenment of the Mind, Freud, Adler, and Jung, were so different from each other that it appears impossible to believe that they were all contributing to the same development. However, in the next chapter, I shall show how each of them played a significant role in shaping the movement.

Note

1.   "Creating the universe".

CHAPTER TEN

Clashing swordsmen

"In peace the sons bury their fathers, but in war the fathers bury their sons"

(Herodotus, 2004)

F reud's gift to humanity came from his Oedipus complex, Adler's from his inferiority complex, and Jung's from his God complex, though Jung, himself, only rarely used the phrase "God complex" to describe his particular experience of the "It".

Neither Adler nor Jung *left* Freud: Freud sent them away. Freud would have been twice as great a leader if only he could have assimilated Adler and Jung. That would have been asking a lot, though, like saying if only Judaism had been able to assimilate Jesus and Mohammed. However, it is a pity that the three analysts never came together with a friendly and competent therapist (in the same way as Jung's wife, Emma Jung, and his lover, Toni Wolff) to enable the necessary emotional dogfight, rather than Freud avoid it by sending them away.

I say an *emotional* dogfight because the intellectual clash was only a disguise for the emotional. The splits in the "Movement" were a failure of friendship. Freud was emotional about differences that were supposed to be scientific. He felt them as personal and racial. It was not, in his eyes, that Jung was *mistaken* about scientific fact, but that he was "disloyal" and possessed by "Aryan religiosity" (Gresser, 1994, p. 159). But "the Jew endures" (Frieden, 1990, p. 121), as Freud wrote to his close friend and fellow psychoanalyst, Karl Abraham, when discussing the loss of Jung and the other Swiss members of the Association, following the controversial Munich Conference of 1913.

So, Jung did not save psychoanalysis from becoming a "Jewish national affair" (Blech, 2004, p. 375), as Freud half-jokingly hoped he would. A great strength of classical psychoanalysis was the special Jewish understanding of family, and to be more knowing about the nature and cause of family loves and hates. Jews appear to be more at home than Christians with regard to the family-creating function of sex and sensuality. I remember being greatly struck by an advertise-ment for lipstick in a Tel Aviv cinema in the 1960s—in a matter of seconds the ad showed that wearing the lipstick would lead to a husband and a string of children for the happy user. Where I come from, cosmetics were associated with rape, prostitution, and hell.

The Psychoanalytical Movement itself was like a great big extended Jewish family: bound together by the family emotions aroused in the "transference" by the training analyses to which they all had to submit, they were strongly united against outsiders, while also riven by internal disagreements. From another viewpoint, the Movement continued the beleaguered psychology of the *stetl*, a mind-set where Jews had accepted, and were accustomed to, ridicule by society, while also knowing their own culture to be superior. Similarly, Freud and his Movement felt hostility and contempt from the medical establishment and society, but also knew, as Freud put it, that they "possess the truth" (Steele & Swinney, 1982, p. 257). When Freud's "dear son" (McGuire, 1974, p. 343) Jung looked outside that truth, Freud felt *personally* hurt and betrayed.

To "possess the truth" was essential to Freud's fight for survival, or his sense of existing. He wrote to a friend once that he had just picked up a new book by the psychiatrist and philosopher, Pierre Janet, "with beating heart" (Freud, 1957, p. 250), fearful of what Janet might know, but had put it down again with a quiet mind, reassured that Janet did not have a clue. Similarly, when he had read Jung's *Psychological Types* in 1921, he contentedly recorded ". . . no new idea in it. No great harm to be expected from this quarter" (Paskauskas, 1993, p. 424). Why should someone else's new ideas have to carry such a threat of *harm*? Because Freud's unconscious mind was telling him that someone else possessing significant ideas could indeed have harmed him, in case he found them to be true himself. But these "enemies" could have been his friends if he had had a different attitude towards them. As Horney said, *why* can't we think differently and still be friends?

Jung and Adler had little chance to remain friends with Freud against the power of Freud's Oedipus complex. That complex shaped his relationships into the reciprocal role model of rebellious son *vs.* authoritarian father, competing for possession of women. Freud knew that his mother loved him more than she loved his father. This knowledge gave him the confidence to successfully attract and possess his wife, Martha, very definitively. (During their stormy engagement, Martha learned that loyalty to her future husband had to be total, and blind.) However, when the marriage went dead he had no difficulty drawing Minna, his wife's sister, to him, with whom he went on holidays and might have had an affair. Then, in the third generation, he had a firm grip of his daughter, Anna, seeing off any rivals her own age. So, whatever his fortunes in the world, Freud was never without the constant emotional support of a woman at home, through three generations.

Freud saw himself as subversive, the rebellious son to the authority of the prevailing *Kultur*, and as a son, metaphorically killing the father of the primal horde as in his anthropological fantasy and successfully winning over the women. As Oedipus the son he won, but as the authoritarian father of his Movement, he partly failed, because he rejected his "sons" and alienated the new life that he had awakened and nurtured. So, in that, he did badly. His anxious controlling narrowness forced Adler, then Jung, and another great friend and colleague, Ferenczi, into looking like rebellious parricidal sons, which none of them really wanted to be in the first place.

A Jewish saying goes "Of anyone a man can be envious, except his son or his pupil". One of the most poignant joys of fatherhood is when a man realises that his son, whom he thought to be rejecting his values, is actually tapping into the same sources of life but by a different route that might be as good or even better than his own. Sons can see further than their fathers when they are encouraged to stand on their father's shoulders. When fathers know this, and are glad, then it is good. By rejecting these three "sons", Adler, Jung, and Ferenczi, Freud missed out on the joy of seeing them explore and discover a world beyond what he was able to himself.

When Freud was in the process of rejecting Jung, Emma Jung wrote to him, ". . . do not think of Jung with a father's feeling—'He will grow but I must decline' but rather as one man thinks of another who, like you, has his own potential to fulfil" (Dunne, 2002, p. 39).

But Freud could not hear her. There was too much anxiety in his authority, which made it rigid. He believed that he knew only too well what sons wanted to do to their fathers. On their sea trip to America, Freud refused to give Jung a certain association to one of his dreams. When Jung asked him why not, Freud replied: "Because I would lose my authority" (Jones, 1993, p. 222). Though he often acted diffident, Freud was a tyrant. One or two people told him this, and he agreed that it might very well be so, but evidently he did not feel anything needed to be done about it. He described himself as a *conquistador*, meaning a combination of explorer and dominator—a very apt portrayal.

Freud was unaware of the fear behind his need to be on top and in control. It was not exactly an Adlerian fear of failure, nor was it his fear of instinct, which he *did* know all about. The fear of being murdered by his "sons" expressed, rather, another fear that only came to be understood later in the century: a primal panic over possible loss of separate identity, loss of boundaries, and loss of self. If his sons showed a deeper grasp of truth, then he would be undermined, dissolved. To his fearful mind, if they had a different view they *had* to be wrong. (It was said that Freud had such a fear of having his mind taken over that he would not read much Nietzsche, although Nietzsche's books sat on the shelf in his study in Hampstead.) His defences were a mental rejection of other men's truths, control, mastery, authority, and success.

Not long before he died, Freud made a recording for the BBC about himself, where he spoke about how, although he had been despised and rejected at first for his theories, he had become the respected creator of a great international movement—that was the kind of worth he needed in order to feel like himself.

If only, earlier in the century, Freud could have believed in his "sons'" love for him, and accepted the truths they offered as gifts, not attacks, then everything might have been different. Their gifts to him could have made him a happier and more effective man. If Adler had been allowed to suggest to Freud that he was too anxious in his pursuit of power and superiority, then Freud might have been able to consider this, and allowed himself to be let off the hook for his neurotic drive for exclusive control. He also might have been able to pacify his alarmist superego and learn, not intellectually, but heart to heart, from Adler the satisfactions of social feeling. Then he might have worried less about the future of psychoanalysis, and more about the future of humanity, and, consequently, become a greater leader.

Thus, treated with more trust and friendship, Adler, in turn, might have relaxed and become more open to more of Freud's feeling for the unconscious mind with its hidden treasures of aggressive and erotic instinct that empower social feeling. Adler the extrovert remained suspicious of anything inside himself, and believed that we only think when frustration forces us to. For example, during war service, Adler found that he was unwilling to send a recovered soldier back to the front line. Then he had a dream that he had murdered someone, which he took to mean that his psyche was thinking up excuses for him being "soft" and wanting to spare the soldier. He said that after that dream he never dreamed again, having decided that dreams were only temptations and undermined the dreamer. *Never dreamed again? Really?* The Anglo-Saxon monk, Aelfric, wrote, in tenth century England, "Some dreams are indeed from God, even as we read in books, and some are from the Devil for some deceit, seeking how he may pervert the soul" (Skeat, 2004, p. 467).

Adler could have believed only the second, and, after the break from Freud, his view was fixed and he was no longer accessible to any different theories coming from his former master.

As for Jung, it has to be said that Jung was someone that Freud was right to fear. When he got into his stride, following the loss of Freud's friendship, Jung's mental exuberance and force did undermine and overwhelm everyone near him. He rarely kept men friends. The Jungian analyst, Mario Jacoby, told the biographer, Deirdre Bair, in 1994,

> Jung was such an enormous personality that it was difficult to have one's own space when with him. He could not help it, it was just his personality. But I also believe it was the reason why women fused with him and men had to quarrel and leave. (Bair, 2004, p. 543)

Perhaps, had Jung and Freud stayed friends, it might have given Jung a better model of friendship.

When Jung finally confronted Freud about his anxious over-control, it was not in friendly candour, it was too late for that. In a letter to Freud in 1912, Jung wrote,

> I am objective enough to see through your little trick. You go around sniffing out all the symptomatic actions in your vicinity, thus reducing everyone to the level of sons and daughters who blushingly admit the existence of their faults. Meantime you remain on top as the father, sitting pretty. (Shwartz, 2003, p. 124)

Again, if only! If only, when Jung revealed his spirituality in *Transformations and Symbols of the Libido*, Freud had not taken it as an expression of personal hostility towards him.

Freud had his own sublime emotions too. In his "History of the psycho-analytic movement", he referred to the "mighty and primordial melody of the instincts" (Freud, 1914d, p. 62). Perhaps if Jung had not been so cautiously secretive for so long, then their thoughts would have gradually unfolded to each other in friendliness; in this case, would Freud have admitted that the awe of the "mighty and primordial melody" was, perhaps, not what other Viennese would have called religious, but what Jung believed as a religious emotion?

Whether it was called religious or not, it was the same emotion that moved both men to create their theories: Freud, who thought that the sexual instinct was a life force, and Jung, who dreamt at the age of three that God is an erect penis. Surely, together, they could have built a better bridge of understanding between them than they did. They were both leaders in a mighty enterprise that had begun with thinkers like Rousseau in the late eighteenth century, and pre-Romantics such as William Blake, and then Nietzsche, continuing through the twentieth century—ideas through which over-civilised man in Europe was recovering instinct. Freud showed the destructiveness of the prescriptive morality of civilisation (*Kultur*), which, to him, was at least partly just mental tyranny justified by religion, while Jung's historical–political background was one in which religion was on the opposite side, the anti-authoritarians, the rebels, the Protesters. ("Extreme Left-wing Protestant" (Parrinder, 1977, p. 92) he once said when pushed to state his own position.)

But both men were actually fighting the distorting value systems of what European culture had become. Freud, like many others, fought by claiming that the God of the churches and synagogues was just a wish-fulfilling illusion, and Jung raged against society by stating that its picture of God was wrong. But the harness was chafing them both in the same place, though they exhibited, apparently, different ways of throwing it off. Similarly, Freud spoke up for the sensual end of the spectrum of love, and Jung *lived* it, and found spirituality in it, too. Freud also knew that sexual instinct was a terror, but from the age of three Jung knew it as a *holy* terror.

Their attitudes to religion seemed opposite, but they were not so much opposites as two generational phases of the same great cultural surge—again, they were like father and son. Freud belonged intellectually to the phase of Nietzsche and Marx and other great liberators of European culture, who tried to free man from the imprisoning husk of a religion that was dead, killed by a nineteenth century civilisation's view of righteous morality and goodness. Jung belonged to the next phase, the rediscovery, in each of us, of the living instincts that created religions in the first place, and that affect us whether called upon or not, and which are better to cultivate than ignore or suppress. These two phases seem to us contemporary because they have taken centuries of overlapping lives to work through.

Today, there are still millions for whom the piety of the old-time religions is enough, because their grip on the sources of vitality and the meaning of life is good and in working order and does not need to die and be reborn. Their deepest heart's desires are confirmed and strengthened by their religion.

Then there are the millions who are flourishing in the exciting realism and freedom of the no-God phase and who will die without ever needing to get past it. They find as much meaning for their lives as a man can handle through family, friends, and politics, as well as in the ongoing awesome discoveries of science.

Or, the millions of people who choose to explore their own spiritual realities. Perhaps, the latter group might say that you have to lose your faith before you can find God.

Others find atheistic spiritualities—after all, Jung's pragmatic interaction with "God" was a kind of atheism if looked at from the point of view of traditional Christianity. Most of the tens of thousands who gave their religion as "Jedi" in the 2001 British census were joking, of course, but not quite all of them. It is a *spiritual* joke. Being a Jedi, relating to the Force, with its Light and Dark sides, can make life more fun, even if it is only taken a quarter seriously.

You might say, stretching it a bit, that Adler (the baptised Christian) represented the first phase of encountering God, the collective unconscious, or whatever you choose to call it, through accepted religion, while Freud was the second, refuting it wholeheartedly, and Jung was the third, by making a creative personal quest for spiritual and, yes, religious fulfilment. (You could see it as a kind of Hegelian thesis–antithesis–synthesis.)

Though each was engaging with his personal complex, all three were fighting on the same side. All of them were exploring the darkness of the unconscious mind, finding great things, and freeing us from being puppets without even knowing it, exposing desires and fears we did not even know we had, and opening our eyes to previously unimagined possibilities of restoration to the true, free, whole, unpredictable surge of natural life and growth. Surely, closer to each other and supported by each other, they could have got through the pangs of anxiety that each would have suffered during the release of the emotional defences that were responsible for keeping their minds and hearts apart. But, by talking about them like this, we are doing it for them; we can see how the things they discovered were more mutually illuminating than mutually incompatible.

I have described the three great originators of the Enlightenment of the Mind. Before we leave the period in which these building blocks were laid down, in the next two chapters I shall look at contributions from philosophy, and the ideas of two existential philosophers of the nineteenth century, Kierkegaard and Nietzsche. Their ideas about religion and how man should see himself and his world seeped in to the popular culture of the twentieth century, and with it our Enlightenment in ways that, I believe, are still not understood.

CHAPTER ELEVEN

Kierkegaard and existential psychotherapy

"People understand me so little that they fail to understand when I complain about being misunderstood"

(Attributed to Soren Kierkegaard)

A good thing about existential psychotherapy is that it encourages the therapist to respect the reality of the patient's actual predicament in the world without interference from psychoanalytic or any other theory. A bad thing about it is that it sometimes respects the patient's conscious mind too much, to the neglect of the unconscious. Ludwig Binswanger gives such an incredibly respectful, empathetic account of his patient's mind in *der Fall Ellen West* that the reader is swept away by respect for her spirit—her defiance, her persistence, her greatness—but after thirteen years of treatment for anorexia, Ellen poisoned herself and died at thirty-three.

The grandfathers of existentialist psychotherapy were two great emotional cripples: Soren Kierkegaard and Friedrich Nietzsche. They were emotional cripples not only because of what death did to their families (Kierkegaard's mother died young, which badly affected the family, and Nietzsche's only brother died when he was four years old, closely followed by his father), but also because the culture they grew up in had a tremendous impact on both men. They took in the culture so totally that it nearly extinguished them, and then, by a very public superhuman convulsion of ridding themselves of it, they changed the course of civilisation (hard to calculate just how much, but they did) and influenced the lives of billions who will never know they existed.

Søren Kierkegaard 1813–1855

Do you remember awesome crossroads in your life with exact recall of place? I remember Thin's bookshop in Edinburgh, in 1947: untidy, busy, opposite the Old Quad of the university; me a teenage art student (also reading philosophy for a Fine Art degree), reaching up and taking Kierkegaard's *Fear and Trembling* (1946) from the shelf while George Ross, a divinity student friend, told me how MacKinnon, the Professor of Moral Philosophy at Aberdeen, had been told by his doctor to stop reading Kierkegaard as the excitement was too much for his heart.

The beginning of the book played with the story of Abraham in different ways and described how the sacrifice of his son, Isaac, might have turned out. I was hooked. I got a real adolescent craze for the Danish Kierkegaard and he appeared in my dreams. In most pictures of him, he looks eccentric and odd, but in one drawing his face is beautiful, with great luminous eyes full of intelligent sensitivity, and that was how I imagined him. I remember a young minister by a field of sheep on the road to the village of Tain, in the Scottish highlands, looking doubtfully at me (with *The Concept of Dread* in my hand) and saying, "Well you're a sensible lad, I'm sure you'll be all right." He was wrong, but it all turned out well in the end, for the mental disturbance brought out by the cocktail of Kierkegaard and the rest of my over-exciting environment took me into my first analysis as a patient at the Davidson Clinic in Edinburgh five or six years later.

With my teenage admiration for my father and attempts to outgrow my mother, I was too ready to be carried away by Kierkegaard's similar mindset. He repeatedly referred only to his father, as though he never had a mother, while a brother of his who went to Canada talked to his hosts only of his mother, as though he never had a father.

Kierkegaard was born in 1813, in Copenhagen, Denmark. His father was the pivotal point in his childhood and youth, whose "crazy upbringing" (Chamberlain & Ree, 2001, p. 326) of him made him unhappy. Michael Kierkegaard was a pious, melancholic man who possessed a deep love for his son and often shared with the child his frightful, melancholic Christian faith. These conversations had a great impact on the young Kierkegaard: on one occasion, his father showed him pictures of great men like Napoleon, Alexander the Great, and others; among them there was a man being tortured to death on a cross: "Who is he?" "That was the most loving person who ever lived" (Rohde, 1963, p. 24), his father replied.

His imagination was extraordinarily developed by his father, who would take him for an imaginary walk in his study, describing imaginary street scenes and incidents so vividly that little Søren was left as tired as if it had all been real. He learned to join in the game and they would invent the drama of their street adventures between them. A sense of duty, of the ethical, was taken for granted as basic, but creative emotional reflection became his life, and he poured it into a literary output that expressed the conflict of his heart and mind (as well as his avoidant hiding-away from others.) He published mostly under different pseudonyms. But these multiple personalities were never for a moment out of his total control, though they were deliberately mutually contradictory; indeed, sometimes his name appeared on the title page as publisher.

His father once told him that when he was a little boy in dire poverty, he was responsible for the lonely job of herding the animals. He climbed a little hill to curse God for his miserable life. However, later on, when he became rich, he suspected it was a kind of divine punishment, and that his children would all die young. However, Kierkegaard was more shaken by another earthquake when his father confessed to impregnating his wife, Ane, out of wedlock. What passed between her and her youngest child we shall never know; maybe it was nothing much, a mutual non-understanding, or maybe she was envious as she was excluded from the love between her son and her husband.

Kierkegaard was a student for a long time, and lived a seemingly extroverted popular social life as a young man about town, somewhat spendthrift and dissolute (possibly just one visit to a brothel, not enjoyed), always highly entertained and brilliantly entertaining to others, belying his inner state. He fell in love with Regine Olsen, got engaged to her, then realised he could not marry her. He could not share with her his tortured inner self, his melancholy, his sexual guilt. Five years earlier, he had written in his journal that he needed to understand what it was that God wished him to do, the "idea for which I can live or die" (Chamberlain & Ree, 2001, p. 15).

So, maybe he had still not found his "idea" and that had to come first, before Regine. Kierkegaard had not the first notion how he could harmonise a love life with what he regarded as his life's work, but he knew God was forbidding him to marry Regine.

He broke off the engagement. What Kierkegaard wrote about God telling Abraham to kill his son was really about God telling him to give up Regine. In one of the versions, Abraham pretends to Isaac that he is just a selfish monster who *wants* to kill Isaac, so as to protect Isaac from knowing that it is God who wants it done, which could have turned him against God. That was what Kierkegaard did with Regine; he pretended he was just a self-indulgent playboy who had tired of her, saying that perhaps when he was older he would want a young thing to rejuvenate him, but not right now, thank you. "She fought like a tigress" (Rohde, 1963, p. 59), he recorded. A man's spirituality is part of his sexual attractiveness to women, and Kierkegaard must have been powerfully attractive to her if she divined the spirituality behind his mask. Her father sacrificed his pride to plead on her behalf. Kierkegaard cried all night for some nights, mourning that he was not allowed to live the good universal human joy of marriage, but had been marked off by God as a separate individual who had to be different. And, yet, perhaps even then he also knew that nothing else would satisfy him than to be the individual called away from the ordinary to a special life adventure, to be the one that will "venture far out, where God can get a hold of you" (Carnell, 1965, p. 62).

God, it seemed, gets hold of you by telling you to do whatever it is that you most dread doing: that is, killing your only son or breaking off your engagement to the girl you love. At seventeen, I wanted a life of dangerous adventure, too, and the thing I could not *ever* imagine doing at that time was to start a certain conversation with my father about sex, so *that*, I thought, was what I would have to do to be like Kierkegaard. I did it in a limited way, but just enough for me to understand what Kierkegaard was thinking.

The *acte gratuit* of the French existentialists is not far from this, but neither Kierkegaard nor I knew that, and still less did we know of the simple psychiatric observation about "antithetic thoughts" which bubble up unwanted in the minds of people who adapt to others too much. For example, this new baby Mary has given me to hold, what if I throw it out of the window? What if I swear at the clergyman when he asks me "Do you take this woman?" etc. What if I jump off this balcony? What if I smashed that priceless vase they are so proud of? What if I . . . ? (unspeakable). It is natural to need to assert ourselves against others, even absolutely mandatory at age two—I WILL open the door myself and you shall NOT help me; and at age fifteen—I WILL wear a miniskirt tonight. It is part of becoming the "I" we have it in us to be.

Sometimes, the antithetic thought demands to be acted out. I used to see a lad, aged thirteen, obese and mother-bound, who had the compulsive impulse to spit at people in the street. He described excitedly, with a scared but beaming face, the delicious dread as he came nearer to his victims, closer, closer, and then DID the forbidden thing! Then he bemoaned and gloated, what a terrible thing to do. Similarly, I once treated a really nice and very talented girl, who could not help peeing from time to time on the floor; it just happened to her, and after a thorough investigation by the genito-urinary specialists she was referred to us. It turned out that she had a dominating mother who owned every cubic inch of every room she was in and every person's thoughts in that room, too. How could she assert herself against her mother? Not by anything she could do or say or even deliberately think.

Even if our environment—Mother, or school, or the Emperor Franz Joseph, or George W. Bush's administration in the White House, or whoever—has hijacked God to support *their* wishes, we can still feel a categorical impulse to assert ourselves, as proof that God is telling us to act out our own wishes for ourselves. It was as unethical of Kierkegaard to dump Regine as for Abraham to kill Isaac, but ethics do not inhibit God, and Kierkegaard invented the phrase "teleological suspension of ethics" (Kierkegaard, 1946, p. v) to cover this situation (which does sound rather like a fancy way of saying the end justifies the means).

The unconscious mind tells people to do terrible things. A friend of mine was stabbed to death in his clinic by a stranger, who later explained to the police that Allah had told him to kill doctors. The Yorkshire Ripper said Jesus had told him to kill prostitutes. In 2003,

Mijailo Mijailovic killed Anna Lindh, the Swedish Foreign Minister, and claimed Jesus had told him to do it, but the examining psychiatrist said he was not insane. Jung, aged twelve, *knew* God wanted him to think of Him shitting on the Cathedral, and Jung did think it. According to *The Washington Post*, President Bush told the Palestinian Prime Minister, "God told me to strike at al Qaeda and I struck them, and then He instructed me to strike at Saddam, which I did" (Kamen, 2005).

We know that young Jung agonised over the command that came to him, and worked through everything he knew before deciding that God did want him to do it. Kierkegaard simply agonised over it. How much did the others worry about it? Would President Bush have been so sure without Rice, Rumsford, Wolfowitz, and Cheney praying with him? In deciding what God wants we might be simply obeying the expectations of our culture, or our family and friends. Or it can be part of the artistry with which our psyche invents and creates our life for us (with our conscious choice or without).

It is part of that artistry to give the highest value, almost at random, to this, or that, or the other. It is like a kind of whim to attribute an impulse to God's will, such as when an artist thinks he will paint in more green leaves here—no, there. It is like the amazing variety of the things that can be holy: a book, a building, water, a woman, a man, a family, a community, a country, a totem animal, a piece of the Dalai Lama's shit, a piece of bread or wafer, a picture, the moment of sunrise, an erect penis or its symbolic representation, anything. Holiness and sacredness are an attitude of reverence taken up by a person looking at something, then secondarily an attribute of the thing looked at. You can confer holiness on things at will; you can garland with flowers whatever your whim tells you. You can do it half for fun, like a friend I had when I was twelve, saying that under his kilt, behind his boy-sized furry sporran, was a god. He must have just discovered masturbation. Obsessive–compulsive disorder can make something an overriding value against our will, in effect holy, though not called so. And there is schizophrenia. How can you *know* when an impulse really is a sacred duty, a command from God?

You cannot, and Kierkegaard believed we could only proceed with fear and trembling and dread and angst, etc., and hope we get it right. The examples above show how much difference it makes if you subject "God's command" to careful critical examination in your head and with your friends, reconciling it, or not, with everything else you know. Schizophrenics lack a cleared inner space for reflection (Jung got it about right), and political disagreement continues as to whether President Bush and his friends gave critical examination long enough. (The French, for example, who have more cultural suspicion of God since 1789, thought definitely not, although it might be that they did not even realise where President Bush's certainty was coming from.)

The Enlightenment of the Mind tells us to make the unconscious conscious, and to wonder if there is an *unconscious* reason for deifying a particular whim, and if possible to get a good hard look at the God who is speaking. Did whoever spoke to Kierkegaard from within have, by any chance, a *reason* in mind for the command that he (or she, or it) did not mention to Kierkegaard? Did a submerged part of his not very integrated personality really *need* him to leave Regine? For a good reason? Or bad? He did acknowledge that losing Regine had made him an author. Losing her supercharged his fantasy. Creative imagination blossomed to fill the empty space. That sounds like a good thing. But was that sufficient reason?

Making a tour of Kierkegaard's different selves as expressed by his different pseudonyms and in his own name, you find in one place a picture of marriage as an ideal state of happiness and goodness, especially when he was complaining at God forbidding him to have it, but in another region there is a clear contempt for women. Woman is *joie de vivre*, he said (not his highest value), which man finds mainly in her as he has not much in himself. In another place she is the sexual bait that traps men; in *The Seducer's Diary*, the seducer congratulates himself for living only on bait and never getting caught.

In his last writing, known as *The Attack on Christendom*, written under his own name, he openly attacked the culture of his society in a series of articles against the Church in Denmark. His hostility, like Nietzsche's attack on *his* culture, was against his own Christian community, whom he accused of being feeble, but, unlike Nietzsche, he attacked it from the standpoint of a religiousness that was more intense, totalitarian, and, as I shall suggest presently, a bit mad. He saw the Danish State Church as being so hypocritically bourgeois and comfort seeking as to be effectually anti-Christian. He said the church was evil to allow young clergymen be seduced by the supreme happiness of "the soft arms of a blameless wife" (Lowrie, 1961, p. 207), as Don Juan puts it to Zerline, so that he seeks first a Church living to support a wife. Then, when that is safely secured, he preaches a fine sermon about seeking first the Kingdom of Heaven, which is what a real Christian is supposed to do, and what he has not done. The cunning venal Church knows "what every politically wise government knows . . . that man is reduced to insignificance by marriage . . ." (Kierkegaard, 1968, p. 215).

One blinks. Is that what Kierkegaard really thought after all? *Man is reduced to insignificance by marriage?* Yes, that was exactly what he thought.

But a man is only reduced to insignificance by marriage if he has too submissive or over-adapting an attitude to women; that is, if he has not outgrown his mother as he should. So, this is why Kierkegaard never mentioned his mother. To the ordinary reader, his writing aches with the absence of a mother's warm embrace that could have softened his lonely agonies. He thinks like an unhappy little boy who needs a good cuddle, but is too proud or mistrustful to accept one. He would flee a woman's compassion. He wrote about himself and Regine in his journal when he was brewing up to leave her, but he wrote in the third person, unable and unwilling to engage directly.

A woman's compassion would have unmanned him, and reduced him to insignificance, he thought. He could never have allowed himself to realise how much he needed the mothering he never had. His whole mother complex was unconscious.

It is easy to understand why Jung could not stand him. Jung saw him as a grizzling whinger, finding excuses to live in the world of thought and not in reality. He thought Kierkegaard talked and talked about fulfilling God's will but actually avoided the encounter with God both inside and outside of himself:

Jung was too normal to be able to empathise with the emotional cripple who did not have the emotional muscles to do anything other than pursue a devious avoidant course back to life (picking up some deep truths on the way). Some of us just cannot grow in a strong way like Jung, and we have to do it in a weak way. Later on, Jung did admit, however, that Kierkegaard could be useful to some people.

As a man, Kierkegaard was a poor thing. Womanless, solitary, and suffering (he once told a Jewish friend how lucky *he* was not to be tortured by Christ), he was laughed at and caricatured in the press for his oddness and his hunchback (he said the ridicule was like being "trampled to death by geese" (Rohde, 1990, p. 78)). He was content to be ailing; he even thought that to "lead a spiritual life while physically and psychically healthy is altogether impossible" (Miller, 1960, p. 90), and he died in 1855, at the age of forty-two, of an undiagnosed illness just as his inherited money ran out. In spite of his grand words about wanting Regine to marry someone else and be happy, he was furious and insulted when she did, as though he expected her to remain some kind of nun in his memory. At the end, he revealed that his entire output was dedicated to her, and he even tried to leave her his possessions, but by that time she and her husband just did not want to know.

His philosophy had nothing to do with reason; it was a tumult of emotional reactions and re-reactions of terror, angst, grief, spiritual lightning, erotic feelings of Mozartian beauty, flashes of joy, and more. He came to hate Hegel's ordered reasonable system. Hegel said that a philosophy is no good unless you can explain it to your cook; Kierkegaard's could not even be explained to an Einstein (being essentially inexplicable), still less to someone like his uneducated mother, who looks out from her portrait like a slightly tight-lipped, bright-eyed—cook.

But, by the way, he gave ideas to those among the dismayed, the defeated, the "beat" generation who wanted to have a real go at life; he was something special, as he was to me. He originated the insight that has been diminished by the silly name of "existentialism": that when I face you *now*, the unpredictable, the unknown *as yet uncreated* present and future between us must override all previous understanding and knowledge, and can shatter it, whether it is what we learnt from our mother and father, or a Hegelian or other system of thought or ideology or a religion, or life attitude or life goal, or anything. We can live on only by signing and handing to the next moment of future an unlimited—but *really* unlimited—blank cheque of blind trust, *unconfined by any previously recognised truth whatever*.[1] Here, we must add another truth so richly and profoundly grasped by our Enlightenment through the century, that for us humans, *being* is, in practical reality, never simply being, but properly means *growth*. To be is to grow and change. *"Being-in-the-world"* is growing and changing along with those we love and hate.

People interpret Kierkegaard's message in different forms. This is the way I saw it: at God's command he resigned himself to doing without Regine, but when Kierkegaard used the word "resignation" it meant *suffering* as deeply and completely as possible the loss of whomever you most love, your only son or your fiancée. Not only the loss of him or her, but, if that person means everything to you, then the loss of everything.

Kierkegaard's Knight of Resignation can, by the famous "leap of faith", become the Knight of Faith. But "faith" did not mean what it means in English religion (i.e., "believing something you know isn't true," as the English schoolboy is supposed to have put it). It meant living as though, however bad things look, everything is going to be all right.

Although Kierkegaard used religious language ("the absurd" is the idea that "with God all things are possible" (Kierkegaard, 2008, p. 32)), he was describing emotional (psychological) processes, which include losing our reason. If you can lose your reason and sense of concrete reality (which he called "finiteness") you can then find a new attitude, which he called "faith", and *return to reality* with it. He defined faith as "spontaneity after reflection". He said, "If I had had faith, I would have remained with Regine" (Kierkegaard, 1946, p. 171).

Plug this into the rest of our Enlightenment. We have talked about the psychotic basis of mental life as it is uncovered in schizophrenia: the schizophrenic's belief that he is Jesus comes from the same root as the ordinary person's confidence that he or his vision of life has something to contribute to others. "I am an experiment to find out if sex is all right," a schizophrenic told me. He was patiently living the experiment he knew himself to be.

We all have somewhere in us, however it may be suppressed and lost, such an irrational assurance that our existence is worthwhile, and has meaning. We need it especially if our unique original vision clashes with the culture that contains and permeates us, so that, if we are to be ourselves, we are forced to transcend our culture (even if only a little). Our culture soaks most deeply into us from the ages of five to fifteen (incidentally, a period when we are most easily hypnotised). We see reality as our culture makes us see it, but we do not know that; we think we are just seeing reality. But our sensations of reality are just as surely determined by the dead who created our culture as the taste of delicious orange in a man's mouth is determined by the hypnotist who gives him an onion to eat, telling him it is an orange.

We can only hope our perceptions are not as falsified as onion into orange, but they might be in some areas if, for example, our culture includes an institutionalised cynicism, or stupidity, or anxiety inter-fering with spontaneous love. *To some extent all cultures do.*

Our culture, for example, hypnotises us to see kindness as a chore and an effort, but in a state of nature it is as much a relief of impulse as sex or eating. Naturally, we can see the distortions more clearly in other cultures than our own. In some North African societies, mothers condone female circumcision as if they know, instinctively, that love for their little daughters must include this operation, or else they will feel unforgivably guilty if they neglect to do it; but *we* can see, as these mothers cannot, that if the little girls scream and complain they might have a point. But if it is something in our own culture, like, say, coming down heavy on children's sex play, our eyes are not so clear.

If the conflict in us turns out to be a conflict between our inborn original vision of love *vs*, "reality", then, if we are to love as we have it in us to love, reality has to give. We can transcend our culture if we are able to draw on the madness in us that we need, and instead see, in some way, that *the reality around us is not real*, and that the absurd might be true: love may somehow be able to work in ways our culture rejects as unreal. We do not need to *know* that what we are doing is insanely rejecting reality, though it is useful for the psychotherapist to know.

What Kierkegaard describes might be a normal growth thing that we would all go through if not hindered by our culture; indeed, every culture has a strong motive (anxious social cohesion) to suppress orig-inality and imagination in most people, especially the least powerful. Some cultures actually do encourage madness in psychotherapy; for example, I once heard of a tribe who would hang their soon-to-be shaman over a fire all night, which encouraged a bit of abnormality, something that was considered useful to him as a therapist.

The second really useful plug-in from Kierkegaard is his observa-tion that the most deadly thing to us is despair, *The Sickness Unto Death*, as he called it. He quoted Shakespeare's Richard II:

> Beshrew thee, cousin, which didst lead me forth
> Of that sweet way I was in to despair.
>
> (Shakespeare, 2007, p. 334)

This is the very crux and heart of psychotherapy. Remember how Adler said psychotherapy is always about encouraging the patient, and Jung said he lends the patient his courage; others, in their own way, have said the same.

My friend John Layard, a Jungian analyst whom we will meet, said what saves us is a change in the direction of our attention. When we have no energy, or good feelings of any kind, and feel the pull of the "sweet way" into despair, we can still choose where to look, whether inside or outside. In other words, we can still choose the direction of our attention. Although hope and despair are infectious, at bottom *the choice to hope or to despair is the purest choice we have, and* can *be made against every influence upon us*. Maybe it is the only real choice we have: all other choices are conditioned by all sorts of influences. It is a choice that needs no energy to make, unlike the "choices" others usually demand of us. (It is nicely symbolised in Coleridge's *The Ancient Mariner*, when, following weeks of helpless hopelessness, he looks at the sea snakes and their beauty awakens an unexpected involuntary reaction in him, and that is the turning point of the poem.)

The effect of all natural impulses and emotions depends on whether they are being used by hope and faith, or by despair. Hate wielded by hope creates love; hate used by despair just kills. The reality around us is decided by choice, because reality *is* and consists of responses to our initiatives. We are in a certain reality if we perceive people, such as Hitler and Stalin or suicide bombers, as simple embodiments of evil (as a baby in a paranoid–schizoid fit sees his mother). But we are in another reality if we take a good look at these evil figures and, instead, see them as pathetic, conflicted creatures too scared to live out the hopeful confidence of the instincts that are trying to live them. Their response is to torture everyone else with their reactions to their own instincts. Your choice really is yours, believe it or not, because it will be what your initiative makes it, and your initiative depends on your choice to hope or to despair.

Faith and despair are infectious, and psychotherapist and client infect each other like patients on a ward. The job of a therapist is to infect his client with enough hope to be able to *feel* despair, to feel his unconscious hopelessness, and to be able to describe the reality of his environment (external or internal). That is the beginning. Then we just might insanely hope. Hope and faith are touched by the irrational roots of the id (or God, or the collective unconscious) to live and create at all costs; despair, on the other hand, is rational and sane. A person choosing the hoping direction sees that life is hell, people really *are* nasty, because in hoping he is allowing his suffering to tell him what people are not, but could be. Hope feels pain, but despair avoids it. Despair says everything is well, all is for the best in the best of all possible worlds. If that's all there is my friends, then let's keep dancing, let's bring out the booze and have a ball, if that's all there is. Hope is willing to tell us that everything is wrong, because it is looking at something despair does not want us to see, in case it would "lead me forth of that sweet way I was in" (Shakespeare, 2007, p. 374).

Kierkegaard's contemporaries did not see anything wrong with Denmark, but he saw the culture and society as full of unconscious despair. However, Kierkegaard was not the only one to perceive his reality differently from others. Nietzsche, often heralded as the grandfather of existentialism, had similar views to his predecessor.

Note

1. This is what Sartre was trying to say by "existence comes before essence", hence "existentialism".

CHAPTER TWELVE

God is dead!

Nietzsche, *The Gay Science*

"After coming into contact with a religious man I always feel I
must wash my hands"

(Nietzsche, 1908)

F riedrich Nietzsche, born in 1844, was grandfather not only to
the existentialists, but to the whole of dynamic psychotherapy.
Every young man in Europe with the least instinct to rebel was
inspired by Nietzsche at the end of the nineteenth century. He died in
1900, but his influence persists: I was so pleased at the television
episode when Tony Soprano's teenage son shocked his parents by
appealing to "Nitch", as he called him, as the authority that God does
not exist. "What!" they chorused, scandalised. Nietzsche's disillusion-
ment, the scathing acid that he poured over traditional values, and his
almost ribald delight in uncovering the *unconscious*, savage, self-
deceiving, and sentimental mess under the *conscious* culture of nice
Christian citizens like his father and both grandfathers (all clergymen), is at the root of the whole Enlightenment of the Mind. Our
Enlightenment, like every other, is partly subversive. I remember a
psychoanalyst who once said that the only reason the English allowed

the Psychoanalytic Movement to take root in London was because the English did not realise how subversive it was.

Nietzsche also continued with an older, subversive perception that came from the French pre-revolutionary *philosophe*, Diderot, who must, therefore, be acknowledged as the *great*-grandfather of our Enlightenment: the perception that civilisation is bad for you. It stunts your normal natural instincts and damages the noble savage in you. I wonder if any of Diderot's ideas influenced Carter and his theory about hysteria as "one of the misfortunes entailed upon the civilised female by the conditions of her existence" (Carter, 1853, p. 93).

Freud avoided reading Nietzsche so that he would not be over-influenced by him, although that would have been difficult, as he was the talk of Viennese café society, and frequently discussed in the popular press.

The unconscious mind, with its disguises, inhibitions, repression, and sublimation of basic instincts, the reaction formations to them, its self-deceit and the contrary hostile emotions, are all ideas found in Nietzsche. Adler's insight about the will to power, and the drive in man to transcend the self are also in Nietzsche.

Like Freud, Nietzsche recognised the force of sex, but, whereas Freud was all about the thwarted mother-incest, Nietzsche was all about sister-incest, acted out with his little sister, Elisabeth. When the book *My Sister and I* was printed in 1951, over fifty years after Nietzsche's death, prominent Nietzsche scholars rejected it because they said it was a fake, or that he was mad when he wrote it. There might be signs of mental disturbance in it, but remember Hughling Jackson's view: mental disturbance no more creates the emotions and thoughts it reveals than a cut creates the blood that spurts from it; this book is the life-blood of genius, and tells us more about Nietzsche than his dissociated sub-personality, Zarathustra.

The book begins with a dream in which the young Nietzsche and his sister are burying their mother (whom Nietzsche hated). The box went into the earth and that was the end of her, but the actual beginning of an incestuous relationship between brother and sister. Nietzsche described how it was the "impotence of Christian love" (Nietzsche, 1951, p. 145) that pushed them into incestuous love, but what he really meant was that he was driven by his mother's destructive nature and Christian repressiveness.

This was how he knew that civilisation and morals—whose highest summation at that time and place was Christian love—were becoming impotent. Ordinary child sex play grew, in the absence of the normal counter-attractions, into passionate love between him and Elisabeth, and their culture could not free them. A tribal culture would have rescued them, no trouble: the older men would have taken the boy in hand and told him, quite specifically, that "you must stop having sex with your sister". Then they would have arranged all sorts of bigger excitements for him and other boys of his age, which would have helped to take him into adult life.

Elisabeth married later (a man who was anti-Semitic, very alien to Nietzsche's views), but Nietzsche did not escape from her control. He had an adolescent affair with a Countess who used him for sex, and, for a while, he was strongly attracted to an Asian girl in a brothel, but the worst threat to Elisabeth's power over him was when he fell in love with Lou Andreas-Salomé, and his sister made him give her up.

His adult life was a neurasthenic nightmare: at first, he was precociously successful, becoming a professor at twenty-four, but resigned nine years later because of ill health. He went to live an avoidant life behind the most concealing moustache of his generation, usually in exile, emotionally solitary, chronically ailing and dependent on chloral, until his final big breakdown in 1889. Zarathustra's triumphantly dominant Superman was the very opposite of Nietzsche in his real life. Significant friendships—Lou Andreas Salomé, Richard Wagner, Paul Ree—did not lead to fulfilment. But he used the tragic illumination given him by his crippling incestuous love to set his generation free from a stifling culture, enabling them by his writing to admit that the God around whom their fathers and grandfathers had built their minds, hearts, and lives was dead.

The function of a culture is to enable love, but the culture of Christian love in the nineteenth century, when Nietzsche grew up, was too shallow and dutiful to contain and cultivate real emotions of love, such as pity, sex, and (as we shall come to see later) hate. You could not have expected it to; you might as well have expected Beethoven to express his feelings in plainsong. It had got too out of touch to nurture his and Elisabeth's sexuality and direct their passion outside the family. It was too weak to digest a person's heartbreak at the suffering of the world.

Nietzsche finally broke down one day in 1889 when he threw his arms around the neck of a horse being beaten in the street, as though the heavy cloud of pity had overwhelmed him, as Zarathustra had predicted. The too-sentimental Christian love of his culture (just think of Victorian hymns) could not contain the true deep passion of pity, God's own hell, "Christ's disease of love and compassion" (Nietzsche, 1951, p. 92). It had lost the hardness required for creation, Zarathustra saw, and without it God had died of pity for men; he had nothing hard and aggressive enough with which to attack and mend the suffering.

Being over-civilised Christian men, Kierkegaard and Nietzsche both missed out on those experiences that tribal societies use to toughen up the muscles of masculine love. They had never sacrificed living animals, brutally severing the attachment bonds they had built up with them; they had never been explicitly and consciously detached from emotional dependence on, and incestuous entanglement with, the women. They had never joined a close-knit body of men initiated together into the spirituality of their tribe, or experienced a firm emotional basis in men's society. They had neither these, nor the unofficial civilised equivalents that many civilised fathers pass on to their sons. They possessed only the official conventional Christian culture—the most advanced civilisation of their time. They both committed themselves to it by revolting against it. Neither Kierkegaard nor Nietzsche could relate well to women, not one little bit, but they could find the freedom of pure creative vitality from deep inside themselves, in reaction to the unconscious despair of their local Christianity.

A friend told me how Nietzsche set him free from the confinement of the culture he grew up in, as Kierkegaard did me. We both agreed that we had been set free from the *prescribed morality* of each culture, the morality of "do as you're told". Nietzsche wrote that what goes beyond "do as you're told", beyond morality, *"beyond good and evil"* (Nietzsche, 1966, p. 90), is the impulse of love.

Kierkegaard and Nietzsche grew up to hate and reject the civilisation of their time, that is, Christianity. Nietzsche called himself not just antichristian, but Antichrist. Yet he "remained a Nazarene to the last drop of his blood!" (Nietzsche, 1990, p. 203). They were both very interested in Jesus, because in Him they saw something different, or, indeed, the opposite of the Christianity they hated. True enough, no religion in history has, in practice, so disowned the spirit of its own founder as Christianity. A way of understanding the culture of the nineteenth and early twentieth centuries could be that Christianity had managed to destroy Jesus by trivialising him enough that he could no longer be a living inspiration. By the nineteenth century, although European Christianity had outgrown quite a lot of its un-Jesus-like cruelty and destructiveness, it was still a nasty piece of work in some ways, and had become banal and useless enough to disgust Kierkegaard and Nietzsche.

Earlier in history, its anti-love was aggressive, blatant, and right-eous; for example, when Philip II of Spain got married, two days of the celebrations were spent burning people alive, presumably for the usual things like reading the Bible in the vernacular, or being secretly Jewish, or whatever: two days of screaming! Everyone at the celebration must have felt a deep moral joy (I am not being sarcastic—right-eous cruelty makes people feel *genuinely* good, a triumphant emotion) and a sense of holy vindictiveness, which Christianity understands very well.

Verdi put the scene of the macabre wedding celebrations in his opera, *Don Carlos* (the first performance took place in 1884). After the massacre, or *auto-da-fé* (act of faith) is all over, a little soprano voice from above reassures the audience that the victims are in heaven now, and feeling fine. True, there was booing on the first night, so not everyone was willing to go along with it, but no wonder Kierkegaard and Nietzsche were revolted by European Christian civilisation during their time, if that was all it had to say about its earlier crimes against the spirit of its founder.

A prescriptive morality, doing what you are told, only works in some cultures if enough people disobey it, like the way the economy of post-war Italy only worked because of the flourishing black market. Again, a sexually repressive morality only works if a sufficient number of people are naughty enough to keep sexual forms of love alive. But if everyone obeys, it sends the id (Freud's name for the instincts) underground and makes the suppressed energy explosive with despairing hate. A prescriptive morality is perhaps a necessary stage in the growth of a culture, as for young children. It is often negative: "don't do that!" and handed down through some form of ancestor worship. All the Ten Commandments are "don'ts", except the one that promotes submission to the ancestors: "Honour they father and thy mother".

If *sex* is too suppressed, then that is bad, but, similarly, if the free *spiritual* initiatives of the id are suppressed by too many "don'ts" (don't dare to look for God outside the Church, etc.), then they become dissociated and act themselves out as creatively imaginative and ingenious forms of hatred and cruelty.

The eighteenth century Enlightenment did not see a need to civilise and use the *non-rational* and emotional energies, which had been, up until then, classed as religion. Thus, now we are threatened by the uncultivated, and only half-civilised, energies and enthusiasms of Christian, Jewish, and Muslim fundamentalism: religion disguised as wisdom, handed down from the ancestors but comprising too much of the bad kind of hate, *justified righteous* hate, the hate that kills dialogue, and, well, just *kills*.

Freud started the Enlightenment of the Mind but he could only take it so far. His "superior" view of the world was largely derived (though hardly acknowledged) from Nietzsche, but his attempt to distance Christianity and all religion as neurosis, and *Kultur* that caused the discontents of European civilisation, were not enough to supply two things that were needed: a radical attack on Christian civilisation, and then a way of managing the destructive impulses of the unconscious which drive us. The contributions from Kierkegaard and Nietzsche helped with both, showing how Christian civilisation had shrunk, unable to contain and express the new surges of the ancient emotions that are life.

Jung's contribution may be summarised as follows: if we listen to, and civilise, what used to be called gods in our psyches with appropriate fear and respect, then we will no longer be at the mercy of mad gods, and will have a tap into the deepest vitalities of the id that lives us. How our new Enlightenment achieves this becomes clearer when we explore the subject of dreams.

In the next chapter, I will focus more selectively, because of the vastness of the field, on the next new insights of the century, beginning with the continued development of the Freudian tradition of psychoanalysis in the next generation.

PART III

THE HUMANISATION
OF PSYCHOANALYSIS

CHAPTER THIRTEEN

Anna Freud: new tricks

"To unpathed waters, undreamed shores"

(Shakespeare, 1623a)

J anet called what he did "psychological analysis", Freud called what he did "psychoanalysis", and Adler called it "individual psychology". Jung used the term "analytical psychology", but there is no doubt which one had the catchiest brand name. For a while, psychoanalysis was to psychotherapy as Hoover was to vacuum cleaner.

As Freud got older and more famous, he became the philosopher and prophet he had really always wanted to be, and lost interest in helping patients. Ferenczi, one of Freud's followers, and eventually his best friend, recorded in his diary in 1932 that Freud, then aged seventy-six, had said to him that patients were rabble (*"ein gesindel"*, Ferenczi, 1995, p. 93) only good for paying the analyst and for research: "It is clear we cannot help them" (Webster, 1995, p. 354). If what Ferenczi wrote was true, what a different Freud that was from the Freud who wrote so interestedly, almost affectionately, of his hysterical patients in the 1890s, and who was so kind to the "Rat

Man", assuring him of his liking and esteem, while patiently sitting through all the negative transference, and responding only with kindness and helpfulness, and, moreover, apparently *curing* him.

How did Freud get so bitter during those twenty years? Thus, it was up to the next generation to save psychoanalysis from Freud, and his daughter, Anna, born in 1895, was one of the first who quietly reintroduced hope and caring.

Anna came to lecture to us at Guy's Hospital in 1972; she was seventy-eight, and by then had spent a lifetime working with children (she died a decade later). As she blew her nose in an enormous man's white handkerchief, which she plucked from her *dirndl* skirt pocket, I wondered if we were looking at an actual relic of the man most mighty, her father, who had solved the riddle of the Sphinx. She talked as though she really felt for children, for example, noting that people always sympathised with sick children for their illness and not for the treatment, which is what the children really minded. She also told us that children needed to have their crying listened to and not hushed, especially when they experienced traumatic events like losing a parent, or suffered other big disasters.

I thought she showed real empathy, and my impression was of a sympathetic woman, infused with her father's ideas but not his later bitterness. However, her nephew, André Freud, had an opposing view and said that he found her not at all warm when he was a child. But, to me, she seemed to have more heart, professionally at least, than her father. Anna certainly cared for the great man most devotedly, and was very close to him right up to the final injection that ended his misery (from cancer) in 1939.

Anna became an analyst after being analysed by Freud, and the mind boggles at what he might have said to her while interpreting her Oedipus complex: "You want sex with me as a way of not admitting that you wanted sex with your father—all right yes I *am* your father but . . ."

Freud blocked her chances of marriage (which, in the case of the rather aggressive courtship displayed by her father's biographer, Ernest Jones, was probably lucky for her), but Anna did experience some family life by partly living with her divorced friend, the psychoanalyst, Dorothy Burlingham, and her two children. Anna analysed the children, but they did not turn out well in the end. They both grew up and married and had children of their own, but the son died of alcoholism, and the girl, Mabby, committed suicide in the Freud house in Hampstead where she had gone back for a top-up of analysis with Anna.

In her book *The Ego and the Mechanisms of Defence* (1937), Anna described state-of-the-art psychoanalysis as it was in 1936. In the early days of psychoanalysis, the aim was to uncover the childish, sexual, and aggressive wishes hidden in the unconscious, and make them available to be dealt with by the conscious mind. Study of the conscious mind alone, "ego-psychology", as it is called, was despised (Adler was castigated for it), but as the century went on, interest turned again to the ego and to the tricks that "I" *unconsciously* use to avoid facing unbearable memories and wishes. The most obvious trick is to dissociate them—*repress* was the word Freud used; an active deed, but it *feels* as though you just lose these traumatic thoughts without noticing, like relatives you do not like who emigrate to America without telling you. That and the other tricks were called *defences*, another way of describing what Adler called the "arrangement" (Adler, 1956, p. 284) which is made in our minds for us by our fear.

The submerged, unconscious end of the "I" is a sort of imp who acts behind our backs to protect us in ways we can choose not to know about, like a king who calls for the execution of a troublesome priest and is then shocked when he hears that his wish has been granted. But though the defences might be lifesaving when they are first induced, and should not be given up too lightly when discovered, in the end, they just make things worse. In fact, it is the *defences* that make us ill when they inhibit us; they impede our growth and give us symptoms.

Anna Freud listed eleven of them, showing the different ways our mind ducks and dives to avoid pain, for example: *projection* (only seeing our own prohibited impulses in others—"why are you in such a bad temper?"); *regression* (reverting to the mental state of a younger age, like a woman who bursts out crying when she realises she has been queuing at the wrong till, which evokes sympathy from the girl at the till, who lets her through); *reaction formation* (being very holy because of fear of sexual impulses, or being terribly polite because you want to hit people); *siding with the aggressor* against ourselves, and so on. There is just one *good* defence, and that is *sublimation*: when a person diverts sexual impulses into creating art.

In her book, Anna Freud described how psychoanalysis was effective in drawing out our defences so they could be dealt with and, eventually, given up. The process took place through free association, something the patient had to agree to from the very beginning of the session. But Anna turned the original idea upside down: now the whole premise was based upon the exact moment the patients were not able to further engage in free association, that is, the therapeutic alliance was *intended* to break down. When the painful or shameful matter that had been dissociated came towards the surface, the patient *resisted* remembering, and defied the analyst's efforts, using the defences he had developed as he was growing up. However, by resisting the therapist's efforts, the patient was showing his defences in the same way as the enemy reveals his position at night by shooting at a patrol.

Freud had his own theories about defences: for example, he believed that a woman who fell in love with her doctor was a defence against admitting that she really wanted sex with her father. Then she could stay emotionally anchored in the past (with the childish wish for a man who would be both father and lover) while pretending to have moved on.

The good old classical Freudian analysis was, and still is, a powerful therapeutic tool, with the right patient. Five sessions a week on the couch with the analyst was designed to enable the patient to regress to childhood, or even infant, mental states. This can be done more quickly through hypnosis, but it works with fewer patients, or by using intravenous drugs, such as barbiturates or benzodiazepines, or it can be done through psychoanalysis.

The Freudian psychologist, Charles Berg, gave a good account of classical psychoanalysis in *Deep Analysis* (1947). In the first months, his young male patient, whose father had died when he was a boy, talked and talked: "The uncovering of infantile memories, *emotionally still active in his everyday life*, continued apace, and the sessions became consequently more and more interesting (Berg, 1947, p. 181).

But that only provided the material for the decisive emotional battle to come: the young man had not smiled when greeting Berg at the beginning of this session and remained, uncharacteristically, silent for five or ten minutes on the couch. Presently, he told Berg that it was a waste of time coming, and he would come no more: "I don't trust you. I don't like you. This treatment is getting me nowhere. It is just a useless fraud" (Berg, 1947, p. 183).

Rather than being deterred, Berg saw that now they *were* getting somewhere, and that at last the young man was encountering his emotional life.

The patient talked on, though at first reluctantly, and described his hopelessness in the situation, the hopelessness of life, and his anger at Berg. Gradually, as he talked on, he sank back into child feelings and the irrational emotional knot (the autonomous complex, or, as Janet would have said, the *idée fixe*) came to the surface as he recovered memories of happiness when his father was still alive. He remembered the delight of being taken to bed by his father and tickled until he was hysterical . . . "a bit frightened at the same time, but what a thrill!" (Berg, 1947, p. 186).

"Good God!" he exclaimed, as it dawned on him that *that* was what he had unconsciously been wanting with Berg. "Good Lord! I believe it is. How positively ridiculous" (Berg, 1947, p. 186). His father's premature death had prevented the gradual development of his child emotions into adult forms, as would have happened if his father had lived. Berg explained how he had become stuck, father-fixated, and the patient realised that this was why he habitually walked out on emotional situations: ". . . which reminds me that I walked out on Gladys at the dance the other day" (Berg, 1947, p. 187). Berg then described how the patient had tried repeatedly to gain satisfaction from others, but had been repeatedly disappointed; this had resulted in him rejecting others and, instead, retreating into isolation. This repudiation of the once hoped for happiness is an attempt to reconcile oneself to disappointment, but can eventually become depression.

Berg summed up that what I call the Battle of the Patient

> . . . would probably have to be fought over again and again [called *working-through*] before the domination of these blind, semi-unconscious emotional patterns over the patient's reasoning life will be undermined and finally destroyed. (Berg, 1947, p. 189)

As Anna Freud would have put it, Berg's patient's inability to keep up free association led to the uncovering of his defence against hopeless disappointment, which had always led to him giving up, leaving the scene, and falling into depression. The patient had come at the therapist, unconsciously, expecting to draw him, too, into this old despairing dance of habitual disastrous interactions, but when it came to the point of his angrily quitting the scene in hopelessness, Berg would not let that happen. He did not respond with an angry "all right, go away then", but persisted in listening and understanding until the anciently wounded desire came up from the depths, and was understood. So, at least this time, through the Battle with the Therapist, the patient got it right at last.

For Berg, as for Freud, the "all-important matter" was for the therapist "not to react emotionally" (Berg, 1947, p. 189). But there was quite another way it could be played, and what that led to we shall see in the next chapter.

CHAPTER FOURTEEN

Melanie Klein: child's play

"Play is the highest expression of human development in childhood, for it alone is the free expression of what is in a child's
soul"

(Froebel, 1826)

The wonderful technique of classical psychoanalysis paid off by
uncovering depths in us that no one had imagined were there,
and, moreover, made it possible to heal previously hidden
wounds and restore life and growth as never before. However, the
whole process of psychoanalysis at the time was a grossly one-sided
and artificial way of two human beings (therapist and patient) having
to do with each other—and it fitted Freud's narcissistic neurosis like a
glove.

It allowed Freud to sit, above criticism, in his own world of pure
thought at the end of the couch over the head of the supine patient,
being the superior one, totally in control of everything in the room,
including the patient and the dog under his chair (although the dog,
occasionally, would jump up and lick the patient). Freud never had to
look the patient in the eye, receiving all the patient's emotions while

giving none in return, and dispensing his "superior view of the world" (Freud, 1895d, p. 282) as he called it, at his own leisure before taking the money.

A trainee analyst once exclaimed to me, "And the beauty of it is, *the patient is always in the wrong!*" When I was being more classically correct during psychoanalysis, a few shrewd patients pointed out how well this situation suited *my* neurosis, and actually they had me well sussed.

In Freud's generation, at first, psychoanalysis was the only game in town for psychotherapy. But then Adler and Jung brought in their very different psychotherapies that Freud could not accept, closely followed by new ideas from the object relations theorists (ORTs), a group made up of some of Freud's own followers who introduced a new transformation of dynamic psychotherapy.

"Object" is the unfortunate psychobabble term for "the other person", or what Adler referred to as the *gegenspieler*. ("No one's going to call my mother an *object!*" protested the rebellious psychoanalyst, Charles Rycroft.) By accepting the awful word "object", however, we can discuss a big new change of direction found in the work of Melanie Klein and others.

The ORTs were psychoanalysts who never set themselves up as a separate organisation, but they shared the same views and said similar things. The more famous of the ORTs were Melanie Klein, Michael Balint, William Fairbairn, and Donald Winnicott. They introduced three new theories: a focus on what goes on between the self and others; an emphasis on babyhood rather than just the toddler (Oedipal) stage; and a shift in perception about love. As Fairbairn was to discover, the most fundamental need of a human being was not Freud's "gratification of libidinal needs" (Harriman, 1946, p. 147), but someone to love. Thus, the ORTs brought about a renewed focus on human relationships, babies, and love: the humanisation of psychoanalysis.

Melanie Klein, or "this inspiring and appalling woman" (Wright, 1995, back cover), as she was cited in *The Times*, is a strong challenger for the position of most mentally disturbed of all the great psychoanalysts. However, her contemporaries were divided in their opinion of her: "What an awful woman she must be. I pity the poor kiddies who fall into her clutches" (Strachey, 1985, p.174), said the British psychoanalyst, James Strachey, while, on the other hand, the Austrian psychoanalyst, Ilse Hellman, had a different view: "She was like a jolly, nice granny" (Segal, 1992, p. 26). When Virginia Woolf saw her at a conference, she described her as "a woman of character and force, some submerged . . . like an undertow, menacing" (Abel, 1992, p. 19). Then there was the psychiatrist, R. D. Laing, who disliked her so much that, as a young trainee psychoanalyst, he sat through the whole series of her seminars without saying a single word.

It was said that Melanie Klein was as easy to loathe as Anna Freud was easy to love. Indeed, she had a ruthless streak: after Freud's death, Klein and her followers made such a serious bid for control of the Psychoanalytic Society in London, against Anna Freud, that in the end the training had to be split to avoid the division of the Society itself. Klein claimed to be more true to Freud than Anna, but Anna knew a radical revisionist when she saw one.

On the surface, Klein did not seem specially warm or loving— almost the opposite. She beat Freud at control-freakery. Her followers, the Kleinians, not only regarded themselves as an elite, but were also perceived in this way by some others; they were like the SAS or shock-troops of the Psychoanalytical Movement, surpassing all others in rigour. Michael Balint did not like their cocksureness and was suspicious that their published papers never seemed to mention failures, as other analysts' papers did. A Kleinian analysis consisted very strictly in interpreting the transference, nothing else. The patient was not greeted on arrival, and the offer of a cup of tea would have been unthinkable. In fact, the rules were so rigid that Kleinians often used to ask for monthly payment *in advance*.

A friend of mine, at the end of his first Kleinian session, after the fees had been settled, asked for the quickest way to his destination from Sloane Square, and the question was interpreted, never answered. A Kleinian colleague once remarked to me in the 1970s that patients having a classical Freudian analysis wish they were having a Kleinian one, but people having a Kleinian one wish they weren't having analysis at all.

Since she had so much to say about the first year of life, it is a pity that we can only conjecture about Klein's own babyhood, although we do know that she was not breastfed. Born in Vienna in 1882 of Jewish parentage, Melanie was the youngest of four children, and her mother, Libussa, was twenty-four years younger than her father. Her father blatantly liked her elder sister better than Melanie, and Melanie could not forgive Emilie for this. Melanie also thought she detected signs of sexual aversion in her mother, and believed that her mother had never recovered from the love she had for a student friend who had, subsequently, died. Melanie as a girl was beautiful, clever, ambitious, and was, socially, remarkably self-assured. She adored her big brother, Emanuel, who, despite being a major influence on her, turned out a waster. As Grosskurth wrote,

> It was a family riddled with guilt, envy and occasional explosive rages, and infused with strong incestuous overtones. Melanie's impending marriage was the prelude to Emanuel's death through disease, malnutrition, alcohol, drugs, poverty, and a will to self-destruction. Melanie Klein was made to feel responsible for his death and she carried the guilt with her for the rest of her days—just as Emanuel had probably intended she should. (Grosskurth, 1986, p. 20)

Melanie married at twenty-one to an industrial chemist, Arthur Klein, and the marriage night horrified her. Did it *have* to be, she asked, "that motherhood begins with disgust?" (Grosskurth, 1986, p. 41). However, during her married life, she had a daughter, Melitta, and two sons, Hans and Erich. In the early years of her marriage, her mother moved in; a self-centred, intrusively manipulative force, she got between Melanie and Arthur, and between Melanie and her children, keeping Melanie away from both, often advising her daughter to spend time in health resorts which were supposed to help Melanie's battle with depression.

In 1914, Melanie Klein read Freud's *The Interpretation of Dreams*, and from that moment became increasingly committed to psychoanalysis. After her own analysis by Ferenczi, she began to develop her own ideas. Melanie also took an analytical interest in her own children; in fact, she analysed them herself and published their case histories under pseudonyms. As a consequence, we learn that the seventeen-year-old Melitta was having difficulties with algebra because of inhibitions caused by thoughts of her parents' sexual intercourse. We also find out that Hans had problems with hostility towards his father, and that little Erich found relief from his anxiety when his mother gave him the sexual information he needed.

The relationship between Melanie and her daughter, Melitta, was "puzzling and disturbing" (Grosskurth, 1986, p. 111), according to Grosskurth, suggesting that although there was a close bond at first, later on, Melitta, who also became an analyst, also hated her mother. When her brother, Hans, fell off a mountain in 1934, Melitta claimed he had committed suicide and blamed her mother for his death. Her animosity towards her mother proved to be a lifelong bitterness; indeed, Melitta spent the day of her mother's funeral lecturing to some group in London, wearing bright red boots.

When analysing her youngest son, Erich, Melanie Klein did not seem to take into account other external factors that might have influenced his behaviour, such as moving to Berlin, and being separated from his father and siblings, his mother's own depressive illness, his brother being sent away to boarding school, the anti-Semitism he faced, and his parents' eventual separation and subsequent divorce. Instead, she concentrates on his sexual and aggressive phantasies. For example, when Erich was anxious about walking down a tree-lined road on his way to school because rough boys tormented him there, she interpreted the road as a symbol of his desire for coitus with her followed by castration anxieties. She interfered in all aspects of his life: stopped him seeing an older girl because of "the identification he was making with the phantasy of his mother as a prostitute" (Grosskurth, 1986, p. 98), and made him break off a "homosexual" friendship: "It must have seemed to the boy that he had no area of privacy from his mother, who knew the innermost secrets of his soul . . ." (Grosskurth, 1986, p. 99).

Melanie's husband was also not a great admirer of psychoanalysis, and Grosskurth writes that Arthur Klein saw it as driving a wedge between himself and his children.

But what an advantage it was for Klein that she was the first of the great originators so far who was actually a mother. When asked to work with a child, Klein got some of her own children's toys and let the child play with them, thus inventing her special analytic technique. Allowing the child patient to play with toys was like using free association in adult therapy. She discovered that playing brought out what was in the child's unconscious mind. What Klein reported was so violently crude it shocked Anna Freud and some other psychoanalysts in the same way Sigmund Freud had shocked *his* contemporaries.

While Anna and the other Freudians, on principle, would begin interpreting at a surface level and then gradually working deeper, Klein went straight to the deepest and most terrifying fantasies in her patients, whether they were adults or children. There was an anecdote about an instance where Klein was dealing with a difficult and emotionally inaccessible child, and said to her young patient something like "you want to kill your mother and you are afraid she will kill you for it". Later on, witnesses were shocked at the unexpected sight of therapist and child, with the child, trustingly, hand in hand with Klein. Although her interpretation sounds shocking, it can come as a great relief to the patient if the therapist gets it right.

In 1924, at the age of thirty-two, she presented a paper in Wurzburg (later rewritten circa 1932) about a six-year-old she called Erna, who suffered from depressions ("there's something about life I don't like," Erna said (Grosskurth, 1986, p. 116)), which involved rocking, head-banging, compulsively masturbating, being over-affectionate to her mother, but also veering to hostility.

Erna's neurosis had first appeared before she was quite a year old. As an infant, she had become trained in the habits of cleanliness unusually early. There is only room here to give brief snippets of Klein's account of the analysis, which, however, do show how this amazing woman, unbearably bossy in ordinary life, became in the analytical playroom permissive, unjudging, obedient to the child's slightest whims of play, supernaturally patient, listening and listening, day after day, totally undemanding of anything from the child and offering nothing but expression in words of what the child's play expressed in drama.

After the early sessions, Erna left the room looking like a battlefield, but Klein's response to this was to remain completely impassive and show the least possible emotion in response to the outbursts of the child.

Erna's games revealed an astonishing secret imaginary world of love and hatred, and sex, violence, and sadism. In fact, Klein's child patients all played games that involved attacking and destroying toys used in play.

Melanie also observed role play in her patient, Erna, who often used to play at being mother, with Melanie Klein as her child. Klein could see excessive fear of her parents, especially her mother.

Indeed, Klein believed that envy was at the heart of Erna's neurosis. But under Klein's unshakeably patient interest in her, Erna began to change. At first, she had perceived her father as only a pawn in the wars between Erna and her mother; in fact, if Erna role-played as her mother and was kind to the figure representing her father, then it was only to make Erna jealous; similarly, if Erna married Father during role-play, it was only to torture Mother. As Erna's hatred of her mother diminished, she gradually began to have genuine positive feelings towards her father. Somehow, normal love was becoming possible for Erna. What exactly did it? What exactly was it about Klein's treatment of her that changed her?

Like William Blake's fool, Klein persisted in her folly until she became wise. She began by driving her own children to despair until they hated her, but she persisted until she had discovered powerful manoeuvres for the salvation of lost small souls.

Her finding, which not all therapists have found, was that in the very first months of life we are full of hatred, of savage sadistic impulses born in us, and our tragedy is that we feel these things towards the person we love. If we cannot work it out somehow, and, therefore, have to dissociate (repress) the dogfight in us between the hating self, which offers irresistible delights of vindictive cruelty and mastery and possession, and the loving self, with its opposite delights, it just goes on and on inside us unchanged, in a cycle of desire to destroy, and desire to be punished for it and to make reparation. This cycle ineluctably comes out from its unconscious source not only into our play as children, but also into our actions and behaviour as adults throughout life.

Erna's games in Klein's playroom were often horrific—horrific crimes with horrific punishments. Klein commented on the similarity of these games to the behaviour of some criminals, ripping up their victims like Jack the Ripper, or raping, torturing, and dismembering people and eating parts of them; the things that we read about in the newspapers. I once exclaimed when a multiple murderer in England was found with a house full of hidden, decaying, dismembered bodies of victims, but a Kleinian forensic psychiatrist friend, who was experienced in dealing with the minds of real criminals, pointed out, "But that is what his unconscious mind is like—he has only externalised it."

A big part of the Enlightenment of the Mind was the great shift towards the value of imagination. Something imagined that gives you an appetite for your dinner is better than a rational fact that gives you a depression so you cannot eat. The truths given by imagination are life or death to the living human organism because they inspire and enthuse and cause our metabolism to turn food into energy and lust into children. The meanings of life are told to us through our imagination.

Imagination and play speak in symbols. Klein was accustomed to her little patients effortlessly pouring out rich symbolism in their play. But, in 1930, she came across a four-year-old boy called Dick, who challenged her in a way she had never been challenged before, and the story of his treatment is a real cliff-hanger, as he nearly did not make it.

Unusually for Klein, she mentioned the part Dick's mother had played in his illness, describing her as over-anxious and unable to give any real love to her child. Dick was worse than neurotic, severely retarded to about the fifteen-month stage and indifferent to his mother, nurse, and everything else in his world. Why? It turned out that it was because he could not symbolise, and was prevented from doing so by his psyche in order to defend him against an overwhelming terror, the one described by Klein and Winnicott as the child's fear of his ruthless aggression towards his own mother, in Dick's case, with too little available love to contain it.

Dick was so terrified by his desire to attack the organs and contents of his mother's body (babies, faeces, his father's penis entering his mother, etc.) that he dared not imagine what these might symbolise. To the little extent that he talked, it was as though he had no imagination and no interest in anything at all apart from one tiny area: *doors*, which Klein interpreted as the child's attempt to connect ideas, with the doors symbolising the entry of Dick's penis into his mother's body. He could not bite food, or use scissors or tools, or language, or even want to *know* anything or anyone.

For Dick, symbolism had not developed, so he was unable to play, and if he could not play, how could Klein analyse him? How on earth could she reach the unconscious depth of his mind where symbols are formed before they appear as play, and restore the flow? He looked at the toys without the faintest interest. She had to make the first move: she described how she took a train

> put it beside a smaller one and called them 'Daddy-train' and 'Dick-train'. Thereupon he picked up the train I called 'Dick' and made it roll to the window and said 'Station'. I explained: the station is mummy: Dick is going into mummy.' He left the train, ran into the space between the outer and inner doors of the room, shut himself in, saying

'dark' and ran out again directly. . . . I explained to him: 'It is dark inside mummy. Dick is inside dark mummy.' (Klein, 1975, p. 225)

Again Klein's intuitive genius--whatever you think of her theory—had hit the bull's eye. They were off! This almost finished-off little invalid was not beyond reach after all! His anxiety became conscious and accessible and, as she "lent him her courage", step by terrified step he recovered play, affection, language, and a self. Thus, aggression came into his play. He began to examine the toys and used them to enact, unconsciously, until she explained to him what he was doing: that he was re-enacting the drama between himself and his mother and father.

This and similar cases convinced Klein that *without symbolism we cannot live*. Without being able to symbolise to bring emotions into the unconscious imaginings (which she called *"ph*antasy") on their journey to consciousness, we are radically stuck.

With typical psychoanalytic undervaluing of the unconscious, Klein believed that symbolism was only about equating emotions about breasts and penises, etc., with toys that aroused similar feelings: for example, the red headlight of the toy motor car which little Erna asked Melanie to suck, she interpreted as a symbol for Erna's father's penis.

However, many of Klein's contemporaries had different theories about symbolism and imagination. Later we shall see that Winnicott was disappointed when psychoanalysts could not accept his opposing view. His idea connected the mingling of imagination and reality (which is play) with art and religion in a *spectrum* between imagination and reality: on this spectrum, dreams are at the most subjective (imagination) end, ranging through fantasy, play, the arts, religion, etc., right along to work with others in shared reality, and with science at the most objective (reality) end. Balint also observed an "area of creativity" (Kohon, 1999, p. 103) in the infant psyche. And, of course, Jung thought dreams and symbols were the word of God (to put it crudely), channelling vitality into us from the collective unconscious in the form of the archetypal imagery that lives us.

Dick was blocked because his environment could not facilitate the growth of his archaic and infantile animal instincts, basic sex and aggression, into human love, until he met Melanie Klein. What is shocking is that his instincts were blocked from even communicating symbols to his own *unconscious* mind. In Klein's other young patients, the symbols passed easily from the unconscious mind into the children's play, and then she could offer them words to express them. Yet, even Klein was strangely incurious about where the symbols began on their journey—where do they come from? They are not just decorative, poetic metaphors, similes, and verbal toys, they are the indispensable hands we need to grasp and change our instincts and our emotions, and each other.

Klein's great ability was to enable the child's unconscious hatred and resulting terror to become conscious.

Erna's troubles had really begun in her first year of life. Klein saw that our adult world has its roots in infancy, not just in the toddler stage, as Freud believed. The baby explains the child *and* the adult. Her key concepts come from the nursery: envy, greed, gratitude, love, and reparation. It is the conflict in us between our love and hate (or life instinct and death instinct, as Klein often called them) that is the basic cause of anxiety. There is one difference in the way this conflict is experienced by boys and girls: boys have a fear of being castrated while girls are afraid of having their insides and unborn babies scooped out of their bellies, which Klein believed was what angry and envious little girls wanted to do to their mothers (as if they think of females as, essentially, containers). But she had one really wonderful advance on Freud: she recognised that there were *natural spontaneous impulses* present to repair the injuries the child has caused, natural impulses, *not* just good behaviour enforced by fear of castration or of ruthless emptying: impulses to *"reparation"* (Klein & Riviere, 1964), as she called it. Children in play, if left to it, literally try to repair things they have broken. Therefore, while Freud thought we suppress our hatred out of fear of punishment ("resolution of the Oedipus complex" out of fear of castration), Klein thought *hate can be overcome, resolved, made useful, by* spontaneous *love*; and her kind of psychoanalysis, of children and adults, was her way of releasing that spontaneous love.

You can see why this sort of thing scared Anna and other Freudians, who believed the latent murderousness and licentiousness of humankind were only precariously controlled (by fear) and needed no encouragement. Furthermore, they were not reassured by the fate of the very first child analyst, Hug-Hellmuth, who was murdered by a teenage patient, whom she had adopted. Anna Freud feared that making children conscious of their ruthless, hating phantasies (Klein spelt conscious imaginings as "fantasies", unconscious imaginings as "phantasies") could undermine their weak superegos and make them uncontrollable. Thus, Klein shocked them, much as Freud shocked people when *his* ideas were new, but the impact had a much darker side to it.

By watching the inexhaustibly inventive and creative outpouring of children's play for hours and hours and hours, without interfering, Klein discovered some remarkable things. She realised that they were disturbed because of something that had *not* happened to them, a development they had not properly gone through, so that they were still, in some ways, reacting emotionally like little babies in the first few months of life, hardly knowing where they ended and mother began. The children were confused about hate and love and tried to cope with them by splitting things up and projecting bad feelings into mother and introjecting good things, like a loving breast, into them-selves, and vice versa. This is a confused and savage war, because, as well as trying to put bad things into mother, at the same time, in the attempt to still have a good mother, the child might, for example, take into himself the breast damaged by his hate and have "damaged objects" revengefully active inside him. Klein called that earlier period the "Paranoid–Schizoid Position" (Doane & Hodges, 1993, p. 8). The child is in pieces and does not know which bit hates or loves. It is like being mad.

Clearing up psychotic remnants from infancy became central to analysing adults, too. Klein and her followers were—are—more ready than most analysts to work with schizophrenia. But the brilliantly useful thing about her observation is that it opens our eyes to infan-tile paranoid phantasies actually at work in ordinary families and couples, and we realise that in quite ordinary people (you and me, for example) the things we believe with regard to the feelings and intentions of other people towards us are, sometimes, no doubt about it, just mad—unreal, not true. We think they hate us, and that their central motive and delight is to maliciously persecute and torture us, when really they are, say, only careless and unthinking, or fearfully protecting themselves, or momentarily annoyed, or naturally envi-ous if we have more than they and show no signs of sharing, or perhaps even innocently doing their job and thinking no harm against us at all.

Klein believed babies arrived with hate prepacked in them, and in the hardware, not just the software. Did she believe that her daughter, Melitta, had hated her from babyhood onwards? That most babies were saved from their hatred but Melitta was not? Believing our children hate us when they do not is the most heart-breaking example of hate misattributed, but common enough, as described in that indispensable textbook *Alice in Wonderland*:

> Speak roughly to your little boy
> And beat him when he sneezes.
> He only does it to annoy
> Because he knows it teases.
>
> (Carroll, 1993, p. 39)

Then there is the tragedy that arises when our mistaken feelings make us behave so provocatively that our worst, mad fantasies become real, and the other person ends up *genuinely* hating us, and so our mad thoughts come true and we are proved right, but with terrible consequences: war, crusade, divorce, or whatever. You can see this level of misattribution happening, constantly, between spouses, parents, and children, and between nations.

However, I have met people who seem to have worked through this phase a little too optimistically, which means they are unable to recognise or deal with a person who really does mean them harm. Thus, it is of fundamental importance in families and in nations to get it just right and be as accurate as possible about how much other people hate us, the nature of their hatred, why they hate us, how mixed their feelings might be, and what we can do about it other than killing them. The utterly necessary thing is to spot how much of the mutual hatred begins from some unnoticed, imperceptible, tiny seed, left over from infancy, of madness *in ourselves*. Getting it wrong is disastrous in families and in the world—see what happened in the past century when the West underestimated Hitler's hatred and overestimated that of the Communists. Science has taught most of us to think quantitatively, but that little seed of madness in us makes us regress to thinking in pure black and white.

Klein could have used the word "attitude" instead of "position", because we can slip into a paranoid–schizoid attitude so easily under pressure. Even an American President's reaction to hostility can be as black-and-white as a four-month-old baby's. Indeed, such a person can even, quite naïvely, utter words which, if heard on the psychiatric wards, would make any psychiatrist's pen, automatically, write the word *paranoid*: for example, "Who is not for us is against us", that kind of thing.

Erna savagely replaced extreme fantasies of her mother with a more realistic picture, instead seeing her mother as a more ordinary kind of human being mixed with both good and bad. Klein believed that we should reach this conclusion about the middle of the first year of life, and if it fails to happen, analysis can help to get it right later on in life, whether it is at the age of six, like Erna, or older. Klein believed that this crucial development occurred when babies appear to look sad around the middle of the first year because they have realised that Mother is good and bad, both; the same person is bad and good to us, an average human being really, rather than two (at least) people, one evil and persecuting, and one ideally devotedly loving. She called this phase of adjusting to reality the "depressive position" (Miller, 2004, p. 94).

If well worked through at six months, or even eventually at sixty years of age, the sad feelings become less of a reason for discouragement and more an acceptance of, and adaptation to, reality. So, sometimes a depressed adult does not need to have the depression "cured" exactly, but simply recognised as an awareness of reality that can be dealt with by a change of attitude or action. For example, I often feel discouraged because I could not win against my mother's moods (even as a baby, probably) and so I picked up a habitual attitude of defeat; but one week I decided I was not going to be defeated by my discouraging psychotherapist in the same way I was by my mother. I decided that I was going to examine whether he really was maliciously determined to harm me, and if he was—and he might well, unconsciously, have needed to keep his patients down for neurotic reasons of his own—I decided he was not going to win without a fight. If he undervalues me he is wrong and I am right, actually. It is not me that is unlovable; it is him that cannot or will not love!

And the same goes for any discouraging boss at work, or discouraging wife or husband at home. Then, having done that, I might get even more real and realise they are not putting me down at all as much as I think, and maybe also that I am giving back as good as I get in ways of which I am unaware.

But this way of putting it goes beyond Klein, because she assumed discouragement comes from inside ourselves, from our own death instinct, and she was comparatively uninterested in the real relationships with real other people. She only cared about the internal: for example, Erna's imaginary relations with her phantasy image of mother, the mother whose image she had herself distorted and then taken inside herself as an "internal object" (Klein, 1975c, p. 30), like the internalised strict father who was Freud's conscience, or the internalised unsatisfactory husband of Freud's depressed woman. Erna's real family situation was only of secondary interest to Klein, and she was just as disinterested in the relationships of her adult patients and the real people in their lives.

Klein's "depressive position", that is, recognising that mother and ourselves are both a mixture of good and bad, was an emotional attitude similar to Jung's recognition that God is partly evil, like ourselves. Some London Jungians felt such an affinity between Jung and Klein that they started working in what was referred to by the Jungian psychoanalyst, Michael Fordham, as "the Jung–Klein Hybrid" (Fordham, 1995, p. 9).

Analysts of other schools sometimes act dismayed by what they read in Kleinian papers. In practice, she seems to have got it right more often with very disturbed rather than with less disturbed children. Karen Horney sent her two daughters to be analysed by Klein on the basis of the belief at the time that everyone ought to be analysed for their own good. But the girls hated it and successfully resisted it, though one of them did sort of like the dirty bits. It was said that, one day, neighbours came to Karen to complain that the girls were putting notes through their letterboxes which said things like "Greetings from your fart" (Quinn, 1987, p. 183). In the end, Karen's initial consternation gave way to laughter and hugs and the analyses were terminated. But that all took place in Berlin, in the early days when Klein was still a beginner.

In the right hands, whether with children or adults, there is real power in Klein's ideas. Melanie Klein made a diabolical mess of analysing her own children and destroyed her own family happiness. But by the time she was analysing children like Erna, she had discovered something awesomely effective. Her practice required quite extraordinary patience and attention, almost daily, for years if necessary, paid to each single child, releasing the child's mind tiny bit by tiny bit from under the ruins of a terrified and sadistic madness, devotedly nurturing the child's latent capacity for normal affections. Whether she was a nice woman to adults of her own age or not, her behaviour to her little patients can surely only be described as love. What else than love could have so steadily and acceptingly, even tenderly, contained the hatred she found in them, without anxiously hastening to deal with it in ways that would have interfered with the child's own inborn capacity to do so for himself once it was listened to without punishment or even blame, and so made conscious?

Working throughout the first half of the century (she died in 1960), Melanie Klein began the most awesome revelation of the Enlightenment of the Mind: how to hate. One of my students found and paraphrased a wonderful bit of Klein for her essay, and then lost the reference, so I can only quote to you what my student wrote, in her lovely foreign English:

> The difference between Klein and Freud is well observed in the theory of sexuality. For Freud, sexuality concerned pleasure and power. In contrast, Klein saw sexuality in terms of love, destructiveness and reparation. The intercourse was a highly important act where love and hate interplayed, where the capacity of one's own reparation, by giving enjoyment and pleasure and one's ability to receive pleasure, were all encountered.

"The intercourse is a highly important act where love and hate interplayed." I could not have put it so well. We shall now go on to explore what three other object relations theorists, Fairbairn, Balint, and Winnicott, discovered about love and hate.

CHAPTER FIFTEEN

William Fairbairn: the isolated Scot

"All children have a list of unkind things done to them by their parents, some of which will have happened"

(Anon)

I used to envy Fairbairn his house in Edinburgh. It was so perfect for seriously introverted personalities like him and me—at the end of a little loch in the middle of the wilderness of Arthur's seat, protected by planning law from anyone ever building near him. Yet, it was actually in the middle of Edinburgh, less than twenty minutes from Marks and Spencer.

Born in 1889, he was a contemporary of Anna Freud and Melanie Klein, but had little to do with them, spending all of his professional life in Edinburgh. As a young man, William Fairbairn was religious and took a degree in philosophy, intending to become a clergyman. However, following military service in the Great War, he opted to become a doctor instead, reading Freud and Jung during his training. He had visited the famous hospital for shell-shocked officers at Craiglockhart in Edinburgh, where Siegfried Sassoon and others in the First World War had been treated by the psychiatrist, W. H. R.

Rivers. He had been so impressed by what he had seen that it had encouraged him to pursue a career in the same field.

Like so many of the great psychotherapists, he was not good at being married. His son, the famous MP and Solicitor-General, Sir Nicolas Fairbairn, said of his parents in a newspaper interview in 1992: "She was a widow from the day she married him. He was the wrong man for her. Terrifyingly withheld. He never had any money because he only ever charged one shilling an hour."

The interviewer then asked Sir Nicholas, "So you had an unhappy home life?"

"I had no home life," Sir Nicholas replied (Davies, 1992).

I should add, though, that the brilliantly talented and ebullient Sir Nicholas was a bit of an exaggerator; inclined to talk for effect. When I knew him as a lad at university he was the biggest show-off in Scotland—maybe one way to get noticed by a withdrawn father. I also do not believe that remark about his father only charging one-shilling fees.

However, Sir Nicholas did speak up for his mother and her plight, contrary to Fairbairn's biographer, J. D. Sutherland, who was more inclined to see Fairbairn's side in the marital war. When Fairbairn's wife died, he married his secretary, and that proved to be a more successful union.

Fairbairn had one curious symptom—a phobia of urinating in public. He really required two locked doors between him and the world to urinate at ease: the phobia was connected to a family drama when Fairbairn was a boy, and his father needed to pee in a train. This was a major crisis for Scottish propriety at the time. In desperation, they opened the carriage door and . . .

Sutherland described how Fairbairn learned emotional distance as his defence. He was the only child in a terribly respectable and Scottishly religious family in Edinburgh, where he was subject to "devoted loving care combined with oppressive strictness" (Dobbs, 2007, p. 87). His mother's attitude towards him was aggressively controlling. She liked his cleverness, but not his sexuality, and, as we shall see later, this conflicting behaviour towards him had a major impact on him for the rest of his life, affecting his relationships with his wife and his children.

As a doctor, Fairbairn was inspired by the influential psychoanalyst Melanie Klein and her writings, although he did not agree with her about very much. In turn, Klein thoroughly disapproved of him and believed that Fairbairn had not undergone the appropriate amount of analysis himself before expounding his theories.

At a very early stage in his career, Fairbairn wrote such excellent papers that he was made a member of the British Psychoanalytical Society, but he did not do their formal training.

More than any other major psychoanalyst, Fairbairn got away with original, un-Freudian thinking about personality structure. As he lived 350 miles from London, he was somewhat isolated from his colleagues in the Psychoanalytical Society and had more freedom to propose his theories without fear of retribution. It also helped that Freud was dead and, at the time, the Society was enrapt by the dispute about child analysis between Melanie Klein and Anna Freud. Thus, Fairbairn worked quietly, building his theories without distraction, and, with his philosophical training, he proved to be a very, very good expositor of his findings.

He learnt his insights the same way as all the other great contributors to the Enlightenment of the Mind—from his understanding of himself and with the help of some particularly instructive patients. Fairbairn was very interested in patients who were withdrawn, just like himself, and he championed their cause against analysts who thought them unrewarding cases. He knew these patients would have fallen into the category of introverted, as described by Jung, but he preferred to use the word "schizoid" instead. All his schizoid patients had the same things in common, such as

- an attitude of omnipotence;
- an attitude of isolation and detachment;
- a preoccupation with inner reality.

"Schizoid" is one of the worst words in psychobabble. It sounds as if it should mean "a wee bit schizophrenic", that is, emotionally disengaged from others and living in a world of one's own, and so it did to Fairbairn. But, by derivation, it means "split", and he thought being mentally in pieces was the significant thing. This got complicated for him, because he soon saw that it was not just withdrawn people who appeared to be divided in themselves, but everyone.

Fairbairn believed that a person is all "I", all ego: it is not my id that wants things, it is I. I might be in *two* minds about it, for example,

I might want sex but fear the consequences and be in conflict, but that is one bit of *me* against another bit of *me*. (This is actually not far from how Freud put the I-versus-my-conscience conflict in "Mourning and melancholia".)

Fairbairn wrote, (1) "An ego is present from birth". (2) "Libido is a function of the ego" (Scharff, 1995, p. 155).

He went on to say that it is only when I do not get what I want that I turn aggressive—my aggressiveness does not come from some "death instinct" (Fairbairn, 1952, p. 79) in some "id", it is just me getting angry at frustration. So, (3) "There is no death instinct, and aggression is a reaction to frustration or deprivation" (Scharff, 1995, p. 155).

Yes, all right, but I wonder whether we turn nasty *only* when frustrated? What about little boys who spontaneously delight in serious fighting, and killing and torturing helpless creatures? Or little girls who spontaneously delight in social cruelty—I'm having a party and I'm not inviting you? Is it that we all, as children, have to learn to use cruelty just in case we need it some day? Or are we all only reacting to some frustration caused by the universal malfunction of all families?

As a boy, I had a friend who had fun shutting the door with the cat half way through. In hindsight, I think his aggression was a result of his overly strict father and a reaction against the oppression he felt. Also, I cannot agree with Fairbairn that aggression is a wholly bad thing. Encouraging, cultivating, and civilising one's aggression (rugby is one good way) is of the essence of growing up, and if one has plenty to start with, then all the better.

Fairbairn's third theory led naturally to the following point: (4) "Since libido is a function of the ego and aggression is a reaction to frustration or deprivation, there is no such thing as an 'id'." (Scharff, 1995, p. 155).

But, to me, the biggest relief and satisfaction came from his fifth article: (5) "The ego, and therefore libido, is fundamentally object seeking" (Scharff, 1995, p. 155).

Although he could not or would not use the word, here Fairbairn, too, is declaring for love. He is saying that I do not just need gratification of instincts, or pleasure rewards, or the tension relieved by sex, or sex and aggression just for their own sakes, etc. That is only how I am if things have gone wrong and I have retreated from natural life and cut down my hopes. Love is reduced to its instinctual core of lechery and anger if I lose my nerve and try to settle for less than I really want. What I really, centrally, fundamentally want and need is *you.*

Fairbairn thought that this was what Freud must have really believed in his heart, and, like a scholar who seeks to find a text in the Bible to support practically anything, he searched Freud's writings, and concluded that the intentions within Freud's *Civilization and its Discontents* (1930a), with its discussion about love and objects, were somehow about the same thing. But whatever Freud really believed in his heart, he claimed that it was the ego's fear of instinct that was at the heart of neurosis. In contrast, Fairbairn believed it was the object as the cause of neurosis; the wound that a child feels when it is not the object of real, true love from its mother.

Fairbairn believed that people can react to such a wound by withdrawing emotionally from the mother, relating only to a small part of her: for example, a baby who feels unloved might give up hope for anything more than just milk from the breast, so its mother is reduced in his mind to merely a feeding object. Possessive mothers and indifferent mothers, especially, can provoke such a regression because they fail to give genuine expressions of love for the person as a child.

I wonder if this last bit is autobiographical. One must consider for a moment that the difference between Fairbairn's views and Freud's might only reflect the differences between an Edinburgh Christian mother and a Viennese Jewish mother.

Dealing with such a mother by withdrawing and expecting little from her is one way of managing. If Fairbairn, through force of habit, went on behaving like that when he was married, it must have driven his wife frantic.

Unlike Klein's theory that babies have an inborn hate, or death instinct, Fairbairn (like his contemporaries Balint and Winnicott) believed that something had gone wrong very early between mother and baby: that the root of a schizoid personality lay in the failure of the mother to be felt by the child as loving him in his own right.

Fairbairn's view was to lead to a painful, shaming phase in the Enlightenment of the Mind—Blame the Mother. Even today, this approach can have a marvellously wide field of reference. For example, we could blame Barbara Bush for her son's foreign policy: it was her fault for being too bossy a mother.

A woman analyst I knew used to exclaim when some new atrocity of mother–child behaviour came to light, "Mothers ought not to be allowed!" She was joking, but there were others who were not. Among the guilty was the psychiatrist R. D. Laing, who had such an awful Scottish mother—in Glasgow in his case—that his personal analysis did not enable him to recover fully from her.

There is a great deal to be said about this topic, but there was one major viewpoint worth noting within this particular theory. The mother Fairbairn mentioned in his own writings was "determined at all costs not to spoil her only son" (Fairbairn, 1952, p. 13). Thus, it can be the parent's *good* intentions that have bad effects. The other thing to be said about "blame the mother" is that although poor mother may be the channel for life's first attacks on us, she is most often a victim herself.

Later, Fairbairn came to reject the terms "good object" and "bad object", preferring "satisfying" and "unsatisfying" objects (Fairbairn, 1952, p. 111).

However, he did think, as Klein did, that the trouble starts right at the beginning with the baby as a suckling infant. The baby somehow picks up the mother's attitude and reacts by withdrawing from her emotionally, which affects its ability to grow up naturally. The baby learns to exist on the basis that he is not loved for himself as he is, and that his love is not acceptable to his mother.

You might wonder how Fairbairn can assume that a tiny baby can sense and react to its mother's attitudes when it is not yet capable even of thinking or consciously knowing. You might choose to go along with this assumption, or disregard it; I certainly agree with it.

I once saw a heartbreaking video made by a researcher in Oxford, in a study of clinically depressed mothers. The mother was saying things like "Give Mummy a smile!" rather than the more usual "Aren't you wonderful!" The baby, of course, could not possibly mentally understand the emotional dependence its mother was betraying by the words, but it was sensing something and rejecting her; it just would not meet her eyes, but looked everywhere else. Normally, babies fixate on their mother's face—but not that baby.

Fairbairn felt that separation anxiety is the first and deepest anxiety of all; the fear of loss of the other. If one withdraws and distances oneself and gives up one's grip on the other, it puts one in a dangerous situation. If the baby takes the introvert path and partly gives up on the outer world (mother), he has to find his main support and comfort in his inner world. Consequently, he keeps good things inside, and feels a sense of loss if he expresses his emotions to others. Fear of such loss makes him suppress his emotions. What he feels is a secret—often even from himself. This defence system lays the foundation for a wealth of symptoms later on in life.

Fairbairn cited a student who always failed oral exams because he could not allow himself to give the right answers; he knew the answers perfectly well, but they were precious things he had to keep inside himself. He cites artists who either treat their productions as worthless once completed (Cézanne comes to mind), or behave as though their paintings still belong to them after they are sold. In fact, was there not a twentieth century French painter whose patron jokingly padlocked his purchase to the wall because the artist kept taking it away to improve it?

The withdrawn (introvert or schizoid) person feels secretly superior because he thinks the best things in his world are all inside him. His inner fantasies are better than reality: "I prefer masturbation because you have to do with a far finer class of girl."

In more disturbed cases, the secrecy fails and the superiority leaks out. I remember a patient in a case conference who defeated six psychiatrists' attempts to find something abnormal in him; he was so friendly, natural, confident, open, and normal, except for one single remark that gave him away. He told us he was sorry he could not tell us who he really was, as the time had not yet come.

Alfred Adler's idea of a normal person was one who felt a boost to his self-esteem through giving to others and by sharing his feelings, and so on. This is because the love-objects who really matter to him are all real people outside him. However, the introvert feels impoverished by giving, and *loses* self-esteem by it. He may get through life by acting a role, pretending to be concerned or sincere, for example, or by showing off—exhibitionism that might be highly expressive, but avoids actual social contact. I cannot remember the name of the playwright who said he could expose his soul to a theatre full of people but never to a single person, but I understand what he meant. He can be the life and soul of the party while emotionally giving nothing true at all. A skilled performer in this way can even give the impression of total unreserved self-exposure, while invisibly in control of every hearer's response.

Fairbairn also maintained that schizoids learn from the mother that their love is not welcome, but, on the deepest level, they fear their love is actually destructive, and can kill. Fairbairn thought this terrible fear belonged to the earliest baby state, rather than to a later one when one thinks it is one's hate that kills: this insight that the baby's love has the capacity to destroy was a deeper insight than that of Freud, who would have seen it only as a death wish. Fairbairn's awareness that *I* basically need *you* showed that our need to exchange love is the deepest urge of all. So, the schizoid person keeps his love withheld inside him not only because it is too precious to part with, but also because it is too dangerous to let loose on others. That is the first great tragedy of the withdrawn person. The second tragedy is that, to be safe, he might even take pleasure in driving people away from him, making them hate him. The third tragedy is a combination of the first two; the feeling that since love is barred to him he might as well enjoy hating, and if to love is to destroy, it is better to destroy using hate than love.

Here our skins might begin to tingle with a certain horror when we sense we are approaching one of the most war-torn areas of the Enlightenment of the Mind—*understanding* evil men and women.

If we put our minds to it, we could understand them in a way they could never bear to understand themselves. Then we are in danger of feeling compassion for evil people; an emotion that could incur the wrath of many. So, for the moment, we shall quickly look away again, and go back to describe how all the above is connected with "being in pieces".

Fairbairn agreed with Freud and Klein's theories that, in some kind of way, we take significant people inside ourselves; a controversial viewpoint at the time. However, Fairbairn had his own take on it. If the mother keeps instructing her child to say "thank you", her suggestion becomes a permanent inhabitant of the child's mind, who will eventually act on it forever without noticing. If she is a normal, kind woman, she herself becomes an internal support for life for her children, or in death for that matter, such as when dying soldiers scream for their mothers.

In the darker world of Melanie Klein's young patients, the mother who lives at the back of one's mind is distorted by one's own hatred into a menacing persecutor, or by one's infantile love into an unreal, ideal, total gratifier. When these internal ambassadors of loved and hated persons appear in dreams, they are never quite like the real person, and might, indeed, appear as hardly recognisable things. For example, an anorexic's mother might appear as a giant devouring slug. They have a life of their own because they are living bits of oneself who have been given the job of speaking for one's mother or father when the real person is not there, just like other autopilots or autonomous complexes we evoke inside us. They are somehow active in their own right, unlike the maps of one's physical environment that one also internalises.

Fairbairn's internalised mother spoiled his marriage. She became his conscience and inhibited him from using his sexuality and aggressiveness to love his wife, thus leaving his son, poor Sir Nicholas, as a child with no home life.

Our internalised mothers can come in dreams to scare us into conforming, or, if benign, to encourage us to be ourselves. They check or supercharge our impulses without our knowing it, and they can sometimes be the reverse of helpful. Difficult internalised mothers are not at all easy to straighten out; they have a kind of permanence that is uninfluenced by external reality.

Fairbairn, like other psychoanalysts, believed that there is nothing else in us but bits of self and representatives of others. As he was so withdrawn himself, he never noticed in himself any intrusion of alien persons through the back door of the mind from the collective unconscious, in the same way Jung did.

Klein believed that we internalise others through our phantasy of eating them—not an easy idea to take on board. But Fairbairn had a different idea of how we do it:

> At one time it fell to my lot to examine quite a large number of delinquent children from homes which the most casual observer could hardly fail to recognise as "bad" in the crudest sense. . . It is only in the rarest instances, however, that I can recall such a child being induced to admit . . . that his parents were bad objects. (Fairbairn, 1952, p. 64)

I cannot help imagining the conversation between the doctor and patient: "Whit dae ye mean, ma Mither's a bad oabject?"

But Fairbairn was on to something important; he understood that the child would rather be bad himself than think this is so of his mother or father. In fact, in the eyes of a child, a motive for him to carry the burden of badness is that this can seem to purge otherwise abusing parents.

It is a common finding that physically abused children think it is their fault. That is a desperate way of adapting and trying to keep some harmony going with the abusing parents, some sort of love. We can even be tied to such a parent by love. Social workers are used to abused and neglected children saying that, given the choice, they would rather remain at home with the abusing parents, but for the abuse to stop.

Unconsciously, one sacrifices one's integrity to the cohesion of the family. For example, if mother tells you that your sexual desires are wrong, and by this you feel she is being bad to you, you can make her good again in your mind, by telling yourself that she is right, sex *is* wrong, and it is you who are bad to want it. But only a *bit* of "I" can agree to that and there is a lot of you that cannot. However, you cannot see how you could ever get agreement between the two sides, so your main central self simply splits off and dissociates the internalised hostile mother along with the bit of ego that agrees with her. What is dissociated is like a couple; the anti-sex mother keeping you in order alongside the bit of you that has submitted to her. Both parts agree with her view that sex is bad and are ready to collaborate in putting it down with as much harshness as necessary. But as these bits of you are split off and unconscious to your central self, they affect your behaviour without you ever knowing about it until you get into therapy. Of course, these split-off parts can be against all sorts of things besides sex: childlike self-confidence, say, or impulsiveness, or passive contentment, or persistence in folly, or anything at all that mothers might find hard to take.

Fairbairn called this sinister hidden couple the "rejecting object" (Fairbairn, 1952, p. 121) and "antilibidinal ego" (Fairbairn, 1952, p. 129), the latter of which he named the *internal saboteur*. This is the traitorous bit of self, the hidden internal obedient child who has agreed to hate love in cahoots with the internalised rejecting mother. He believed the *internal saboteur* to be responsible for all sorts of inexplicable disasters that happen to us, and for things that we need that seem to be too far out of our reach. This goes far beyond just sexual inhibitions, as illustrated by Carter's patients' inability to ask for sympathy openly, or Freud's hypnosis patient's inability to feed her baby, or Fairbairn's student patient's inability to pass oral exams, or the thousands of traffic accidents or other snags and disasters.

The *internal saboteur* overlaps with the notions of Freud's cruel superego, and Jung's shadow. It sides with the rejecting mother and sabotages one's life from the unconscious. The rejecting mother is only one side of one's real mother. One's real mother usually has two sides to her, even two opposite sides.

A colleague of mine also had a Scottish mother who was more than usually Scottish. She married into a family, some of whose members were good and not very interesting, and others naughty and interesting. She married one of the good ones and despised him, while responding with lively interest to the naughty ones. Once, when my colleague was a little boy, the concrete pavement outside was being relaid. She told him, "If you had any gumption you'd be out there writing your name in it." When he did, she was furious and outraged and gave him hell, and even denied ever having said any such thing. I believed him, not her, at least to the extent that she was generally giving him a double message.

Similarly, Fairbairn knew that he was getting not just suppression from his mother, but also devoted love, and more than that, on some level, she excited him. However puritanical she might be, a mother can hardly help stimulating her baby if she handles him lovingly as Freud described, and she can excite him just because she has a woman's body.

Here we are again with the incestuous sexual intercourse between son and mother, just as literally unthinkable in Edinburgh as in Vienna. This causes the main centre of the ego to actively forget and split off from the unbearably exciting interaction with the mother, resulting in the "I" being split into three:

1. A central ego relating to the real mother in reality and/who is manageable and comfortable to live with.
2. A split-off bit of ego in a fantasised sensual heaven with the internalised exciting mother (love-object).
3. Another split-off bit of ego colluding with an internalised anti-life mother (internal saboteur).

This is like the three bits of Freud's Rat Man: his normal kind, cheerful, and sensible self, his childish passionate and evil impulses, and the third self that paid homage to religion and asceticism. Fairbairn completed the picture by showing how these three related to the aspect of mother and illustrated how one has to split into these three parts to cope with a mother who can be sometimes more exciting and sometimes more rejecting than one can bear.

The psyche of one of his patients put it well in a dream about her father, in which she was in a corridor. At one end, her father wielded his stick in an erotic suggestive way, and at the other end was her father again, but was raising his stick to hit her. In the dream, she felt at her wits' end, trying to find the best way to react while people watched her through a window, thinking what a silly person she was.

You might think of "rejecting object" (mother) and "internal sabo-teur" as mere fantasies, except for their power to influence and take over one's behaviour. For example, a man taken over by either one of them could find himself behaving to his wife like the irresponsible dependent child who passively takes from the seductive mother, or acting like the internalised hostile mother to his daughter in her blos-soming teens, and so on. To the onlooker, the split-off parts of the person's self are not necessarily invisible at all; they may be quite clearly running his life. Therapy can help him see it, too.

Yet, these split-off parts of self are not really relating to the real people around us, but to fantasies: the fantasy of the exciting mother and of the rejecting mother that is projected on to one's father, sister, wife, daughter, son, boss, subordinate, etc., so that real love is foiled. But marvellous to say, love *can* begin to grow when *released by the external life disasters that the false projections themselves actually cause.*

In Notting Hill Gate in the 1960s, I saw a show where Botticelli's *Birth of Venus* was projected from a big old slide through an ancient projector on to the cinema screen. Then they set light to the slide and it gradually burned away, leaving the unobstructed light flooding out to show a real naked girl posing where the image of Venus had been. I never saw a better image of projections being destroyed by disaster to reveal the real other person.

I have paraphrased Fairbairn's own words "libidinal attachment" as "love" in order to point out something rather staggering suggested by his findings about the origin of the destructive internal saboteur. It is this: the need to love is the most basic thing in our being, and *it is in our determination to love our parents that we become like them, that we take in their own hopelessness and hate from them, and then we act it out like them*. As the song in *South Pacific* puts it, we learn to hate whom our family hates, and what our family hates, and that might be love.

Freud maintained that the superego, ego, and id were three mutually co-operating parts each with its own function, whereas Fairbairn saw them as a pathological splitting of the "I" into three "I's", all of which we can suffer from. He rejected Freud's Oedipal conflict between mother, father, and child, instead believing that there was an initial pattern between infant and mother, which would later transfer to a three-person situation with the father.

So, if we are all split apart, how can we get ourselves together again? One of my students wrote something brilliantly relevant to Fairbairn: "Internal integration of the personality is due to choosing to relate honestly to another".

The "another" could be a psychotherapist. To Fairbairn, psychotherapy was not a science, but "a *human activity transcending and using science* . . . You can go on analysing forever and get nowhere. *It's the personal relation that is therapeutic*" (Guntrip, 2005, p. 64).

Here is something Fairbairn does not pick up on, but which is crucial: what if one did *not* submit and agree with mother's values but stood up to her and told her she was wrong? Escalating mutual rage is what would happen, with Mother always able to get angrier than oneself! For example, "if I were angry with her, she would get more angry". The words "She would go ballistic!" are nowadays often heard in this context. Someone in you wants to speak and someone else in you has to tell him to shut up.

So, the corollary to my student's magnificent statement that *integration of the personality results from talking honestly to someone* is that *conflict avoidance disintegrates the personality*. When you should be having a fight with your nearest and dearest, but you avoid it, it becomes a fight inside you against yourself—as good a definition of neurosis as there is.

How does a baby, child, or adult stand up to the angry Mother? And if one has made it an internal fight against oneself, how does one get it back outside again where it should be?

The split-off bit of ego (or sub personality or autonomous complex or whatever one wants to call him or her) is infantile in that it soaks up all the gratification that comes along, and the anti-love bit is infantile in just thinking exactly the same as mother. As long as the two remain split-off from central daily consciousness they will never grow up. The central "I" is hindered from growing up too, as well as it might, having lost parts of itself.

Fairbairn thought the essence of growing up was to develop gradually from infantile dependence on others to adult dependence.

At all stages of life, it is amazing how we can become fixated on someone who rejects us. Rejection is very bonding. Sometimes we seem to seek out someone to love, and get fixated on those who repeat the very kind of rejection we suffered from a parent, as though the repetition compulsion is a need to return to an old unsolved problem to worry at it once again and see if, at last, we can get what we were deprived of back then. If it is something we need for our growth, of course we cannot just let it go and forget it.

How can one possibly complete the gaps in one's growth without somehow going back to infancy and getting the emotional food indispensable for emotional growth? To that question, Michael Balint found the answer.

CHAPTER SIXTEEN

Michael Balint: a Hungarian bastard

"'With my body I thee worship', says the bridegroom in the ancient Anglican Sacrament of Marriage. 'With my body I thee console,' says the prostitute. 'With my body I thee heal,' says the psychotherapist"

(Derry Macdiarmid)

I once asked Michael Balint's widow at a party what he was like as a person. "He was a Hungarian bastard," she said, straightforwardly. Uninhibited aggression came naturally to Balint. He was a bombshell of energy, assertiveness, and originality. His obituarist, Sutherland, recorded how, at the end of his frequent quarrels with Balint, after good humour was restored, Balint would refer once more to the proverb "If you have a Hungarian for a friend, you don't need an enemy" (Sutherland, 1971, p. 332). Sutherland went on in true obituary style, "[H]is challenges and impatience were part of his zeal in sharing his genius" (Sutherland, 1971, p. 333).

Born in 1896 in Hungary, Balint left in 1939, as it had become a place of considerable political unrest, and lecturing on psychoanalysis was almost impossible. Indeed, it was not unusual for the police to turn up at his seminars. So, Balint moved away from his homeland in search of a more peaceful environment. It is sad that Scotland lost out as a second home to him, because, though Fairbairn's hospitality in Edinburgh had taught him much about the varieties of Scotch whisky, he also learned that "Scottish culture tended to foster a greater readiness to endure suffering rather than to pay for its relief" (Sutherland, 1971, p. 331), so he and his wife and child headed for Manchester.

Michael Balint was one of the few great psychotherapists who *was* good at being married. His first wife, Alice, died tragically from a ruptured aneurysm only a few months after arriving in Manchester. There was a brief second marriage that did not work, then, in the later 1940s, he married a colleague, Enid, an active leading social worker, who worked closely with him until he died in 1970. They became well known, worldwide, for setting up "Balint groups" which trained GPs in the doctor–patient relationship. Challenging and, indeed, confronting in style, it enabled GPs to help problem patients by focusing on their own emotional reactions to those patients.

Balint had been analysed in Hungary by Ferenczi, one of Freud's followers, whom he loved and admired, and he was inspired by Ferenczi's interest in regression to early infantile states of mind. Balint knew about the infant stages not only from his own childhood, but also through his thesis on individual differences in the way infants behave, for which he received a Master's degree from Manchester University in 1945.

Being a baby is hell, according to Melanie Klein, but in Michael Balint's account, it is heaven. Where Klein saw early infancy as a mad confusion of bits of hatred and love, Balint saw infancy as a "harmonious interpenetrating mixup" (Siegelman, 1993, p. 179) of primary love, where you never *need* to know where you end and mother begins, and where all needs are gratified. The baby's demands and claims (food, glorious food, cuddling, sleep, soft devotion in every touch, paradise) are paramount. Mother creates total harmony by preventing any lasting distress.

In direct contradiction of Klein's idea that inborn hate and suspicion is present from the beginning, he described the baby's attitude at this stage with an untranslatable German adjective, *arglos*, meaning something like innocently trusting, guileless, unsuspecting, describing someone who feels "that nothing harmful in the environment is directed towards him, and, at the same time, nothing harmful in him is directed towards the environment" (Balint, 1979, p. 135). This is the attitude that we start off with as a baby, which is, subsequently, lost when things begin to go wrong. It is the attitude that we should try to recover in therapy in order to make a new beginning.

Like other natural extroverts among psychotherapists (Adler, for example, and quite a few family and group therapists), Balint was not so interested in people's internal structure or internal conflict or inner world, but deeply interested in what actually goes on in the outer world between people. For this reason, he is the perfect complement to Jung and Fairbairn. Balint did mention the inner world, briefly, as what he called the "area of creation" (Balint, 1979, p. 24), when a person is alone, yet *not completely alone* because in solitude the mind gives birth to things, like art, thought, insights, awareness of health or illness (the latter being very important). Because he thought that language had no words to describe such thoughts, he merely called them "somethings" (Balint, 1979, p. 25).

No words? Jung filled eighteen thick volumes with words describing these "somethings"! Add Balint to Jung and you get a good whole picture of outside plus inside. As we shall see, Balint described people in terms of their interactions with others, not their internal structure.

Because we are so happy as babies, it is not surprising that we often yearn to go back to the baby stage. Balint thought we all try to do this when we get a chance, for example, when at the fairground. In the fairground there is endless food and rewards for aggression (shooting gallery, coconut shy, etc.). He evidently assumed that an ordinary mother is delighted by her baby's aggressiveness. On the Big Wheel and other rides, we can venture to dizzy heights but always return safely to earth. In fairgrounds, some prefer the safer pleasures, like staying with mother, while others prefer the adventure of being away from mother up on the big dipper, or whatever, with the additional pleasure of returning to the safe place later. This gave him a metaphor for describing Jung's extroverts and introverts in a new way. He mentioned Jung but did not acknowledge he was talking about the same thing, which increases suspicion that half the time the great men of that century did not actually read each other's books very thoroughly.

Balint focused on how immature extroverts need other people in a dependent kind of way, calling them "ocnophils" (Balint, 1959, p. 52), meaning they shrink back from venturing away from mother and cling to the safe, comforting end of experience. They trust to other people's helpfulness and care. The introverts he called "philobats" (Balint, 1959, p. 52), because they like to be away from mother in the friendly (as they feel them to be) open spaces. The philobat (introvert) thinks "hell is other people", but trusts in his skill to manipulate others if he has to.

This is reminiscent of Fairbairn's description of the schizoid's skill in acting lovable. I remember a man telling me that if he were lifted by helicopter from my room and dropped in Wormwood Scrubs, he knew that by the end of the day he would be accepted, liked, and feel at home.

You will never have heard the words "ocnophil" and "philobat" because they just did not catch on. There are many words in psycho-babble that refer to this same polarity:

>   narcissistic–anaclitic (Freud);
>   independence–co-operation (Adler);
>   introvert–extrovert (Jung);
>   schizoid–hysterical (traditional psychiatric, including Fairbairn, but now less used);
>   philobat–ocnophil (Balint);
>   disengagement–enmeshment (family therapists);
>   avoidance addict–love addict (Pia Mellody).

The proponents of each set of names would say they refer to different things; please do not believe them; the overlap is greater than the difference, and more useful. I especially like the last pair, though "avoidance addict" does not so well express the self-sufficient *adventurousness*, which Balint observed, of the socially unconnected "philobat". I knew a young man once who drove the latest exciting sports car, but it was the only one I ever heard of that had a little trailer carrying all the spares he could possibly need in case of breakdown—an idea to thrill the heart of any philobat like me or him. He could have safely taken it across the Sahara, let alone to see me in South London.

Jung was a well-balanced introvert living an exuberantly outgoing, extroverted-looking kind of life, while finding his primary source of stimulation inside himself. He probably saw quite a lot of similarly well-adapted uninhibited introverts, not too introverted to be unable to socialise and launch out into life, as well as adapted thoughtful extroverts, not too extroverted to be able to be alone sometimes and look inwards. So, Jung saw extroverts as plunging boldly into life, while Balint viewed them as shrinking back. Balint was seeing introverted patients who were morbidly self-sufficient and too detached, like Fairbairn's schizoids, and extroverts who were like Freud's hysterics: clingy and over-dependent.

In the Introduction to *Thrills and Regressions* (1959), Balint gave clinical descriptions of two young women as examples of the two types. They were not exactly opposites, he said, because they branched off from the same stem (meaning they were two ways of being neurotic). One, the ocnophil (extrovert, love addict), absolutely needed objects (i.e., people *and* things, and even ideas) to hold on to. As she always needed help, she was well practised in activating the kindness of strangers but, nevertheless, people repeatedly let her down. He described the other woman as a philobat (i.e., introvert, avoidance addict) who preferred to be alone, and who dealt with people as (not uninteresting) nuisances. Several men wanted to marry her, but she rejected their advances while still keeping on good terms with them; she also refused to possess more than could be carried in two suitcases. She was a psychiatrist, unusually gifted in her management of patients. Balint concluded that "Both women were ill, indeed very ill" (Balint, 1959, p. 16).

Jung saw extroverts as leaping too fearlessly into socialising, but Balint saw that also they tended to timidly *shrink back* from adventure whenever it meant going it alone, and he saw how they timorously looked all the time to other people for supply of needs. Being so dependent on the other, an ocnophil has to accept and preserve the other person, but can never really trust him, and has to cling and not let the other out of his control. Development of skills of independence is inhibited. This is what the clinical adviser, Pia Mellody, would call love addiction, but Balint asks, is this love or hate?

Jung believed the introvert was living inside himself, but Balint saw how the introvert feels free and brave when away from others. The intimacy-avoiding philobat (introvert) puts freedom before love, prefers friendly open spaces, avoids independent objects, and prefers those over whom he can feel superior, and can control. He is one who might love a long walk alone in the country that will only be spoilt if he bumps into someone. The philobat leaves and rejoins objects without expecting them to resent being put down and picked up; objects are hardly allowed to have freedom of their own. Again, is this love or hate?

Clearly, Balint wrote, *both are ambivalent*. The ocnophil despises himself for so desperately needing the object, and hates the object for it. The philobat is on guard against his own need for the other, which he denies having at all. The ocnophil behaves as though really mistrustful, critical, and suspicious. The philobat is superior, self-sufficient, condescending, and distant (again reminiscent of Fairbairn's account of the schizoid).

Unconsciously, both wish they had never grown up. They are actually longing to go back to the bliss of infancy and both try to recreate it. The ocnophil does it by acting on an unrealistic faith that everyone, or at least the chosen object, will "click in" with him like an ideal mother. At first, Balint thought that the clinging of the ocnophil was like normal infant behaviour, but then he realised that normal babies do not cling; they let themselves be held. By anxiously clinging, and disguising or denying the fear that he might be dropped, the ocnophil actually prevents himself from getting *held*, which is what he really wants. Similarly, the philobat acts on an unrealistic faith that the whole world will also "click in" with his needs like the ideal mother, while he pretends to himself that he does not need anyone. Both act on an unrealistic faith that, at bottom, they cannot really believe in, and both really unhappily fake the feeling of the harmonious mix-up of primary love.

The philobatic attitude needs skill, and a basic acceptance of the depressing fact that objects are separate. (Later, Karen Horney was to describe the *resignation* of the morbidly independent person.) Though the philobat has the same aim as the ocnophil of rediscovering the harmonious mix-up of primary love, he does it in a more roundabout way, perfecting his skill in distancing and manipulating others until it becomes effortless and *therefore unnoticeable*, so it feels as if the whole world *is* fitting in with him, like a mother.

It was a stroke of genius that Balint saw how the two attitudes arise: if things go wrong between mother and baby in some frightening way, the infant has a choice: to *panic and withdraw*, or *panic and cling*, and the choice they make leads either to the introvert–schizoid–philobat–avoidant life-style, or to the extrovert–hysterical–ocnophil–love-addict way of coping.

What provokes these two opposite desperate manoeuvres? Klein thought things are wrong for us from the start; hate and confusion are in us before we come through the birth canal, and we begin to cope with that, with terrible effort, during the first year. Fairbairn, Balint, and Winnicott thought the opposite: that we are born all right and then things go wrong, which raises the question: *what* goes wrong and how?

Fairbairn thought that the deepest anxiety was separation anxiety. But gradual separation is what being born and growing up is all about. However, separation is normally accompanied by the development of bridges—after birth comes physical affection exchange, mother and infant seeing and feeling each other. The baby knows he can summon her back by crying when she is absent, and learns she is still there even if he is left for gradually longer absences; he also learns speech as a bridge to mother, and so on. If mother is too emotionally detached or absent for too long at a time, and the bridges are *not* making up for it by constantly growing in reach and flexibility and reliability, then separation threatens to become loss, which can cause panic. Conversely, if the bridges cannot grow because mother is too close and intrusive and never allows enough distance or freedom, (feeds the child before he is hungry, or is too pushy in play), then there can be an opposite basic terror of *not* being able to separate, of feeling overwhelmed by mother. In this instance, the child is in danger of being taken over and swallowed up by her emotions with no room for any of his own, which can cause the child to lose his sense of being a separate self, and that is an opposite cause of panic. So, there is both separation anxiety and engulfment anxiety: in early development, either loss of the mother or engulfment by the mother can equally extinguish the self.

Fairbairn, being an avoidance addict himself, who discovered his hidden unconscious dependence as a revelation, thought separation anxiety the more basic, which was reinforced by his work with soldiers in the Second World War, who were naturally suffering from separation. But, later in the century, others, for example, family therapists working with anorexics, added to our knowledge of the terror of engulfment and suffocation. You would think that the child of an engulfing mother would become an avoidance addict, and the child of an over-detached mother would become a clinger, but it might not be as simple as that.

Like Jung, Balint saw that to get better, each of the two types had to add in the opposite: the clinger has to stop being so scared of independence and self-sufficiency and discover the delights of freedom, while the avoidance addict has to stop being so scared of intimacy and affection, of real love and hate, and discover the joys of them. However, if we had a bad experience very early on that gave us good reason to be scared, mistrustful, watchful, and complicated, how can we stop being scared?

Balint's ideas focused on the extraordinary capacity we have of returning to infant states of mind (regression). This is a really strange thing that we human beings are able to do and can be dramatically demonstrated through hypnosis. By regressing *emotionally* to a situation we think we have remembered perfectly well, we can discover that there was much more to it than we thought. I recall a woman whose agoraphobia was getting worse and worse. She remembered that it had started when she was six after she had been frightened by a thunderstorm on the way home from school. Hypnosis regressed her to the event where she was, once more, trudging home through the storm; she was able to recapture the panic feeling—the real problem was that her parents were separating and she was terrified of what was going to happen to her and them. That was what it was really all about.

Balint saw how, in psychotherapy, a person really can *go back to the bad place and start again.* But we do not have to be hypnotised to regress to child states of mind and, indeed, we do it quite often, given the right circumstances. We may become childish in a love situation and it is delightful. Similarly, being in hospital arouses infantile dependency; I remember when I was discharged after an appendectomy when fully adult and I had a momentary flash of feeling, wondering how they could cast a little creature as vulnerable as me out into the harsh world. Similarly, regular sessions of psychotherapy, especially if they are frequent and the patient is lying on the couch, can enable them to drift back to very early states during the session. I have noticed that patients in regression, sometimes change the way they speak: for example, they stop talking about "my mother" and, instead, start referring to her as "Mummy". Thus, through this process, we can go back to where things first went wrong.

Some of Balint's patients talked about a "basic fault" in them that resulted from something they felt must have gone wrong very early in life. In his book *The Basic Fault*, he wrote all about this sense of becoming flawed somehow in infancy, and how it can make us feel that, because of it, we can never live a normal life. But he found how, through regression in psychotherapy, that we *can* go back and deal with it and make a new beginning, even if we have to go very far back. Thus, like the other object relations therapists, he carried the Battle with the Patient back past the three-person drama of the toddler (Oedipal) stage to the two-person drama of the mother–baby stage. At that stage, something can go wrong which is not a conflict, like the Oedipal stage, and which language may be useless to describe, because it happened before speech.

Balint found that sometimes a patient who had come to feel relaxed and secure enough would tentatively offer a form of reaching out to him that would previously have been too scary, or even "impossible, distasteful or repulsive to him", and if Balint responded to it in a human kind of way "an immediate break-through occurred with signal therapeutic developments" (Balint, 1979, p. 128).

An example he gave was of "an attractive, vivacious, and rather flirtatious girl in her late twenties" (Balint, 1979, p. 128) (he was just over thirty or so when he was seeing her), whose main complaint was an inability to achieve anything. A number of men wanted her, but she could not respond. Gradually, he uncovered in her a "crippling fear of uncertainty whenever she had to take any risk, that is, take a decision" (Balint, 1979, p. 128). Balint pointed out to her that the influence of her forceful father and intimidated mother had convinced her that the most important thing was for her

> to keep her head safely up, with both feet firmly planted on the ground. In response, she mentioned that ever since her earliest childhood she could never do a somersault; though at various periods she tried desperately to do one. (Balint, 1979, p. 128

If Professor Freud had heard her story, he would, perhaps, have made an interpretation from on high, but the less inhibited young "Hungarian bastard", not one to smother an impulse, said, "What about it now?" She got up from the coach and performed a somersault with no difficulty.

This proved to be a real breakthrough. Many changes followed in her emotional, social, and professional life, all towards greater freedom and elasticity. Moreover, she managed to get permission to sit for, and passed, a most difficult postgraduate professional examination; eventually she got engaged, and married.

This and other experiences showed Balint that it was possible for the patient, once he was used to being with and talking to the therapist, to risk a return to the naïve (*arglos*) trust of the time before mother scared him, and to trust that the therapist was *not* going to disapprove of childish spontaneity or squash the trust, and would neither over-stimulate or under-stimulate, or be too close or too distant. With this knowledge, the patient could try again, and make a new beginning.

This can mean going back a long way, if the basic fault happened in the very first years or months. Balint became skilled at recognising when his patient had gone back to a really early stage. He noticed certain signs, such as how his interpretations felt like personal slaps or caresses to the patient, and that his words or gestures might carry a wildly disproportionate charge of meaning.

In this situation, classical psychoanalytic technique will not do. Balint based his new technique on the discoveries described above, and on some beliefs, which might be cause for some dismay.

Like Fairbairn, Balint did not believe that hate was a primary instinct or a death instinct, but a reaction to frustration. Instead, he thought it to be the flip side of the unconditional dependency of primary love, which comes out in the form of the total hating, yelling, fury of babies when frustrated; the infants recover from this through normal growing up. But the basic fault *fixes* you in it, or at least in some of it. This is where a dismaying bit of Balint's belief comes in.

> [T]o liberate the individual from the fixation to his hate, the cooperation of the environment is indispensable . . . The only situation in which the environment can be expected to comply intentionally and systematically . . . is the analytic situation . . . (Balint, 1979, p. 71)

I profoundly hope this is not true, and that psychotherapy is not the only way to stop hating, but that does not take away from the genius of the rest of Balint's approach: to cure our fixation with hate, we must *grow up* from the place where we first became fixated, and part of growing up is to *become the equal* of the parent or the therapist, not the subordinate.

The clash with Klein about whether hate is inborn or reactive begins to matter less if maturation is the cure in either case. But the way Balint puts it implies that the function of hatred is to assert ourselves and make things more fair and equal between us and other people, by getting rid of "oppressive inequality" (Balint, 1979, p. 71).

Refusing to be superior to the patient was essential to Balint's treatment. He especially criticised Klein and her followers for getting this wrong. He said they assume that the baby in the patient (whose experiences are preverbal) can be understood not only by words in their normal meaning, but also from the special meaning Kleinians give to words like "breast", "split", "damage", etc. This exclusive language creates the impression of a super-confident, knowledgeable, and, perhaps, overwhelming and omnipotent analyst, an impression only too easy to pass on to their patients.

By contrast, Balint talked as though his *behaviour* in reaction to the patient, as well as the behaviour of the patient to him, was almost more important than words. He watched the patient's behaviour to ascertain whether the patient was looking for tentative experimentation with emotional involvement or free independent adventurousness. He observed the way the patient feels the couch and whether he finds it a safe place or as constraining, or how they look around or close their eyes, and whether they feel safe enough to try a little adventure, etc.

He believed that changes could be observed in the patient's fantasies about the couch, from the way he lies on it, or whether he keeps his eyes closed to feel safe. So, Balint was watching all the time for the little movements of trusting spontaneity coming from the recovered *arglos*, the guileless open trust (reminiscent of Fairbairn's image of the frightened mouse venturing out and retreating) which would dare try out again the lost impulses of separate free adventuring on the one hand, and reaching out to relate, on the other.

When a patient previously scared of relating began to try spontaneous outgoing movements, Balint felt it was often right just to *be there*, and indestructible, like the primary substances earth, air, or water for the patient to act on, or be there offering himself as someone for the patient to love, in a baby way at first, "unconcerned about keeping up proper boundaries between himself and the patient, etc." (Balint, 1979, p. 167).

It is remarkable how just being in the company of a therapist who is not persecuting can somehow free us for a while from the power of a chronic internal persecutor, in this case, an internal sub-personality, always "telling him what to do" (Balint, 1979, p. 142).

If he had a patient who was previously a clinger but showed signs of independence, Balint gave him space. Similarly, if the previously pathologically self-sufficient person showed signs of needing him, Balint responded. His response could include physical warmth, and though he does not mention kissing or cuddling, he was defiantly assertive that physical contact with the regressed patient could be "definitely libidinous" (Balint, 1979, p. 145).

So, here we are back to Freud's question: *how far do you go?* Balint had a wonderful answer, which leads to the next part of Balint's genius: his distinction between *two kinds of regression*.

Balint saw that some patients regress to an almost vindictive, passionate, and ruthless (like a baby) demand for gratification of their infantile needs, like Anna O, who ate Breuer up emotionally while not showing the slightest consideration for him as a person, nearly destroying him, as he acknowledged later on in a letter. We know people who do this in ordinary life. Others, however, like the somersaulter mentioned above, remain civilised and considerate in behaviour even at the infantile level of emotion, and are satisfied and changed and released by the therapist's *recognition* of their basic failing, of the pain and deprivation originally unacknowledged by their environment. So, Balint recognised a *malignant regression* aimed at gratification, and a *benign regression* aimed at recognition. And the pinnacle of his achievement as a therapist was to work out how to change a malignant regression into a benign one. Part of this approach depended on doing the opposite of Freud's technique of dispensing his superior view:

> The more the analyst's technique and behaviour are suggestive of omniscience and omnipotence, the greater is the danger of a malignant form of regression. On the other hand, the more the analyst can reduce the inequality between the patient and himself and the more unobtrusive and ordinary he can remain in the patient's eyes, the better are the chances of a benign form of regression. (Balint, 1979, p. 173)

(You could say, by the way, that being steadfastly more ordinary than the patient enables the therapist to infect him with normality and health.)

Balint gave an example of a patient who felt especially awful at the end of one Friday session and asked for an extra one over the weekend. Balint had provided the patient with such extras before, and they had made him feel better, but had not advanced his cure. Was Balint to refuse and seem cruel, or give in and foster the patient's dependence?

He responded by acknowledging the request, but explained that it was his wish for the patient not to feel further weakened by such dependence. Balint tells how the patient did ring later but only to let him know how he was feeling, and not to repeat his request.

This episode shows how the analyst's response turned a process that started in the direction of a "craving" for satisfaction—that is, a possible malignant form—into a benign one, that is, a regression for recognition. Balint managed it by avoiding even a semblance of omniscience, while he also demonstrated his willingness to accept the role of a therapist, whose chief function is to recognise and be with his patient.

So, should the therapist be as emotionally detached as Freud recommended? Klein was adamant that therapists should not allow themselves to display ordinary human reactions to the child's hostility. But Balint had found another way: he was selective among his own emotional responses, allowing those which he thought would do the patient good and disallowing those which would do harm. The rule (which I do not think he ever tried to state explicitly) in practice was: express and act out those responses in yourself which will encourage the patient's trust in life and in self and in others, that is, healthy enterprise, adventurousness, freedom, and sincere emotional bonding, and use all other responses only to understand the patient and yourself, without acting on them.

This is what I am taking money for in my work. The patient can see the therapist as an authority exacting financial tribute in payment for his leadership and guidance. What is really going on with those of us who follow this line is that we are selling the use of our emotions, which really means our bodies.

Balint thought we needed a two-body psychology to understand what happens in psychotherapy. He counted physical, including subtle sexual ("libidinal" was his word) exchange among those responses of the therapist that can be good and useful. In any case, even if the patient and I never lay a finger on each other, if I allow myself to respond emotionally to the patient, my emotions are reactions of my body. My muscles, heart, salivary, adrenal, pituitary, and thyroid glands, and gonads, tearducts, sympathetic and parasympathetic nervous systems, and all they control, the adrenalin, serotonin, and other chemical carriers of emotion flowing in my blood and cere-brospinal fluid, etc., are open for my patient to play on. He awakes reactions in my body that send truths about the interaction between us back up from my guts, or wherever, through the stem and palaeo-cortex of my brain into the neocortex and I hear them.

If I feel the hairs on the back of my neck stand up, I know I am getting angry at the patient's unfairness to me when assuming the role of baby, whatever it may cost me. As far as the patient is concerned, I am to blame for any distress or inconvenience he may feel because I am totally responsible for him feeling good, now and forever—that is the deal he is counting on: the malignant transference. Or, sometimes, a patient's anxiety sort of gives me uncomfortable tingles as she radi-ates it at me from her rigid body in her chair, poised ready to attack if either touched or ignored, while I in my chair take in her tenseness; however, I do not react with tension, but wait and let its vibrations gradually die down as it drains away from her into the shock-absorber of my calmer body. Then I feel like Elisha in the Bible lying on the widow's dead boy, eye to eye, mouth to mouth, hand to hand, and warming him back to life.

Of course, you can get it wrong. A certain well known London psychoanalyst happened to be with a patient when he had his first heart attack; "What are you doing to me!" he exclaimed at her. Maybe she *was* doing something to him. Although it is unlikely she had silted up his coronary arteries, patients do have the ability to make a thera-pist physically ill.

I remember as a young man being in a session with Jung's close associate, Jolande Jacobi. I was telling her about some sexual adven-ture, and I saw her tummy quake under her dress, and I knew this was a sign that she was empathising with me. Our body *is* our emotions. "With my body I thee worship," says the bridegroom in the ancient Anglican Sacrament of Marriage. "With my body I thee console," says the prostitute. "With my body I thee heal," says the psychotherapist. So, I am taking money for making my body available to the patient. Does that make me a prostitute? Yes, it does. I heartily accept that it does. I once saw a gentle Australian prostitute being interviewed by Alan Whicker about what she did for her clients: "It's got to make you a better person," she said, and I know how she felt.

But I claim to be a *sacred* prostitute. Like the sacred temple prosti-tutes of antiquity in India, I am married to the god (like nuns, too, come to think of it). So the god's demands come first: I will not fake orgasms, as it were (in order, for example, to *guarantee* unconditional positive regard or non-possessive empathetic warmth), or pretend to feel anything I do not. I will not excite the patient for *my* satisfaction, but only respond to his or her needs, and my spontaneous reactions will be either acted on or used only for information and then allowed to die, according to Balint's rules. I will not do S&M or anything phys- ical that would only be avoiding emotional conflict, and in practice that reduces skin contact to near zero (to less than Balint used—I am Scottish, not Hungarian), but it is still two or more human animal *bodies* in the dances of emotional interactions, and one of them is being paid to subordinate his emotional needs, temporarily, for fifty minutes, to the other's. Selling my body in this way I am hiring out the use of whatever sound vitality my parents and ancestors devel- oped through the ages, plus whatever I have embodied of the lessons learnt from the stupid and cowardly mistakes I have made in my own life, and my training has taught me how to do it, like any other high- class and well-trained prostitute.

Freud charged professionally for his intellectual reactions to the patient, but I and many others, like Balint, are charging for our emo- tional, that is, our bodily responses, as well as for our intellectual training. Itemised bills would vary wildly from patient to patient and session to session, but a careful invoice on one occasion might go:

> Benign indifference . . . 24 mins @ 50p per min.
> Affection or sympathy . . . 6 mins @ £2 per min
> Spontaneous admiration . . . 4 mins, fee waived
> Empathetic sadness . . . 7 mins @ £2 per min
> Existential angst . . . 4 mins @ £5 per min (special skill)
> Anger . . . 3 min @ £4 per min
> Love or hate . . . 2 mins @ £10 per min
> Fear . . . not charged—counted as part of the exhilaration associ- ated with job satisfaction
> Total: 50 min at £90. (Laundry for tears and sweat not charged for but might be claimed off income tax.)

On William Blake's principle that "opposition is true friendship", I would charge more for love and hate than other emotions. It takes more effort to manage. Lola Paulsen, a Jungian analyst, once told us how she paused behind her front door to say, silently, to the patient waiting on the other side, "I *HATE* YOU", with all her heart, and after having established that with herself, she let him in and went on satisfactorily with the analysis.

The psychoanalyst Donald Winnicott, who was an exact contemporary of Balint, commented that the therapist might have to wait a long time for the moment when they can tell the patient how they had hated him and what for. Only too gentle and sweet himself, he had some amazing observations about hate, as we shall see in the next chapter. He carried the understanding of the babies into depths that can only be described as awesome, exploring among the roots of human passions and human culture.

CHAPTER SEVENTEEN

Donald Winnicott:
the compassionate thinker

"All that I am, or hope to be, I owe to my angel mother"

(Attributed to Abraham Lincoln)

D onald Winnicott came to talk to us at Guy's Hospital and told us about a little boy who had been born with toes connected together by skin, which his mother had had surgically corrected. Winnicott played his famous "Squiggle Game" with the child, a game in which the child and psychiatrist take part. Each, in turn, makes a squiggle that the other alters into something that it suggests to him. The boy altered Winnicott's squiggle into a duck with webbed feet.

"When I saw that, I cried," Winnicott told us. This was followed by a startled intensification of attention in the audience. "*Cried*" did he say? But surely it was Freud who said that the attitude of the psychoanalyst had to be like that of the surgeon's attitude to pus: unemotional.

Yes, indeed Freud did. But Winnicott, typically of him, had an intuitive flash of empathy for the child, and felt how the little boy must have wished that his mother had loved him just as he was, and not felt the need to surgically change him in order to make him acceptable. Thus, Winnicott empathised, and he cried.

He evidently enjoyed talking to us in quite a showing-off kind of way, entertaining us as well as informing us. When he asked us where he had put his spectacles, and we told him they were on the top of his head, he said, "Well, if I'm going to be seventy, I might as well act like it!"

There was a charming lack of aggressiveness in Winnicott, and he was a bit shocked at the way Fairbairn had so boldly contradicted Freud. He had an endlessly receptive humility that opened him to a staggering wealth of observation and understanding of mothers and babies and children. Yet, as you will see, some of his observations were more radically subversive of psychoanalysis than might seem on the surface. He started as a paediatrician, and kept on with that when he became a psychoanalyst; he is thought to have known 60,000 children and babies during his career. Melanie Klein valued him and undervalued him; Winnicott wanted her to analyse him but she refused, instead asking him to analyse her son—provided, that is, she supervised the analysis, an offer Winnicott declined.

In 1952, following some bruising clash between Klein and Winnicott at the Institute of Psychoanalysis, he wrote her a long, long letter which said that he knew he was annoying, but he was tolerated by his peers because at least he had ideas, and did she have to insist that it was *her* language that was used for any new discoveries? He also wrote that he believed, from the bottom of his heart, that she was the best analyst in the movement. However, he mentioned that he was unable to write a chapter for her book, as requested by Klein, because she disagreed with a number of his theories, and he was afraid that his theories might be dismissed as mental illness, something he was able to deal with in his own way. (Perhaps Klein had been using the psychoanalysts' debating style, usual at that time, where opponents were told that they needed more analysis.) One could not imagine Fairbairn or Balint writing her such a humble, flattering, reproachful, letter.

Winnicott grew up with little example of good assertive manliness at home. He was born in 1896, and had two sisters, six and five years older than he; he said later he was "in a sense . . . an only child with multiple mothers and with father extremely preoccupied in my younger years with town as well as business matters" (Philips, 1989, p. 23).

The input of his father, Sir Frederick, Mayor of Portsmouth, a merchant of women's corsets, when he *was* there, does not sound encouraging of male aggression, or, indeed, encouraging in any way. His father teased and disapproved of his son; according to Winnicott, when his father heard him exclaim "drat" at age thirteen, he sent him to boarding school. However, Winnicott blossomed at school, and had a great time, and developed a teenage enthusiasm for Darwin, which liberated him emotionally. The mothering he got was also found wanting. I remember forty or fifty years ago, listening to Winnicott being interviewed on *Woman's Hour*; the interviewer asked him about his own mother, and he said, "Well . . . I *had* a mother . . ." and either went on to say, or seemed to imply, "and that's all there is to be said about that". His mother suffered from depression, and when he was sixty-seven, he wrote a poem called "The Tree" about her, in which he wrote ". . . to enliven her was my living" (Philips, 1989, p. 29). So, by insisting on being alive, he cheered her up, a bit. When I read that after his death and remembered him being so lively, cheering us all up at Guy's, I could have wept for him like he did for the little boy with webbed feet, as I thought of his personality being formed by the way he took on the "unnatural", "intolerable" burden of enlivening his mother.

His first marriage, to Alice, was not a success, but he stayed with her for twenty-seven years before they divorced; two years later, he married Clare, who was a social worker. Winnicott did not have any children from either marriage, but twice he and Alice took in disturbed young people, one an impossible nine-year-old boy, to live with them, which sounds pretty admirable of Alice. Of all the great therapists in this book, so far, he was the only one, apart from Anna Freud, who had no children of his own, but he knew more about babies and children than any of them. It was reported that, on one occasion, when someone was driving him home from a psycho-analytic meeting, he said, "None of them can do what I do." And it was true.

His best writing was for mothers, about babies and children. He seemed, almost unbelievably, to be able to empathise with what babies were feeling. In his book, *The Child, the Family and the Outside World* (1964), there is a lovely chapter about the different emotions that make babies cry: the satisfaction of exercising their lungs, or the pain of hunger or fear, or rage, or grief, sad crying with a musical note, or the "crying of hopelessness and despair, the crying that the other kinds break down into if there is no hope left in the baby's mind" (Winnicott, 1964, p. 67). (The latter heard more often in institutions than in homes.)

However, Winnicott said that he learnt more about how babies' minds work from adults in regression than from babies themselves. What he has to say is of special significance for the Enlightenment of the Mind: what he found comes from farther outside our culture than the most remote primitive tribe; it comes from a place where there are *no words at all*: the inner world of infancy. Our culture is word-centred: Jews, Muslims, and Christians are the "People of the Book", and the word is given the highest value: it is God—"in the beginning was the word, and the word was with God, and the word was God". Because Winnicott was reaching into the preverbal, he often wrote in an obscure manner, but it is worth making an effort to understand what he was trying to say. Of all the great therapists, he was the most *original* observer of babies and children, but that does not help to understand him either, and neither does the way he takes pleasure in being mischievously provocative. Trying to make the obscurity of his genius transparent to the common reader is *very* hard work, I can tell you, but well worth it in order to show the preverbal roots of our adult world.

When, as a young man, he started understanding babies, it was still orthodox in psychoanalysis to look to the toddler period, the Oedipus complex, for the origin of all problems. Thus, he was extremely nervous about exposing his own beliefs on the subject; theories that contradicted the great master, Freud. For Winnicott believed that emotional trouble began a lot earlier than the toddler stage.

When he got Melanie Klein to be his supervisor, she emboldened him to believe what he observed: what actually goes on in the intense, twenty-four-hour interaction between a baby and its mother. "There is no such thing as a baby" (Winnicott, 1964, p. 88), he, famously, said. He meant that babies could only be understood if they are with their mother, as a "nursing couple" (Philips, 1989, p. 5). To Balint's picture of the baby in the heaven of the harmonious mix-up of primary love, he added a wonderful depiction of the enormous work and unconscious wisdom of the ordinary mother in making the heaven. "Primary maternal preoccupation" (Winnicott, 1975, p. 302) was his term for the way the mother, in love with the newborn little person, is totally devoted to baby's needs. It develops towards the end of pregnancy, lasts for a few weeks, and "is not easily remembered by mothers once they have recovered from it" (Winnicott, 1975, p.302).

Winnicott observed how the mother was always following the baby's initiative. This is similar to Klein's discoveries when she watched children play and saw them enact phantasies alongside every instinctual impulse; thus, when mother responds to baby's needs, she is giving him what he is already consciously or unconsciously *imagining*, perhaps even hallucinating. Winnicott realised that when a baby is hungry, for example, he has some idea of what he wants, a fantasy of a breast, as though he is hallucinating a breast with milk in it before his mouth closes on the real nipple.

Winnicott believed that what the mother does in those first weeks or months while she is still in love with the baby is to encourage the baby in his feeling that he is creating his world, and that he is omnipotent: he just has to be hungry and imagine a breast and lo! the nipple is in his mouth being sucked. He just has to need to be held and the arms are there. In short, he just has to imagine and reality fits in. The concept of infantile omnipotence was already in Klein's model. (I knew a Kleinian analyst and his wife who used the concept in forwarding marital understanding: "Don't be so *bloody* omnipotent!" she would yell at him.)

The way Winnicott put it was that the baby *creates* the breast, and creates his mother, or at least that is what it feels like to the baby, because mother gives the breast at just the right time to fit in with the baby's imaginings. This, much repeated, starts off the infant's ability to use *illusion*, without which no contact is possible between the psyche and the environment.

Winnicott also cited the case of a baby girl wounded by a red-hot poker that her brother had pushed into her neck; the baby hardly cried and showed no ill effects, emotionally, because "it happened that having a hot poker put next her neck corresponded with nothing already in the infant's mind" (Winnicott, 1975, p. 9). What Winnicott was saying was that there had to be an idea of something in the mind already, before something could affect us emotionally.

That needs thinking about. When we *act* on the illusion that there is a breast which, when sucked, will give milk, our action is magically rewarded with milk. Winnicott believed that it took months and years for a baby to fully grasp that the breast is real, and that it has a real mother, and a real world that it is, in fact, having to relate with. It also takes a considerable amount of time for the baby to realise that it is a complex process, involving at least three entwined achievements: the baby gradually becomes disillusioned about its magical power; it discovers it does not want to hurt its mother; and it learns to hate.

At first, the baby imagines and creates his world, and the real world, obligingly, mostly clicks in. He does not need to know where his fantasy ends and reality begins. The transition from an interaction with mother based on illusion should happen gradually. The unconsciously wise mother who enables the baby to feel omnipotently self-confident at the beginning, which is a good start-off for life, also gradually disillusions him, by being less than perfect herself and letting him encounter the real world around, so that he gradually gives up the feeling of magic omnipotent power over everyone and gears in more to reality, and learns to relate to a real mother who sometimes lets him down or frustrates him. This is rarely a smooth process, and plenty of us have not entirely done it yet, however old we are. Violent emotions are involved.

It is said that there is nothing in human relationships that is more powerful than the bond between a baby and the mother (or breast) during the excitement of a breastfeeding experience. Winnicott views this primitive love impulse from the baby's point of view, as a kind of fantasy, such as it is, of a ruthless attack on mother (or breast.) But somehow, for no reason at all, the baby eventually stops being ruthless, and begins to care for its mother's feelings, not wanting to hurt her, as though it becomes able to empathise with her.

I knew a woman whose baby fed quietly for months then, suddenly, out of the blue, bit her so sharply she yelled and jumped. After that, he would never go to the breast again, and they both accepted Nature's message that he was now ready to go on to less reactive food.

Two years after Klein's death, lecturing in San Francisco, Winnicott said, "I think this is a bad name" (Winnicott, 1975, p. 9) in relation to her term "depressive position", adding, "and the term paranoid–schizoid position is certainly a bad one . . . (Winnicott, 1990, p. 176). Like Balint, he could not believe it *had* to be as awful being a baby as Klein described, and he thought that no baby who had ordinary "good-enough" mothering suffered the "paranoid–schizoid position" (Klein, 2003, p. 187), as described by Klein. Ordinary babies are not mad, he said. However, he did agree that an adult in regression in analysis who belatedly reached this stage might well feel *depressed* by the responsibility it brings with it.

Winnicott thought that we have *two* kinds of aggression: natural instinctual aggression, as exemplified in nice, greedy breastfeeding, *and* aggressive reactive to frustration, and we cannot help either. But it sets us a problem: healthy spontaneous aggression is good, but yet one does not want to hurt mother.

As we look at the infant developing into a person, we can see how the mother is gradually perceived in the quiet times as a person, too, as something attractive and valued exactly as she appears. How awful then to be hungry, and to feel oneself ruthlessly attacking this same mother. No wonder infants often lose appetite (Winnicott, 1964, p. 81).

The basis for eventual health in this, and many other respects, is the whole experience of being carried through infancy by the ordinary good mother who is not afraid of her infant's ideas, and who loves it when her infant goes at her all out. The mother and baby are then launched on an adventure of mutual love and hate. She puts up with being the bad mother sometimes, instead of always the ideal mother, and increasingly the child sees her as the individual person she really is: neither ideal angel nor evil witch. (Klein's child patient, Erna, reached this point, belatedly, in analysis.)

She survives the baby's attacks, and, bit by bit, humanises the extremeness of the baby's aggressive instincts and his terror of retaliation for them. The natural functions of eating, defecation, and urinating are socialised as the child learns to enrich the instinctual satisfaction they give by also giving mother pleasure through them. Taking in nourishment especially gets adapted to the reality of mother as a person, and normal breast-feeding is an "orgy", with violent accompanying fantasies.

Winnicott sees this as the birth of morality. Mother's task is to *allow* and *encourage* (*not* inculcate) the "innate tendencies towards morality" (Winnicott, 1964, p. 81).

Winnicott describes this sense of guilt as the basis in the child for a capacity to feel a sense of responsibility. The continued presence of the mother (or fathering when in the mothering role) from about six months to two years is needed to enable the child to make a healthy fusion of both destroying and loving the same object (mother.) The child gradually integrates these two aspects, and is able to tolerate a sense of guilt about destructive instincts, because he knows about the possibility for repair. As Winnicott might have said: civilisation has started again inside a new human being . . .

So, this is where civilisation comes from—it starts spontaneously in the individual infant in the first few months of life! Winnicott thought of civilisation as a moral state, where "ruth" is the gradual learning of responsibility and empathy by the baby towards its mother and then others. The instinct to repair and make up for harm done, and the urge to make another happy, is all part of this process, and it happens from within, *spontaneously*. This is in direct contradiction to Freud's belief that conscience originates from the fear of being castrated as punishment for Oedipal desires. Conscience, to Winnicott, is not an implant from outside, neither is it caused by stick, or even by carrot; no bribery is necessary, it is born out of nowhere into the ordinary baby, and only needs to be encouraged.

Winnicott list patterns of behaviour by which a child can manage his aggression:

1   A bold child expresses it openly and finds it is limited and expendable—good.

2.   A timid child projects it and is scared of whatever he projects it into in his environment—not so good.

3.   He can hold it inside and become tense, over-controlled and serious, perhaps liable to the occasional tantrum.

4.   He can express it in dreaming:

In dreaming, destruction and killing are expressed in fantasy, and this dreaming is associated with any degree of excitement in the body, and *is a real experience* and not just an intellectual exercise. The child who can manage dreaming is becoming ready for all kinds of playing . . .

5.   In play, symbols express aggression: by losing a toy a child can express the desire that mother's new baby should get lost.

6.   The aggression can be expressed in *construction*.

It is a most important sign of health in a child when constructive play appears and is maintained. *This is something that cannot be implanted* . . . (Winnicott, 1984, p. 95, my italics)

Winnicott believed that you could demonstrate the connection between aggression and construction by preventing the child—or an adult for that matter—from making some spontaneous contribution, for example, a child who wants to give its mother pleasure by doing something useful, even if it is beyond his capabilities. If the child is laughed at for its clumsy attempts at vacuuming the carpet, or something like that, you can expect some frank aggression or destructiveness to follow. This, Winnicott thought, was because *no one understands that a child needs to give even more than to receive.*

Just as the baby magically creates the mother, so the angry baby in imagination magically annihilates the world, which could leave one feeling pretty bad, alone in an annihilated world. It is better to really hit your real mother and find she is not in the least annihilated.

If time is allowed for maturational processes, then the infant becomes able to be destructive and becomes able to kick and scream instead of magically annihilating the world. In this way, *actual aggression is seen to be an achievement.* As compared with magical destruction, aggressive ideas and behaviour take on a positive value, and *"hate becomes a sign of civilisation"* (Winnicott, 1984, p. 97).

Winnicott believed that the "good-enough mother" (Winnicott, 1987, p. 38) enables the baby to hate. By "good-enough", he meant that the mother does not need to be perfect all the time, but needs to have the ability to adapt to the baby's needs; this includes accepting the baby's discovery of hatred, and allowing the baby to lash out. However, Winnicott also believed that the mother hates the baby first, and he goes on to list "some of the reasons" (he gives eighteen) why a mother hates her baby. Here are just a few:

- The baby is a danger to her body in pregnancy and at birth.
- The baby is an interference with her private life, a challenge to preoccupation.
- He is ruthless, treats her as scum, an unpaid servant, a slave.
- He tries to hurt her, periodically bites her, all in love.
- The baby at first must dominate, he must be protected from coincidences, life must unfold at the baby's rate and all this needs his mother's continuous and detailed study. For instance, she must not be anxious when holding him.
- If she fails him at the start she knows he will pay her out forever.

The above are taken from his paper "Hate in the counter-transference" (Winnicott, 1947). Two kinds of patient especially make the therapist hate them: psychotic and antisocial patients. He gave an example of how he hated, not a patient, but a nine-year-old antisocial delinquent evacuee taken in by him and Alice. The boy was well known to police stations far and wide. The Winnicotts found him both lovable and maddening.

Elsewhere, Winnicott spoke of delinquency with great understanding and sympathy, describing the delinquent act, the thieving or whatever, as the "moment of hope" (Winnicott, 1975, p. 309), when the person acts as though he has found the mother who is rightly his to ruthlessly use and take from. Winnicott believed that antisocial attitudes result from the baby being deprived of love from its mother, and that delinquent acts are attempts to find the missing mother.

You will remember how Adler said a child's play should be treated with serious respect, and how Jung recovered from the loss of Freud by playing with his children and then by himself (and how that released in him the pure creativity of the archetypal dramas, persons and creatures that visited him from the collective unconscious). Klein also valued play and made great use of it; Balint described it as the "area of creation" (Balint, 1992, p. 24). Winnicott saw play as the heart of life—or rather the fountain of life, issuing from a source at the core of a person, a source that is itself always safely beyond reach of others, kept *incommunicado*.

I mentioned his Squiggle Game at the beginning of this chapter. At the orthopaedic clinic, he kept a bright, shiny, metal spatula on his desk within reach of the babies so he could see how they would play with it. Like Klein, he saw how a child's play expresses its *inner world*: he thought that the baby begins life in an illusory, imagined world which his mother supports by providing what he is imagining, and she gradually eases him bit by bit into grasping reality.

Winnicott was fascinated by the intermediate stages where illusion and reality mingle. He cited as an example of this the phenomenon of the particularly loved toy or cuddle-blanket, which is treated as if it can exchange affection and comfort like a breast or mother. He believed that the baby was using the bit of blanket, or whatever, as a *transitional object*: transitional between illusion and reality, between the earlier way of relating to the world and the later way, and between mother and the rest of the world—a transitional state where illusion and reality are not defined.

This area of the mingling of imagination and reality is where play happens; this also applies to art and religion: for example, in transubstantiation in the Mass, where the bread is both real bread and the body of Christ. Winnicott was disappointed that this idea was not taken up more by psychoanalysts, though the phrase "transitional object" became a great cliché for a while in the caring professions. He drew some obscure diagrams to express what he meant, that showed a spectrum between imagination and reality with dreams at the most subjective end, ranging through fantasy, play, the arts, work in shared reality, and science at the most objective end. So, the mingled illusion and reality of the cuddle-blanket is another aspect of the dawn of civilisation in each baby.

He believed that therapy is essentially therapist and patient playing together, and if the patient cannot play, then the therapy must teach him to. Play with Winnicott could work like magic, as we shall see in the next chapter.

I mentioned that Winnicott is often obscure because he is trying to describe preverbal states of mind. Words that were supposed to be scientific he used like a poet in startling, enlightening ways: for example, "A word like 'self' naturally knows more than we do; it uses us and can command us" (Winnicott, 1990, p. 158). But his light and playful style can sometimes frustrate the earnest reader, as can his less co-ordinated theoretical structure. A lot of Winnicott's theories were confusing because he was never seriously aggressive enough to stand up and contradict Freud flatly and energetically, as Fairbairn did, even though the "object relations" direction of thinking, as it culminated in Winnicott, did contradict Freud. For example:

1. Where Freud saw neurosis as following from failure to grow out of the Oedipal complex at the toddler stage, leaving the neurotic with an ego afraid of instinct, Winnicott saw emotional problems as a result of being let down by the environment in the first year of life.
2. Freud believed that conscience arose from the fear of being castrated by father for Oedipal wishes, while Winnicott saw conscience as spontaneously dawning in the first months of life.
3. Freud saw the unconscious sub-personality of his patient, the Rat Man, as childish lust and hate as evil and at enmity with civilisation, but Winnicott saw the baby's active aggression and hate as good, and an achievement of civilisation.

Winnicott's description of the child's inner world sounds like Jung's description of the archetypes, but Winnicott thought the archetypes could not be active until the baby had an organised ego.

Writers about Winnicott that try to explain what he meant cannot help putting their own slant on it a little, which I am about to do now, so this is advance warning! Putting my slant on it, I believe that the function of aggression and hate is to assert the creative originality of the true self in the face of opposition. Or, pushing it a bit further, the function of hate is to defend and assert the individual's creative imagination against threat from others. The crucial question is whether one fights fair or fights dirty, destructively or constructively. If it is done constructively, my vision and yours can marry and enhance each other, so that hostility can lead to and create goodness. Easily said, culturally momentous. How does one hate constructively? We shall explore this later on.

In Winnicott's eyes, baby could do no wrong, and the baby in the patient could do no wrong. His attitude was an endless benign tolerance, patience, and acceptance; his second wife, Clare, said he suffered from "delusions of benignity" (Jacobs, 1995, p. 5)! How that affected his treatment methods can be understood from a talk he gave four years before his death to Borstal (juvenile reformatory) staff about the "anti-social tendency", saying that it was a reaction to deprivation.

He believed that a person *steals* in a *moment of hope* (famous phrase of Winnicott's) of recovering what he once ceased to get from mother, and is *aggressive* when hope prompts him to provoke his environment to give him the containing structure that is missing in his family.

So, according to Winnicott, a delinquent in a prison cell, like a patient in a locked ward of the mental hospital, can find the containment they are looking for—but can it feel the same? I used to think that when psychotic patients in an episode of violence were put in the padded locked room in the hospital where I worked they seemed reassured. Sometimes, when a patient (let's call him James) from the general part of the hospital paid a friendly social visit to the locked ward, the staff would say, "James came today to book his bed", because whether James was aware of it or not, he was on the verge of a psychotic episode. By visiting the ward, it was as though he wanted to be assured that the staff he knew from the past would still be there to look after him.

Winnicott pointed out that with regard to stealing and aggressiveness, society is likely to respond "moralistically" (Winnicott, 1986, p. 95) with punishment and further hardening. But if the child receives psychotherapy instead, there is the possibility of recovering the moment before deprivation, and within a creative relationship with the therapist, of reliving this time, and restoring the lost security.

Where does punishment come in? At the end of the century, a British Conservative Prime Minister (John Major) reacted against such soft attitudes to crime: "We need to understand a little less and condemn a little more" (Barry, 2005, p. 12), he said.

You might think that the shepherd who understands wolves will lose fewer lambs, but psychotherapists like Winnicott gave the Enlightenment of the Mind a soft public face so that "understanding" shifted towards meaning "weak".

Winnicott contrasted two ways of bringing up children: allowing them to find their own spontaneous goodness on the one hand, and on the other implanting a moral code in them by coercion. When talking about actual children, he was strongly in favour of the first, but when talking more abstractly about social problems, he would not dismiss the latter, sympathising with the anxiety that causes people to try to coerce children into being good, and saying that for some children who have had a bad start it is the best that can be done.

Winnicott's writing is among the richest of the century, and my brief account can only provide a little of his wisdom. I do urge everyone to read *The Child, the Family and the Outside World*. The great founders of the Enlightenment of the Mind were geniuses, no doubt about it. But after the biographies and diaries are published and the gossip comes out, we can find ourselves knowing more about these geniuses than their friends did, and they can begin to look a wee bit strange. Winnicott's capacity to mother his patients was uncanny, even monstrous in a man, but as an ordinary chap, I was taken aback by two things that he did that I would not have done.

I would not have quit the room if a patient started trashing it. I would have stayed right there with all my antennae out, drinking in the scene and missing nothing of the patient's reactions or my own, ready to stop him if he went too far. And I would have expected reparation in the form of replacement of the vase. I remember when a patient in a therapeutic community ingeniously turned the fire hose on me. I gave her the bill for the cleaning of my suit—she didn't pay it, and I did not expect her to, partly because I sympathised too much with her point of view, but I felt she should know I thought she owed me something.

Also, I would not tell a nine-year-old boy that I hated him (as Winnicott did with the boy he and Alice had taken in) without expressing anger. I would have done the opposite: I would have expressed anger, without saying I hated him and I would not have turned him out (even if there *was* a bell he could ring for re-admittance.)

Another little thing that jars about Winnicott is that he sometimes writes of excitement as itself an unpleasant thing, something that babies and people would avoid if they could. (He said that when a baby is excited it feels like how we would feel in a den of lions.) Balint insisted at both the beginning and at the end of his book, *Thrills and Regressions*, how in the fairground one's destructive aggression is enjoyed and rewarded. I wonder if Winnicott's depressed mother was not able to enjoy that side of her baby in the same way as Balint's mother, instead leaving Winnicott permanently over-sensitive. Winnicott's mother might also have not empathised with the old nanny in Shakespeare's Coriolanus, and her gleeful admiration of the way the infant general tore a butterfly to pieces: "Lord! How he mammocked it!" (Shakespeare, 1623b).

And another little thing: I feel excluded from his collusive intimacy with the new mother when he tells her, "Enjoy all sorts of womanly feelings that you cannot even start to explain to a man" (Badinter, 1981, p. 276). Winnicott's world is too cosy and innocent. He believed that the way the analyst expressed hate towards the patient was by ending the session. Call that hate?

The eighteen reasons that Winnicott came up with to explain the mother's hatred of her baby are mild compared to others that lead to torture and infanticide. Later in the century, in Britain, other paediatricians and social workers swung the opposite way. Whereas Winnicott was well content that his paediatric clinic in Paddington Green should mainly cater for the hypochondria of mothers, others saw mothers as deliberately hurting and making their babies ill in order to get attention themselves—"Munchausen Syndrome by Proxy" (Myers, 1998, p. 244), and made the diagnosis of sexual and sadistic cruelty to children too often. So, in the early years of the new millennium in Britain, the consequence was a reverse witch-hunt, trying to right unknown numbers of cases where the experts might have got it wrong, where heartbroken and bereaved mothers, instead of being consoled, were jailed, their families broken up, etc. I would argue that, in the first instance, these events only ever occurred to satisfy the repressed sex and aggression, projected from the unconscious minds of unanalysed professionals into their innocent clients. I wish Winnicott had taken evil more seriously, more like a man, and brought to it the talents he had that the rest of us do not have; then, perhaps, these incorrect misdiagnoses by our colleagues would have been fewer.

The things that jar about Winnicott add up to an imbalance between his genius as a mother, and the absence of an equal father. It is as if he triumphantly made up for the poor mothering he got by finding in himself the living archetype of the good-enough mother, better than anyone else ever has, but he did not even try to find the father inside him.

Adam Phillips, in his biography of Winnicott, was suspicious about Winnicott's determination to see his own father as benign, only seeing the hostility between them as a conventional Oedipus complex. In the area of father–son hostility Winnicott was actually a conflict-avoider, who failed to thoroughly murder his father (psychologically speaking) and take over and dominate the father territory, as was his due.

In his rare mentioning of fathers in his books, he said the right things, but generally in his writing, authority presents itself as a weak and fearful attempt to coerce and impose compliance by force and fear—no better than Freud's image of authority, the threatening super-ego. It takes over only when mother has failed, and merely contradicts mother's kind of love instead of complementing it. As I said above, he kept the two principles apart in his mind: the deeply understood loving (and hating) mother of his reborn self is kept separate from the father as prison-officer, who sends his child away to boarding school when he hears him saying "drat!"

Winnicott's motherly softness, which was essentially a great truth, needs a powerful good authority of a father to protect it and validate it, rather than a weak father to undermine it, but the development of the stronger image of father had to wait until later in the century.

Before leaving this phase of the humanising of psychoanalysism I shall tell you about a psychoanalyst who found another marvellous excuse for believing in love, although it was something that Winnicott could not see the point of or believe in at all, but many others have found it enormously valuable.

As a child, John Bowlby, eleven years younger than Winnicott and twenty-five years younger than Melanie Klein, hated being sent away to boarding school, really suffered, and no doubt was expected at the time to be British and stiff-upper-lipped about it. He qualified as a doctor in 1933, and shortly after as a psychoanalyst. Possibly because of his wartime experiences as a doctor, including arrangements for evacuating children from London, and the rescue of Jewish children by the kindertransport, he was struck by the terrible effect the loss of a loved one could have on a person. While working at the London Child Guidance Clinic throughout the 1950s, he noticed how badly children were affected as a result of being brought up in institutions, thereby lacking a close loving relationship with a mother of their own.

Animal ethology brought him a blinding light, in the form of the naturalist, Konrad Lorenz, and his findings about the powerful instinctual attachment between bird and animal mothers and their offspring. Lorenz observed how hatching ducklings attached themselves to the first moving object near to them, whether it was their mother or Konrad Lorenz himself, and followed closely wherever the object went, and would not part without great distress. Lorenz called this "imprinting" (Helms & Turner, 1986, p. 52). This supported Bowlby's idea that there is an instinctual need for *attachment of an emotional nature*, for the love and presence of a mother, as important as the need for food, noting the research done with primates which showed the way baby apes need their mothers. For example, the American psychologist, Harry S. Harlow carried out a famous and rather gruesome experiment in which baby chimpanzees were given a wire-netting mother that mechanically supplied food, or a more cosy fabric-covered artificial version that did not provide any food. The baby chimps spent more time with the soft, "cosy" mother, thus demonstrating that comfort was more important to them than food. As they grew up, these chimps were unable to relate to other chimps.

Bowlby pointed out that maternally deprived children cannot themselves easily make good parents. It seems strange now that he had to go to such lengths of scholarship and investigation to get across the idea that it is an *instinctual* need essential for mental health . . . that the infant and young child should experience a warm intimate and continuous relationship with his mother (or mother-substitute) in which both find satisfaction and enjoyment . . . (Bowlby, 1951, p. 11)

He revolutionised the management of children in children's hospitals: after a few years of battle, mothers were finally allowed to stay with their sick children in hospital, and children's teddy bears were no longer taken away from them.

Attachment and loss were Bowlby's themes. Given secure attachment, the child shows confident exploratory behaviour and can grow up successfully; with only insecure attachment, the child shows anxious, clinging, avoidant attachment or hostile attachment. A study of these states turned out to provide a good way of understanding neurotic behaviour.

So much for the soft, mothering side of psychoanalysis. In the next chapter we shall leave Britain behind and jump to America to describe a great therapist who operated as a hard father.

CHAPTER EIGHTEEN

Karen Horney: the gentle rebel

"Why can't we think differently and still be friends?"

(Karen Horney)

I n the first half of the century, a notable rebel against Freud emerged. Her name was Karen Horney, and she was thoroughly fed up with Freud's and his colleagues' attitudes to women. In fact, as her biographer Susan Quinn emphasised in the title of the biography (1988), she was a person who had *A Mind of Her Own* from childhood on.

Karen was born in Hamburg, Germany, in 1885. Her father was a sea captain, a real disciplinarian who clashed terribly with the rest of the family, including her mother. Karen disliked her father intensely and resented his "bible thumping" (Quinn, 1988, p. 404) ways and authoritarian manner.

From an early age, Karen adored her mother but later on in life was put off by her intrusive clinging. As a child, she developed a crush on her brother, but his rejections triggered a bout of depression; a condition that would have an impact on her for the rest of her life.

Karen loved men and they loved her. She was always in love with someone and her adolescent diaries deliciously describe her conversations with her girlfriends about her first encounters with men and sex. Her desires were intense and passionate.

At age eighteen, two days of blissful mutual love and kisses were succeeded by a winter of broken heart when the man moved on. Her pride fought passionately to restore her and, by using her very considerable intellect, she concluded that "sympathy hurts and humiliates me" (Quinn, 1988, p. 73).

Against her parents' wishes, Karen enrolled as a medical student at the University of Freiburg, one of the first institutions in Germany to allow women into higher education. She transferred universities a couple of times and graduated from the University of Berlin in 1913. Following her graduation, she decided to study the pioneering subject of psychoanalysis.

Like all her contemporaries in training, Karen underwent psychoanalysis, with one of Freud's favourite pupils, Karl Abraham. However, it soon became apparent Freud's dogma did not quite fit the spirited Horney. Her unhappy childhood, her parents' difficult relationship, and her total alienation from her father had made her distrust convention as the basis for love. She, instead, associated love with sexual passion.

Despite her rebellious feelings against conventional love, she married Oskar Horney, a successful lawyer with good prospects. They had three daughters, and Oskar turned out to be as strict with them as Horney's own father had been. Although she was soon unfaithful, they stayed together ten years and divorced about the time he was going bankrupt. She went to America with the girls, where she joined the Freudian Institute for Psychoanalysis. She never married again and instead had lovers for the rest of her life.

She was a bit of a love addict, really needed sex, and was obviously much better at pulling men than Melanie Klein, though less of a beauty than Melanie when she was young. She had insight: she knew that her need of a man was too driven to allow her the time to always pick the right one. (The one that was most wildly inappropriate was probably her last; a young candidate in a training analysis with her at her own Institute in New York.) But she did know herself and knew she was not otherwise a dependent personality. Her genius in her work gave her self-sufficiency, power, and influence.

Karen Horney is a strong candidate for the most lovable psycho-therapist of the century. She had a prodigious appetite for enjoying life. Quinn's wonderful biography includes stories of her eccentricity, tactlessness, and occasional striking ignorance of her own great wisdom when it came to her own life. One of my favourite stories about Karen was that she always made a toast to "luxurious and lecherous living" (Quinn, 1988, p. 376) at the annual dinner held by the organisation she had founded.

As an analyst in America, she dared to criticise Freud, which led to her removal from her teaching post in the Institute. In response, she founded her own Institute and training school, which she called The Association for the Advancement of Psychoanalysis.

Karen was the first person who rejected Freud's views on penis envy and his theories on women feeling inferior to men. She drew from her own experiences of being a mother and the overwhelming joy and fulfilment she felt at each stage of her pregnancy. On the contrary, she believed men to be envious of women because of their ability to give birth.

In a lecture she gave in 1932, she claimed that men were actually terrified of women and especially feared their contempt, and that was why men had to keep making such extra efforts to put women down and keep them in their place.

Karen noticed domination and submission in sex, and agreed with Adler's theories on superiority and inferiority. Unlike her contemporaries, Karen had a different perspective on the theory of neurosis, especially when it came to early childhood. She felt that neurosis was something that we continually experienced throughout life, rather than just something that was triggered by negative, external, sporadic events.

According to her, what is wrong with us is *basic anxiety* which starts in early childhood, when "[t]he basic evil is invariably a lack of genuine warmth and affection" (Horney, 1999, p. 80) from our parents. As a result, the child does not develop a feeling of belonging, but instead a profound insecurity. In turn, she believed that children who feel hostility are even more anxious.

A neurotic person is rarely aware of the underlying feelings of their basic anxiety. For example, a sense of basic mistrust may be covered by "a superficial conviction that people in general are quite likeable" or those with "an existing deep contempt for everyone may be camouflaged by a readiness to admire" (Horney, 1999, p. 93).

She was especially good at seeing how amazingly, genuinely, unconscious we can be of our real motives and feelings in ordinary dealings with others.

Horney set out four ways that we relate to people: close, distant, dominating, and submissive, and how, in healthy human relationships, we are able to fluently and freely move between them so that they become complementary to one another. For the child who is overwhelmed by anxiety, this capacity for adaptation is compromised, and is likely to be both rigid and extreme. For example, affection becomes clinging, and compliance becomes appeasement.

In an earlier book, she spelt out the four possible directions of flight from anxiety, summarised here as

1.   If you love me you will not hurt me.
2.   If I give in, I shall not be hurt.
3.   If I have power, no one can hurt me.
4.   If I withdraw, nothing can hurt me.

Gentle, nice Karen did not make much of the fact that each of the four ways of avoiding hurt to oneself can equally be used as a way of hurting others, by intrusion or smothering, treachery, tyranny, and abandonment. In fact, all of Horney's four tricks are means of conflict avoidance. A really useful discovery of our Enlightenment given to us by Horney is that tyranny is a form of conflict avoidance. It can look like naked aggression, but it is really conflict avoidance. You stamp out the other person's vision—end of conflict.

One of the great British comedians, I cannot remember who, said that every comic actor has a comic character who is what he himself would have been if he had not had a sense of humour. Similarly, the great psychotherapists each described his own neurosis, but with an insight that saved them from it and provided a gateway to a deeper general understanding of humanity. Horney saw herself as a love addict. What other psychoanalyst would have come out crying from the meeting where they were horrid to her?

Horney was particularly interested in how these four defences applied to children. For one child, one defence might be predominant, for example compliance becomes over-compliance, so that a child submits entirely to the wishes of all around her, regardless of the outcome or her own desires. Others might experience all four defences as a coping strategy, so that the scared child is driven in all four directions, which results in contradictory behaviour.

Horney's theories were very different from her Freudian contemporaries, who believed a child's inner turmoil to be a great cultural conflict between civilisation and instinct.

If a person narrows himself down to one of the defences more than the others, what does he do with his other impulses? They might continue to split off, almost like multiple personality disorder, and, as a result of these clashing defences, a young person might compensate for his insecurity by developing "an urgent need *to lift himself up above others*", and build up "his personal idealised image" (Horney, 1999, p. 22).

One cannot always keep it up. It is a big task to be perfect, and life can deal blows that show one up. Horney's version of the internal enemy, saboteur, or demon is the *self-hatred* and self-neglect with which one punishes oneself for failing to achieve one's goal of glorious superiority.

I remember, for example, an ambitious girl, aged ten, who told me she would rather be blind than not be first in her class.

You might think that the drive to glory is the same as the need to dominate, but you do not have to use power to outstrip others; you can find glory by being more irresistibly cuddly, or edifyingly humble, or sublimely imperturbable than anyone else.

None of the fundamentalist Freudians in Chicago or New York— or anywhere—noticed Horney's wonderful marriage of Freud and Adler's insights. I am not sure she did herself. She shone a light into the human soul that largely went unrecognised by her contemporaries. Horney showed in detail and depth how defending against one's own wishes and defending against others are not two things, but one mental movement. Maladaptation to others is, at the same time, loss of self: if somebody becomes a tyrant by adopting the third defence above of assuming power over others, he might seem to be getting exactly whatever he wants all the time, but in reality he is only having one need served, forsaking the rest. He is just as alienated from his real self as a doormat type.

Add Winnicott's account of babyhood to Horney's account of childhood and adolescence and one gets a wonderful consistent account of gradual alienation from self.

In *Our Inner Conflicts*, published in 1945, Horney described how therapists should treat patients suffering from neuroses. Her idea of treatment was rigorous. She believed that the unconscious conflicts suffered by the patient could not be resolved by rational decision or willpower alone, but only by changing those conditions within the personality that brought them into being in the first place, such as basic fear, isolation, and helplessness.

Therefore, the therapist must treat the patient with delicacy, tact, and attention and be sensitive to what the patient can bear at any stage. That especially applies when the therapist is dismantling the patient's idealised self-image. For example, if the therapist uncovers the patient's wish to be cruel, it might so threaten his idea of himself that it "fills the patient with terror and disgust" (Horney, 1963, p. 224). Similarly, a patient who has idealised his aggressiveness might feel despair when he realises how much he really needs human intimacy—something which the therapist has to carefully manage.

Strangely, Horney says nothing directly about how to cure the root of the matter—the patient's basic anxiety. She only goes as far as making him conscious of it enough to diminish the alienation from self. She does not say anything about how trusting the therapist can also take away the patient's anxiety.

In fact, she was a million miles from the idea that the physician's love cures the patient, and she does not ever mention the words transference and countertransference. There is nothing about a real mutual emotional influence. In her conscious mind, her particular "Battle with the Patient" was an intellectual one, like a chess game, though it was full of intense and careful management of the *patient's* emotions. That explains why she could write a book about how to analyse yourself without a therapist (*Self-Analysis*, 1994) and how she could have sex with her young male colleague after his training analysis with her.

Analysts like Fairbairn could have a proper formal session with a trainee for an analytic hour and then move on into an informal chat and gossip, perhaps with a cup of tea, without it dawning on them that there might be a serious additional input to what they were doing. I can imagine Karen could also have such an intellectually rigorous and formal session with her trainee before joining him on the couch.

Did the physician's love help to cure the patient? Did sex with her have the same transforming effect on his personality? Or was it kept totally separate from his analysis? No therapist can help but respond warmly to, and encourage any signs in, the patient of whatever the therapist is living for him/herself. In Karen's case, it was "spiritu-alised great sensuality" (Horney, 1980, p. 63), and though that is never mentioned in her books, I wonder if it did ever come into her actual work with her patients.

Part of Horney's genius was her understanding of how the con-science is distorted by fear, not as a result of a moment's mistaken choice, but as a lifelong, gradual knotting-up, like the tangled trunks of a hawthorn hedge on the seashore. The problem of the sick con-science was central to the Enlightenment of the Mind from the begin-ning. Freud's answer was to give his patients the benefit of his superior enlightened view. Down the ages, saints and sages in pithy sound bites, and moral philosophers in tortured tomes, worsened the problem of ethics for mankind by giving us *rules* for how to decide what is Right. Augustine's "love God and do what you want" (Ahmed & Donnan, 1994, p. 20) still said you had to love God. Kant said to act as though your choice could be a universal law; Sartre said to act in good faith—do not hold someone's hand if you do not mean it.

In *Neurosis and Human Growth*, published not long before she died, Karen Horney settled the problem of ethics for our Enlightenment in a few paragraphs. Characteristically, she tabulated three alternative views from which the correct choice issues in a clarion call for *freedom*. In other words: rules? *forget them*. Thus, she played her part in a general trend of Western culture during the century to escape from a prescribed morality of "do-as-you're-told".

This was half way through the century, in America, and Horney was talking about what was wrong with the world and, essentially, redefining ethics. In her eyes, the Enlightenment of the Mind revealed not just that people were being naughty and choosing to "sin", but that we were infecting each other with fear, passing it down from generation to generation; fear of each other, which stops the natural growth of love.

With all that Karen Horney and the object relations theorists have shown us, maybe it is time for the definition of neurosis to be moved on from its Freudian origins of the nineteenth century. My contribu-tion is this:

> *Neurosis:* socially transmitted disease consisting of unconscious fear of each other, causing partial abortion of normal growth and development, unnumbered symptoms, broken families, physical

illness, crime and wars. (Basic cause and cure: see this volume, final
chapter)

Karen Horney was a woman way ahead of her time. Although she
died in 1952, before the feminist movement really took hold, her
contributions undoubtedly helped with the advancement of women in
society. She was also the first woman to introduce the first self-help
book, believing that we could all be our own psychiatrist. Her extensive contributions shaped the world of psychoanalysis and her practices are still in place today.

CHAPTER NINETEEN

John Layard: the divided man

"The man who has no inner life is a slave to his surroundings"

(Amiel, 1874)

In the late nineteenth and early twentieth centuries, the work of anthropologists such as Franz Boas and Margaret Mead caught the eye of several psychotherapists. In fact, a few anthropologists even became psychotherapists, and new theories emerged on the study of human behaviour.

Several books had a major influence on the Enlightenment of the Mind, one of which was Mead's *Coming of Age in Samoa* (1928), causing a bit of a stir at the time. Looking for the best cultural examples for civilised people to learn from, she highlighted how the Samoan girls enjoyed casual sex before eventually marrying and settling down. She felt that their adolescence was far healthier than that of the West, where teenagers were typically raised in ignorance and suffered inhibitions as result. The book caused major controversy among Westerners, who were shocked at this level of promiscuity.

Almost fifty years after the book was published, Mead was to comment that American society had changed so little that she was often told by others that her strictures of 1923 still applied. Later criticism in the 1980s of Mead's original findings did not much diminish their effect for us.

W. H. R. Rivers was an anthropologist before becoming a distinguished psychotherapist, but it is his student, John Layard, that made the biggest impression on me, because I knew him.

I wanted to write about John Layard because, like me, he was a Jungian analyst, because you are not otherwise likely to hear about him (although his findings were revelatory and still not generally assimilated), and because his work is a vast departure from Mead's sunny Polynesia and instead delves into a darker, older world, deeper into the human psyche.

In 1914, Layard, aged twenty-three, accompanied his mentor, Rivers, on an anthropological trip to the New Hebrides (now Vanuatu). He stayed for a year on a small island off Malekula studying the inhabitants, their culture, and lifestyle. When he returned, he had a severe mental breakdown and was treated by Homer Lane, a psychoanalyst who advocated rather unorthodox methods as a cure for his patients.

It took years for Layard to recover from his experiences and his troubles did not stop there. In 1929, he shot himself, but survived, and what I do not know is whether he was miraculously transcending the effects of brain damage most of his life, for the bullet must surely have ripped his corpus callosum on its way between the cerebral hemispheres.

Layard's *The Lady of the Hare* (1988), about a woman cured by her dreams, and *The Incest Taboo and the Virgin Archetype* (1945), about the incest taboo, fascinated me as a young man more than any other Jungian literature.

From his writings, I could not understand how he knew about the things he wrote about, so, in 1959 (as a postgraduate student), I sought him out in Cornwall. He was a tall, striking figure with a great nose like an eagle, set in a noble, weathered head that reminded me of some ancient sea adventurer. He was the kind of genius who was as consumed by his personal quest as any Jason for his Golden Fleece. Later, I learnt he could be a very awkward cuss indeed. He had no sense of humour and could turn vengeful when his often consuming emotional demands were not met.

When I met him, I already knew from his writings that he believed life to be about instinct wanting to be transformed into spirit; for example, if one has spiritual aspirations one must start off with the maximum experience of instinct (sex) that one can get.

"You *must* have irresponsible sex!" he told me. "Look at St Augustine! Look at Ghandi! When Ghandi was visiting houses in England as a young man, if there was an unattached girl in that house, Ghandi had her!"

His message was clear: if you want to be a saint you must start with as much unbridled sex as you can possibly get. There was one brief moment of compunction where he clearly realised the kind of advice he was giving to such a young chap, and said, "You'll be able to tell which girls not to hurt . . ."

By sex, he meant every kind of sex. He never directly urged me towards homosexual sex, but he did mention a middle-aged man he knew who was catching up with homosexual experiences he missed when he was younger. Once, Layard told me a dream he had where he was refusing homosexual advances from a man. There was a women there he badly wanted, but in the dream she told him, "No, I don't want just half a man." Layard took this to mean that she wanted him to first have sex with the man before she would accept him.

When we parted after a week of analysis, I wanted to work with him further, but we could not see how as there were no jobs for me in Cornwall.

"Well go and get all the fucking you can and . . ." he said, and paused.

". . . and we'll leave the rest to God," I finished.

I went off to do my side of it but it was not long before we saw each other again. It turned out that a tanker had met his little mini head-on in a Cornish fog and Layard had to go to London for treatment. Consequently, I decided to move from my homeland, Scotland, to London to continue my analysis with him. When I told my father I was moving to London to become Layard's disciple, my doubtful father asked me, "Is he a *happy* man?" I tried to think I was being sort of truthful when I answered, "Yes", but I knew I was stretching it.

Following my analysis with him, I then became his secretary, helping him write and rewrite his books. For a brief while in the 1960s, he shared a house with me, and my actor and writer friends, in Notting Hill Gate. He was not a popular housemate and never bothered to make an effort with any of the others. My girlfriend at the time, who lived with us, claimed that he was just a selfish old man, while another girl in the house resented his being my "lord and master", as she put it. Another lad, called Tom Stoppard, who had just come from Bristol to London to seek his fortune, also could not wait until Layard moved out.

Layard was the type of person who really enthused about his own sexuality and the sexuality of others. I remember him once complaining about not getting a slice of the action when my girlfriend, not quite dressed, sat on my knee at breakfast. He was about seventy then.

He could empathise with anything, sexual or violent, or criminal or perverse. On one occasion, he returned from some homosexual social event and described to me, with respect verging on admiration, how a man had demonstrated stuffing an entire rubber suit up his bottom.

Layard believed in loving the sin, that everyone had to do something evil as part of their spiritual development. "What bad thing can Derry do?" he would ask friends of mine. I thought I had done plenty.

"Wisdom comes from sex," he used to say. Once, in a little Greek restaurant in Marylebone Lane, he became exasperated with my slowness to comprehend why books are made the shape they are. He pulled out his diary and opened and closed it a couple of times in front of me.

"Look! Look! What is it?" he kept shouting.

Nearby diners got interested. I was still being thick.

"It's a cunt! A CUNT!"

Silence from the other tables. Of course! A man's wisdom comes to him from the genitals of a woman!

To Layard, sex was healing in itself; he claimed to have started the cure of a schizophrenic lad by masturbating him. He often said, "If you can't straighten people out through sex you can straighten them out through piss and shit." In the early days, he told me he was quite mad, but I was never really on the receiving end. I know almost nothing about his background and how he got to be the way he was when he broke down after Malekula. I do not know whether he was destabilised by separation from his own people, and by such deep immersion in an alien culture.

He came from a respectable English family. His grand-uncle was Sir Austen Layard, famous for excavating Nineveh. He grew up in conflict with his mother, was not close to his father, went to school at Bedales, and had a sister and a brother who were killed in the war.

A great complaint he had about our culture was that it makes us into adults before we have been children, so I think that is probably what happened to him. He grew up too fast and missed out on the emotional security of childhood. Thus, he was more of a love addict in this respect, needy and demanding. This behaviour, understandably, seemed to put people off.

He turned it on me only once. It was the kind of incomprehensible reproach one gets from patients sometimes that is loquacious enough, but one cannot make out what exactly one is being asked for, or where one is supposed to have failed them.

He was also quite manipulative, and I remember one time a friend of both of us came to me in the kitchen reproaching me because Layard had told this friend that I had been neglecting him! I got very angry and told our friend that I was slaving to help Layard with his work as well as cooking for us and even washing his clothes, and it could not have been a more unfair accusation.

However, his uneven temperament was nothing compared to the generous and deep gratitude he expressed to me for all my efforts to help him.

His life sounded like a history of people fending him off when he turned his too-hungry love on to them. A week after starting their fieldwork project together in Malekula, Rivers, without any explanation, suddenly took a passing motor launch to Tangoa, and never came back. Layard, who had idealised him, was devastated.

Still, there was something about Layard that disturbed some people. Jung stopped analysing him rather sharply: "He realised I was mad and he did not like mad people so he leapt a mile away," Layard explained to me one day. Instead, Jung passed him on to Toni Wolff (Jung's mistress), who became very starchy when Layard tried to get her to reveal more about her sex life with Jung. Furthermore, the Professor of Anthropology in Oxford took out a legal injunction to keep him out of the Department. I remember a homosexual lad, probably expert at exploiting older men, pathetically screwing a lock to the door of his room in an attempt to keep Layard out, when he realised which way the exploiting was actually going.

However, in 1914, Layard was lucky enough to fall among tribesmen that he liked and admired. Layard's Melanesians might have been murdering homosexual cannibals, but for him they remained the only real gentlemen on this planet. They were just still at an early stage, that was all. His account of the emotional and spiritual wealth of the life and culture of the Melanesians is breathtakingly sympathetic and moving.

When Rivers and Layard set out for Malekula, they deliberately neglected to bring any meat with them, as they already knew that the islands were full of pigs. What they did not know was that the Melanesians regarded pigs as enormously valued religious objects that could never be slaughtered just for food.

Spiritual and social advancement through the fifteen- to thirty-year cycle of rituals was based on the sacrifice and ritual eating of boars. Without boars, a man could not relate socially or grow spiritually. Without boars, a man was nothing. Boars' teeth were knocked out so that their tusks could grow right around, in a circle, white like the moon, even to a double or triple spiral, which visitors to the village would pay to see. Their lovely, awesome, unnatural tusks were kept forever.

For some rituals, it was better to sacrifice and ritually eat a man or a bastard specially reared (unawares) for sacrifice, or a young man bought—for a good price in boars—from another tribe, but boars were the most usual sacrifice. They were reared with intense loving care and fed better than their owners in the way a woman would rear a child. Then the day of the sacrifice would arrive, and as we will see, attitudes changed.

Usually, the loss of any pet is a real bereavement, sometimes very bad. I remember the terrible distress of a little boy when he accidentally trod on his hamster—not a trivial tragedy.

But to kill a pet deliberately! Yet, that is what ritual animal sacrifice is about. In Malekula, boys as young as six years are shown how to sacrifice a boar during a public ritual. Prior to that, the boys would be encouraged to torment and kill worms on the seashore, for sport. The father would initially give him the boar, then help the child tie it up, club it brutally to death, and encourage him to mock at its pain, cries, and struggles. Afterwards, the men would gather around a ritual fire to eat the meat of the dead boar.

Layard wondered why it was only men that were welcome to the feast at the ritual fire. An informant explained something to Layard that suddenly illuminated the whole thing, and Layard told me about that moment. He told Layard, "When we have killed the boar, we must do something strong. And the strong thing we do is not to eat with the women."

This was a revelatory insight for Layard. He interpreted the boy's first sacrifice as a destruction of the infantile animal bond to his mother. His unthinking dependence on her for his very life had become a threat to his development and it was time for it to be killed.

This is similar to Alfred Adler's theory on "social feeling" (Adler, 2005, p. 205). After the sacrifice, the boy lives and eats with the men. Killing the cherished animal pet releases enough cruelty to kill a close emotional family attachment, a childish love, and so make room for a more grown-up and bigger love. Thus, it might come as a surprise that the incest taboo was, in the beginning, a taboo against men and women eating together rather than family members having sex. The new love is more consciously demanding, and includes a larger number of people—the whole extended family, which, under primitive kinship rules, means the whole tribe.

The psychoanalyst Ian Suttie was highly amused to read about the Trobrianders policy on incest. Whereas there might be some room for manoeuvre about sex between forbidden relatives, if the couple were caught *eating together* there was hell to pay. The incest taboo, in general, is not merely a rule against some kind of indulgent naughtiness that is eugenically bad, but a well-justified fear of an emotional tether that can stop a person from growing up and going out into the big world.

In his first sacrifice, the boy's triumphant, aggressive, sadistic vindictiveness against his pet is also directed towards the incestuous darling-mummy-love that is now beginning to cloy and hold him back. Thus, the first sacrifice is a kind of rejection of the mother.

Perhaps, too, by mocking at the boar's sufferings, the boy's sense of humour is being shaped—after all, the pains of growing up and moving on can be funny, not tragic. He becomes less self-centred and more sharing (giving his boar's meat for the others to eat for a start). He has become independent of women and bonded to men. The tusks are religious artefacts, not quite on the level of Chartres Cathedral, but embodying, in the supernatural beauty of the shining moon-like circles, a concrete example of how culture transforms nature and instinct into spirit, and animal attachment into human love.

As the lifelong cycle of sacrifice continues, the vindictive cruel killing of boars (or other men) repeatedly frees a man from too much dependency on his mother, sister, or wife. When the boar dies, he raises his hands high to the hawk, seen as the symbol of spirit. The man's spirit is then released to take on a more responsible and caring attitude to the whole tribe, and to create and invent dances, songs, music, and artefacts (which could, incidentally, increase his wealth by being sold).

After the rituals, there is an opening to infinite, unpredictable possibilities for new behaviour. For example, when the post Stone-Age Hebrew tribesman Abraham, consented to kill his only son at God's command, it was regarded as a cultural advance. Therefore, every descendent of Abraham was emotionally structured to accept that God (or whatever word one wants to use to translate the idea into our language—"something inside", the id, the self, the collective unconscious, the life force, whatever) could demand, with no reason given, the most outrageous crimes, such as infanticide, and expect obedience.

The Malekulans, who were still in the early stages of tribalism right into the twentieth century, never got as far as infanticide; if they were offering a human sacrifice, they chose an enemy or a bastard, nobody too close to home. The victim was sanctified and made holy before eating. The Malekulans understood exactly what it meant when a Catholic missionary told them about the meaning of Mass. The Christian ritual of eating the body of Christ was just what they did.

Layard was intrigued to find out how the women coped with the rituals. After all, they had to rear the boars and treat them like one of their own children. In some tribes, baby animals are taken from the wild and reared by being suckled by one of the women. Even worse, how did the women feel when they were raising bastards for human sacrifice? In fact, how did they react to the constant cruel ritual murders that were intended to sever the link between mother and son? How did they cope with losing their young sons to their fathers?

Layard observed something striking in the way the rituals affected men *vs.* the women. While the men were expected to sacrifice their incestuous ties to their women folk, the women, in contrast, *must keep the myth of the incestuous link between mother and son*. By this, Layard meant the myth of the Terrible Mother found in very primitive tribes, where the mother wishes to retain her son in opposition the father, and so also against the unconscious ethos of the tribe.

The natives, of course, are not conscious of the boar sacrifice as a release of their aggression against childish dependence or incestuous desires for their mothers or sisters. To their conscious mind, boar sacrifice was a way to ward off their most deadly enemy, Le-Hev-Hev (literally meaning, "That which draws us to It so that It may devour us".) Le-Hev-Hev is the archetypal Devouring Mother, pulling one back into the throes of symbiotic contentment. We sometimes find, in times of despair, an inner longing to be comforted, to return to the womb and blissful extinction. Although the Malekulans did recognise a benign and generous God called Thaghar, he was more ignored than worshipped. Le-Hev-Hev was the one the natives feared, made sacrifices to, propitiated, neutralised, and outwitted. She is a hideous creature: a crab-like monster with great claws, a woman and a giant sow, known for devouring piglets. She lurks in her cave demanding endless sacrifices. It was believed that when they died, the natives had to battle to pass her in order to get to the volcano (the Malekulan equivalent of heaven). Le-Hev-Hev would set many traps to thwart the journey. Legend had it that she had a labyrinth drawn in the sand that she would half rub out. If her victim failed to complete it, she would eat them. Only if a man could pass all the trials could he get to his final heavenly destination, the volcano. Layard deduced from this that the volcano represented Le-Hev-Hev herself.

The rites are preceded by great preparation and fasts and abstinence, in which the sacrificer becomes one with the ancestral dead. Singing and dancing "of the most elaborate kind expressing the whole gamut of emotions" (Layard, 1942, p. 13) also takes place.

Layard understood these sacrificial rites to be about rebirth, and about starting again. The boar represents the alter ego of each participant, thus, he is really sacrificing himself.

The culture hero who created the rites was called To-we-we. He was married to his sister, had sex with his mother, and then sacrificed himself by falling into a hollow tree with his boar. Layard compared him with Thomas Mann's *Holy Sinner*, who also offended society by having sex with his sister but made up for it in self-sacrifice.

Now we can finally see what is wrong with incest. It is nothing to do with eugenics, nor was it the cause of father–son conflict (as Freud thought). The trouble with incest is that it forms bonds that hinder the natural growth of love. In Stone Age Malekula, father and son are as one in the son's steps towards adulthood, any lingering ties to the mother or sister are seen to hamper this development.

So, there are many reasons to battle against Le-Hev-Hev, for she is not just the Devouring Mother but also the *Initiating* Mother that sets challenges throughout a man's life. Thus, she is a constant female influence on the man's male personality. World mythology is full of stories about goddesses who wreak havoc on their weak male hangers-on, such as Osiris, Attis, Adonis, Tammuz, Odin, and even my own earliest named ancestor Diarmid.

(My ancestor, Diarmid, too handsome for his own good, could not resist the determined seduction by Grainne, the wife of the High King Finn McCoul. Eventually, poor Diarmid was killed by a boar belonging to a witch called Grey Eyebrows.)

However, the Malekulan men knew better than to let any woman control them completely. Through the rituals, they gained control of the mother goddess's aggression and cleverness, and even took over her motherliness. Although women are excluded from gatherings to discuss tribal affairs, Layard noticed that the head of the tribe acted like a male mother to the others.

The male mother effect of groups of men (*alma mater*) is a reality not too often mentioned, but often found, for example, in good units of the traditional British Armed Forces. During my National Service, I found that older non-commissioned officers (NCOs) would use the term "nannying" with reference to their young recruits, but never call it mothering, which was probably more appropriate. I remember a few of us were given a shaming mass bollocking (as we called it) for letting a young officer go off drunk when we should have been looking after him. We took it to heart and, after that, the Officers' Mess became more of the male mother it ought to be—though, of course, that phrase was never uttered.

In Malekula, although human sacrifice was not practised as frequently as animal sacrifice, it did have the advantage of advancing a man spiritually to an extent that could take half a lifetime by boars. The body was cooked the same way as a boar; there was the all-night celebration and dance, and all the men ate some of the corpse. Joints were sent to other villages. Even Layard himself took part in the feast, chewing gingerly on a bit of arm, and observing it as sweet. To eat a person was considered a brave, dreadful thing to do; a man-eater is afraid of nothing, not even the Devouring Ghost.

Layard once told me about another strange experience he had with a different set of tribesman. He joined them on a long journey where he had to trudge through a desert, weighed down with packages. The tribesmen undertook this expedition to bring obligatory ritual gifts to their brothers-in-law. After a full day of trekking, the brothers-in-law came into sight. Relieved, Layard waited for them to approach, expecting greetings, chat, an exchange of news and perhaps a little refreshment. Not a bit of it. The tribesmen he was with threw the gifts on the ground and, wordlessly, turned back to retrace their path to home. At first, Layard was flummoxed by this strange behaviour but, by adding up all the rest he knew, he got it.

In Malekula, they maintained that sex begins with the sister (meaning sex-play), but when brothers and sisters become nubile, they must avoid each other; if they meet on a path the sister must turn aside, and no sexual matter can be discussed in her presence. When she is older, she is given to another man, her cousin. In these societies, marriage took place by sister exchange. Therefore, the brothers who had grown close to their sisters typically resented them being taken away from them and acted aggressively towards their brothers-in-law, as Layard experienced first hand.

However, what was so breathtaking about the Malekulan culture was the achievement of *turning these mortal enemies into best friends*, not only as ritual and trade partners, but something beyond. This was done by homoerotic love.

When a betrothed girl was too young for sex, her brother supplied her place. Thus, many boys commonly grew up through passive homosexuality with their little sisters' fiancés, then active homosexuality with the brother of their own not-yet-nubile bride, followed by heterosexual sex and parenthood. In some cases, young boys would be "sold" to older men to teach them and mentor them during the course of their initiation rites. When they completed the initiation, they would be expected to return to their sisters' husband-to-be to continue their relationship until she was ready to take the reigns herself.

Still, in spite of all these homosexual relationships, the incest taboo still held; the tutor was never a boy's father, and sex with father, brother, son, etc., simply never happened. In fact, in Melanesia during the initiation process, the tutor was called the husband and the novice the wife.

Layard gave a paper, "Homo-eroticism in primitive society as a function of the self" to the Society of Analytical Psychology in 1959, relating his findings in Malekula, and how they could explain the psychic structure of modern man. However, he did not reveal his thoughts about his own homoerotic side. He had concluded from his dream that his own homosexual side had become his "shadow" (a Jungian term) because he had rejected it. Thus, he felt that side of him had to be joined up with his conscious self in order for him to be a complete person and help him to relate to women normally.

He had seen in Malekula that, in spite of the degenerate forms of homosexuality here and there, homoerotic love was what was holding each tribe together in its elegant complex symmetrical pattern in which the cohesive forces held the disruptive ones in a successful creative balance of tensions.

This is the astonishing thrust of his paper: it is homoerotic love, whether or not it is expressed physically or consciously, that builds society.

"Love" is a word not lightly used by anthropologists, but there is little doubt that it began in primitive society not heterosexually between men and women, but between men and men, in this case between the man-lover and the boy-lover who is his own sister-substitute and the man-lover's wife-substitute. It is much later in the history of culture that such love (as opposed to purely sexual relationships) gets transferred back to women as wives.

As we have seen, the Malekulans had a great repertoire of lechery with which to make relationships: incest in childhood, passive homosexual, active homosexual, heterosexual, and everything else. Layard believed that unlike civilised male lovers in the West, Malekulan homosexual mentors nurtured the heterosexual future of their boy-lover novices, encouraging and strengthening their sexuality in preparation for their future wives.

Once they have completed the initiation process, they are welcomed back into the tribe during a sequence of rituals and rites. They now engage with their mentors as equals. It all seems like a good outcome for an institutionalised homosexual adolescence and homoerotic mentoring system, in contrast with the Western world.

In 1938, Layard collided with Jung, and, developing a strong transference to Jung, as so many people did, Layard had two homosexual dreams. In one they were lying down together with their clothes on in an empty theatre before the curtain had risen. Describing the dream, Layard knew he was asking Jung to pay more attention, but Jung's only response was, "We cannot discuss that."

Layard drew another blank when he told Jung he had once wanted to have sex with Doris (Layard's wife) in a Sussex church. "You can't do a thing like that. That's desecrating the church," Jung told him (Hayman, 2002, p. 354).

Frustrated by Jung's reticence in discussing the topic of sex, the analytical relationship between the two began to deteriorate. A few years after the analysis, Layard tried to do some work with Jung. However, Jung was old and tired and less accessible even than before, especially in talking about sex. In fact, years before, Jung had once mentioned in a letter to Freud about being "betrayed" by someone, meaning they had made a homosexual pass at him. It was an incident that traumatised him and he found it difficult to relate to homosexuality in his patients as a result.

Although Layard drank in Jung's discoveries and ideas, and became a Jungian analyst himself, he also highlighted the great man's limitations through his serious avoidance of the instinctual, sexual and personal.

Layard's discovery of the most ancient evolutionary beginnings of human love among the Stone Age tribes of a little island only sixty miles long in the New Hebrides is still one of the most moving and inspiring to be made, not only in the Enlightenment of the Mind, but in our whole cultural history.

The first sight Layard gives us of these Stone Age men and women shows them as much stranger and more alien than we could have imagined. It requires a serious effort to understand them. But, with his aid, we begin to recognise them as still alive in ourselves, and the endless quest to force the terrifying and tangled roots of primitive passions to yield more and, still more, love. I did not understand all of Layard's thinking, but, knowing the type of person he was, I do think he presented new and original ideas about how to understand our deepest nature, and that his contribution deserves to be known. I am aware that I might be getting him wrong, and if there is an afterlife, I might be in dead trouble.

CHAPTER TWENTY

Salvador Minuchin: family ties

"The touchstone for family life is still the legendary 'and so they were married and lived happily ever after.' It is no wonder that any family falls short of this ideal"

(Minuchin, 1974)

For extroverted therapists, family therapy is the apotheosis of dynamic psychotherapy, as dream therapy is for introverted types. One of my extroverted psychiatrist colleagues says that going from individual therapy to family therapy is like going from black and white into colour. Actually, all therapy is really family therapy, even if you are only treating one person; indeed, it is very gratifying to hear about improvements in the patient's relatives during treatment of an individual.

During family therapy, you are with a family in which the members are making each other ill in front of your very eyes; when you see how they are doing it, you can join in and stop it. In this chapter, I shall tell you about a family therapist from the second half of the century, Salvador Minuchin, an American, who showed the healing power of aggression. But first I want to describe the new environment in which he worked, because it was so important for our Enlightenment.

Around the middle of the twentieth century, family therapists, as well as the military developers of guided missiles, became very interested in *systems theory* (cybernetics). We have already seen what an achievement it is for a baby to work out where he ends and the rest of the world begins. The anthropologist Gregory Bateson (one of Margaret Mead's husbands) became interested in the system in which our sense of "I" works: how far "I" extends, and how "I" is influenced by "you". Bateson saw that, in action, "I" correctly extends beyond us into the environment. (We think nothing of hearing a fighter pilot say "they got me in the wing".) Bateson's image was of a man cutting down a tree: each axe blow is guided by the state of the tree after the last blow; similarly, in families we act in complex loops of feedback of which we are all a part, each of us activated and regulated by the other family members and, at the same time, activating and regulating them, like the feedback system between the complex parts inside a smart bomb as it homes in on its target.

Part of the genius of Bateson and his friends was to see that, in some families, there is an unconscious anxious avoidance of change and development in the family, as though the family fears the children growing up; they called this a "homeostatic" (Bateson, 2000, p. 355) system, designed to avoid change like the thermostat heating system in a house. You can see that enmeshment, over-protectiveness, rigidity, and conflict avoidance are all likely to prevent growing independence in children. The "systems model" is one of the lamps of our Enlightenment.

Salvador Minuchin was a pioneer in family therapy, and he made use of these insights by looking at the family rather as a system, where the actions of each family member have an effect upon the actions of the others. Minuchin was born in 1921, into a family of Russian–Jewish immigrants. He was raised in a small town in Argentina with a population of 40,000. As the town was very close-knit, avoidance was not an option when resolving family conflicts; thus, in his work, he developed the provocation and resolution of family conflict into a breathtakingly powerful therapeutic tool. It had its dangers. As a therapist, he took twenty-four-hour responsibility for his patients, whether it involved a midnight swoop to foil attempted murder in one of the disadvantaged families, Negro or Chiquito, with whom he partly worked, or being at emergency midnight sessions on the paediatric wards when a child went into a diabetic or asthmatic crisis. Such children needed psychiatric care because the usual treatments (insulin, etc.) did not work as well in some dysfunctional families as they did in emotionally normal families. He took a special interest in these cases, and especially in children suffering from severe anorexia nervosa.

In 1978, Minuchin and his colleagues Rosman and Baker published *Psychosomatic Families: Anorexia Nervosa in Context*, which was a statement of the art of their discoveries and practice. The new discoveries of family therapy revolutionised psychodynamics, especially, at first, in child, family, and marital therapy.

Minuchin described a case of a diabetic child: she had been treated by a psychiatrist who had tried to shield the child from family stress, believing that this was the cause of the inexplicable failure of medication to stabilise her diabetes. But Minuchin disagreed with the psychiatrist, and took the opposite approach. He met with the whole family repeatedly, and induced family crises during the sessions to actualise and so help the family to deal with them. During the course of the treatment, over several sessions, the child was also encouraged to engage with the family for the first time as an autonomous individual. After several months of family therapy, the parents were able to negotiate conflicts between themselves without always involving their daughter. The result was to end the chronic pattern of hospitalisations of the child, and this was maintained for nine years after therapy had ended.

Minuchin and his team researched what he called "psychosomatic families"—families that included children with poorly controlled asthma or diabetes, or with anorexia nervosa.

In some families, members are unhealthily disengaged from each other, for example, some criminal families, and the occasional upper class English family where animals supply the emotional support (which I thought was only a joke until I met some of them), but Minuchin's "psychosomatic families" turned out to be the opposite: they were emotionally *over*-involved with each other—"enmeshed" (Minuchin, 1974, p. 55), and also *over-protective, rigid*, and *conflict-avoiding*.

They observed new things that had never before been noticed in the study of anorexia (intense as that research had been in the past), but previously the therapists were only able to report what went on in the family rather than observing the family dynamics first-hand.

Some of it was rather startling. For example, a girl who had hither-to presented herself as helpless and hopeless, dominated and invaded by her mother, could now be seen as tyrannically manipulating her intimidated parents. Similarly, a father whose dearest wish was to have his child eat and grow healthy again could be seen as under-mining his wife's efforts in this direction.

Remember how Karen Horney said the trouble with her four ways of not getting hurt—which are essentially ways of avoiding conflict—is when you get stuck in one way of relating and cannot move flexi-bly through all the different stages? Similarly, Minuchin believed that normal families use the ways of relating described by Horney, but that they use other ways, too, and in the end reach real resolution of their conflicts. Families with anorexic children, however, *get stuck in repeti-tions of a few tricks to avoid fights.* That is the root of the trouble, and *that is the illness—the habitual style of interactions.* Thus, it is tempting to see anorexia as an illness caused by family interactions, but Minuchin was going further, abandoning the traditional linear causality way of understanding illness, and seeing the anorexic symptoms as *only one facet of a whole family system that is sick.* The *whole family* needs the child *not* to eat, however much they may disagree with this theory. This is a new understanding of unconscious wishes: wishes unconsciously supporting a system of family interactions.

Reading the transcripts of Minuchin's treatments of cases of anorexia, you realise that the reason he is a hard act to follow is because his formidable research and theory all come *second* to what he actually *did*, which was to join the family and then react in it with the same violent direct emotions as if it were his own family. When Minuchin was treating an excitable Italian family, the Menottis, who were getting upset about the father's threat to break his daughter's leg if she went out with a boy, an observer asked Minuchin how he knew that this apparently quarrelling family were, in fact, really engaged in conflict avoidance. Minuchin responded that he knew this was the case because they were *not making* him *angry*—yes, he felt frustrated and helpless, but their apparent attacks were never truly provoking; they always slid into appeals for pity or guilt or some other bypass away from true confrontation. I remember when Minuchin came to London in the 1970s, he was hurt by how the London doyens of anorexia treatment did not fully accept his work; I thought he was right to be hurt, but I could hardly imagine many public school educated British psychiatrists at that time ever being able to do what he did.

His programme of treatment of anorexia began when the patient's self-starvation was putting her life at risk; she would then be admitted to hospital for a behavioural regime to increase her weight. Then, usually, the first big therapeutic event was a family lunch with Dr Minuchin. Minuchin knew exactly what he was aiming at: family drama.

"Drama" was the right word. Minuchin rapidly joined the family emotionally, making friendly bonds with each, and supporting the family's strengths and values, keenly appreciating the individuality of each of them, almost as though he liked them more than they liked each other. (Which is not impossible.) He believed that a therapist had to be at home with proximity, and that it was essential for the therapist to feel what it was like to be one of that family, and feel the forces of the family system acting on him. But, as he joined in, he was also assuming leadership, taking any chances to challenge their enmeshment with each other, their over-protectiveness, rigidity, and conflict avoidance, etc., at first, in usually gentle, humorous, friendly ways. The work, Minuchin said, needs a therapist who can be close to people, and be emotionally intimate, but then challenge, and push beyond what the family system is designed to allow. He once remarked that a father being challenged by the therapist should feel as though he has been stabbed in the belly by his best friend. The therapist might even have to be unfair if he is to unbalance the actively self-correcting system.

At the lunch party, menu choices were made and, typically, Minuchin would stir up a fight when everybody was eating (not always; his technique was flexible, and occasionally he would ignore whether the anorexic was eating or not to focus on other conflict). Stirring up a real fight is not easy in a family dedicated to conflict avoidance, but Minuchin was an expert at it.

In my opinion, Minuchin's work was more significant than he, himself, grasped. Sometimes a man does not understand his own genius while we stupid bystanders do, because we feel in such bright distinct colours what we are getting from him. Minuchin described what he was doing as "psychotherapy for a small planet", a "contextual approach" that recognises "the tremendous power of the social system" (Minuchin, Rosman, & Baker, 1978, p. 323); it is a true description, but he was also doing more. He was welcoming hate and turning it into love.

The families he saw were too anxious to be able to hate openly and normally, but Minuchin could make them hate, and make them fight it through. Using Erikson's wonderful phrase, their "shared panic and isolated anxiety" (Erikson, 1959, p. 28) inhibited their growth. Also, their culture could not save them. Thanks to our Enlightenment, we know that hate is designed to assert an individual's God-given unique vision of love, which is meant not to override other individuals' visions, but to marry them to create some group social feeling. (I remember an Israeli politician saying about the Middle East "Life *is* a conflict of just causes.")

Now that we have a better understanding of the unconscious, we can better comprehend that what is never said in a family can easily become what is never thought by anyone there, even though it might still lurk in the shadows. The psychiatrist, Christopher Bollas, had a great way of referring to this: he called it "the unthought known" (Bollas, 1989). And it might take a bold and confident therapist to take them where they do not want to go.

I have told you only about one therapist working in the field of families, but there are others whose wonderful work has contributed so much to changing the experience of family life and marriage from the point of view of all the participants. Virginia Satir in America was pioneering in her work with families, so that, for a time, the USA was ahead of the rest of the world in the field. Then, in the UK, Robin Skynner began teaching generations of mental health workers over decades of practice at the Maudsley Hospital, London. Family and marital work is now considered to be a mainstream technique, and, in the right hands, can allow us to rediscover our capacity to relate to others, to love and be loved.

In the NHS at the time of writing (2005) in the UK, you are likely to receive the treatment your doctor happens to believe in: individual, family, or group, or cognitive–behavioural (CBT). In group therapy, an initial meeting or two of careful polite helpfulness gives way to chaos and mixed emotions, including hostility, succeeded by real relatedness as the work goes on. The changes in each individual are like those in other forms of therapy: each person tries, at first, to relate to the others as he related to his own family of origin and ends up relating to them as who they are, and perhaps with a new understanding of the nature of society. The American psychiatrist, Yalom, believed that a group therapist must never be allowed to choose patients from the waiting list, for *he* will tend, unconsciously, to recreate *his* own family of origin.

The emotional mesh extending from the pathology of families out into the pathology of nations and their cultures is one of the most interesting, and potentially useful, studies of our Enlightenment; something we shall return to.

CHAPTER TWENTY-ONE

The parts of a person

"There is another man within me, that's angry with me, rebukes, commands, and dastards me"

(Browne, 1909)

O f the great early explorers of the territory of the unconscious, exploring different—though overlapping—districts, each was a king in his own country, and each really knew what he was talking about. Starting his career as a conquistador, Freud discovered in our unconscious mind *hurts* we cannot bear to remember ("traumas"), then *desires* we cannot bear to know we have, such as the desire for sex and murder towards family members. He saw how the tricks our minds develop to stop us from thinking of these things— the "defences" that keep them unconscious—do not resolve the conflict inside us but just make us frustrated, unhappy, or even ill. Then he found deeper in the unconscious the basic instincts that give rise to our desires, and noted how these instincts evolve and change as a person grows through childhood into adulthood, and how normal growth can be spoiled by the defences.

Freud's kingdom, then, included these two areas: first, internal conflict and internal structure in a person, and second, development and growth. He could have become an emperor if he had accepted the offered tributes from the nearby territories of Adler and Jung. Adler was a king in the area of the unconscious ways in which we relate to others: the unconscious "arrangements" our minds make for us to evade brave, useful ways of relating, and how we choose—unconsciously—aggressive superiority and power instead of fair dealing. ("Arrangements" was his way of talking about "defences".) This, after all, is just another way of timid avoidance.

Jung pushed the frontiers of discovery deeper *inside* again, right through the inner world and beyond into an inner not-me, the collective unconscious (just traveller's tales?—go yourself and see!), and he carried the study of natural development into the later half of life, and called it individuation.

So, from early in the century, there were these three districts of unconsciousness to colonise with insight:

1.   *Inside us*—internal structure and conflict.
2.   *Outside us*—what is unconsciously going on between people.
3.   The unconscious processes of *development and growth*.

All three look at the same thing—that is, us—from three different points of view, but individual psychotherapists tend to go for one at the expense of the others. In this chapter, I shall start on the first of the three, *internal structure and internal conflict*, and how it was explored around the middle and later part of the century.

We have seen the different ways Freud, Jung, and Fairbairn described the parts of a person. In the 1890s, Freud began with the idea that the psychopathology of hysteria is the same as that of multiple personality. His famous patient, Anna O, flipped between two selves, troubled woman and naughty child, and had memory gaps when the child took over. Then, early in the following century he saw how the Rat Man had fallen apart into three selves: first, a normal sort of chap, second, a religious ascetic, and third, a passionate, evil child. But the Rat Man was not a multiple personality because his three personalities had not grown strong enough skins or I–you boundaries around themselves for that. Multiple personality is like putting your finger on a blob of mercury: the surface tension is so strong it separates into distinct separate blobs, each with its own ego boundary.

When Freud was young, cases of multiple personality were rare and much mulled over, but by the 1970s it began to look like an epidemic in America (estimates varied from 20,000 cases in 1988 to 300,000 by 1990), and by the 1980s there was a wealth of literature on the subject, including textbooks, journals, and documents published by special medical societies. Even more popular were the books and films *The Three Faces of Eve* (1957), *Sybil* (1974), and *When Rabbit Howls* (1988). The cases were mostly female, and very often their history included child sex abuse.

Of the dozen or so cases we saw at Guy's Hospital in London in the last quarter of the century, nearly half were men, and only three reported sexual abuse. I felt sex abuse was only part of the wild mayhem of the dysfunctional families they were so often born into, not a specific cause of the illness.

Until recently, there were psychiatrists who genuinely could not believe in it, saying, "All that is required for a case of multiple personality is a clever hysteric and a gullible psychiatrist." It has certainly been faked by at least one criminal trying to get off; in a case cited by a psychologist colleague in 1987, the criminal was only unmasked because the psychologist who assessed him had an unusual knowledge of altered mental states.

In real cases, it can be disconcerting at first to witness the whole poise and shape of a person change to someone else; a different person takes over the body that has a completely different attitude, different facial expressions, voice, and body language. When a previously quiet submissive person suddenly transforms into a cursing virago, stamping about and staring at you with hate, it can be quite startling. On further conversation, it turns out that this second personality knows things the first personality does not know about him or herself, and has no memory at all of other very important things, and certainly wants *very* different things. It is also possible for each personality to have a different mental illness (there is even a record of one subpersonality being schizophrenic). They can be male and female, one deaf and another not, one needing spectacles and the rest not, one with an allergy so that a bangle rash appears but disappears when the patient comes to again.

In the American cases, it was common for the front personality to have no knowledge of the others, and to come complaining of other things, such as memory gaps. At Guy's, only two of our cases presented thus. One of them, in fact, had not complained of anything at all. She was a young woman sent under a pretext by her GP because he was concerned about her behaviour; she was a terribly well behaved, innocent girl but had been seen being outrageously sexy on the streets and, in fact, had made a pass at the GP, which seemed totally out of character. When questioned, she said she had not noticed anything unusual in her life—except, well, yes, a funny thing: she had found in her wardrobe sexy clothes that she would *never* wear and her mother had completely denied putting them there.

In a series of interviews under hypnosis, the front personality was able to listen in to conversations with the second personality, and although she was a bit shocked by this second entity at first, they grew to know each other and became able to share their points of view and fuse together. Previously, the common sense of the front personality had been dissociated and left at home, and she had been going out dressed in a see-through blouse and split skirt, and making passes in the wrong way at the wrong people, which only led to more trivial adventures than the ones she really needed. After the patient had been treated, I expect she would have gone on adventuring into life outside the family, but now with better goals.

In our other cases, the presenting personalities were aware of sharing life with one or more others, and knew them. In the case of one patient, Alice, her disorder was a result of a split unwittingly drawn by the family between what they liked and what they did not want in their daughter, for example, a family might draw such a line when they are afraid of their children growing up. This young woman told me that while she had been in the waiting room outside my office, her mother had told her to stop swearing. Alice had not uttered a word but she was used to this sort of thing; she knew it was Nicola, the bitch (her word) she was sharing her body and her life with, who took over from time to time, and who was, on this occasion, fed up with waiting to see me. Alice had named her "Nicola", thinking that if she was there to stay she might as well have a pretty name.

Alice was a really nice girl, with a lovely smile and an expression of fun and friendliness, who actually cared and worried about the people in her life. In our very first conversation it became clear that Nicola was Alice's angry reaction to her not very lovable, and separated, parents. Nicola had become split off because Alice was afraid her own rage would get out of control. But, of course, splitting her off was a recipe for just that: Nicola spoke out when she wanted to, split off or not. Once, when Alice's younger sister was being hassled in the street by some girls, Nicola emerged and, with a few choice remarks, put them to flight. Nicola was angry with the parents for not listening or not even being there when she needed to come out and have *her* say about the family discords. Alice had never expressed her rage to her parents and as she had no experience of using it successfully, she was afraid of it. Only she knew about Nicola, which led to further complications in her relationships with others. For example, she could not explain to her boyfriend why she was so unpredictable about sex: Alice liked cuddling but not sex, while Nicola loved sex, so it depended on who was present when she was with her boyfriend.

Good girl and naughty girl—usually good *grown-up* girl and naughty *childlike* girl—is not an uncommon couple in multiple personality.

A case of good girl–bad girl was Eve White and Eve Black in *The Three Faces of Eve*. Eve White was a serious Baptist complaining of headaches and blackout spells, unemotional in interview, as though bound by propriety and inhibition. Her husband described some strange stories where another Eve emerged.

This was Eve Black, who was carefree, enjoying every moment of being alive, in whose gesture "there was something of a pert sauciness, something in which the artless play of a child and a scarcely conscious flirtatiousness mingled" (Thigpen & Cleckley, 1957, p. 27). She denied being married with a child as Eve White was, but it was she who was able to explain how Eve White's husband had received a bill for some sexy expensive clothes. She said of the other Eve, "I like to live and she don't" (Thigpen & Cleckley, 1957, p. 28).

I suspect that the families in the above cases probably changed their attitude towards the girls when they reached puberty, a period when girls can become embarrassingly twice as alive as before. ("Don't come close to me—you're so *lush*," a friend of mine once said to her daughter.) Such families might have been scared of their girls' new thrusting, sexual, hedonistic selves, and the resulting frustration or anger may cause cynicism and alienation to become part of the second self. Often, the second personalities contain those desires that do not fit in with those close to us, or with how we like to see ourselves, and therefore are rejected: what Freud called "the repressed" and Jung called his "shadow".

In Fairbairn's personality, the rejected chunk was in *two* bits, hostile to each other: the "libidinal ego" and the "internal saboteur", but in Eve Black, these two bits were *one* person who was both love-seeking *and* malicious. But Freud's repressed bit of self with its wicked Oedipal desires, and Jung's shadow, though split off from consciousness, did not grow all-round I–you boundaries (like the blobs of mercury), and take separate time-share possession of the body, but Nicola and Eve Black did just that.

One of the personalities, or "alters", within a multiple personality that I saw was "Baby Girl". She described how, once after a couple of glasses of wine, the front personality, in the middle of a perfectly normal adult conversation, heard herself say, "Do you like socks?" and she knew it was her second personality speaking from the background. Baby Girl loved life and when she was out she insisted on being naked, reclaiming a freedom lost under the tyranny of her prudish father. I worried about her visits to a local city graveyard in the middle of the night, naked, with another alter who was an Anglo-medieval witch. She was quite sure she could cope with police or anyone when I asked, and, indeed, the stories of multiple personalities show how amazingly they *can* cope with their adventures.

For most of us, our disowned bits do not usually operate so blatantly as free agents like Baby Girl or Eve Black, but *occasionally they jolly nearly do*, showing that they can be just as powerful and purposeful as alters in a multiple personality, although we are unaware of them. Alcohol, drug use, premenstrual tension, indeed an environment of extreme tension, and, of course, hypnosis, are among the many things that make it easier for our suppressed selves to act in spite of us.

I remember seeing a photograph in a newspaper once which caught a famous capitalist in the act of falling and breaking his leg in the street; he had just left a board meeting in which he had been deposed—the internal saboteur at work. People who lose their temper often say it is like being taken over, and are appalled at what they have done. In a Scottish play, a timid lad gets drunk and challenges a man: "Right, you just come outside!" Then you hear him thinking, terrified, "Who said that? Did *I* say that?" People who are emotionally in pieces, though they are not multiple personalities, often use the phrase "I heard myself say": "He walked in and said: 'How many times have you tried to do yourself in?' I thought, 'I don't believe this question,' so I heard myself say 'Four or five times'" (Morton, 1997, p. 97). (Princess Diana to her psychiatrist. Notice the "so": her usual public self probably forgot (dissociated) her suicidal wishes, but the right question reached them and she heard them acknowledge themselves.)

The cases above illustrate the conflict between how *we* want to love, and how *others* want us to love them. Maybe it really started when they were babies, not at puberty. Winnicott described the conflict in infancy between wanting to love mother the way seagulls love fish, and later wanting to love her another way, which comes spontaneously but is also, incidentally, the way she wants to be loved, human being to human being. If she not only responds encouragingly to the second kind of love but too actively demands it, and perhaps distorts it by only accepting some of it, a part of us resists the pressure and holes up, waiting for better times when it can live in spite of mother. (The part Winnicott called the true self.)

The second personality that is not as nice as mother wants is, sometimes, better at surviving in the world outside the family, because it is harsher and more assertive. This better survivor might appear quite late. A patient of mine once told me, "The trouble is I'm two people, but no one understands that." Tamar, the second personality was erect, strong, proud, and in charge when I met her in the waiting room, but soon changed into Ann, a weeping, gentle, submissive woman, brought up in an orphanage, who had been a complete slave to a bullying husband until she found out he was having an affair, which broke her heart. Thereupon, at age forty-five, she unexpectedly found herself sharing her life and body with Tamar, a competent, forceful woman, not broken-hearted at all but furious, who said to me, "There were too many people telling Ann what to do, so I came along and took over." Tamar had secured a good divorce settlement and was angry with Ann for softening and letting her ex-husband have the house. "If it had been me he would never have got away with it. Never." I was able to talk to each of them while the other listened. Tamar told me she was fed up with Ann's floppy submissiveness. Ann told me she was scared of Tamar and when I asked, then, to speak to Tamar, I found her raging—how dare Ann tell me, a complete stranger, what she had never told Tamar. I asked again for Ann, who said, well you don't tell people everything; indeed, she had been scared of her husband and she had never told him. I got Ann to apologise, which made Tamar soften towards her, and Ann said she would try trusting Tamar, who said she would give Ann another chance. It was like doing family therapy. But by the end of the session they were clashing with each other again, and that was the last I saw of them. I think Tamar thought I was being too sympathetic to Ann, so she would not let her near me ever again. This case made me feel uneasy—Tamar had come into being because Ann needed her, but can a person live out their whole life without *ever* being provoked into becoming their whole self by needing a latent other half to come to life? And, had Tamar really never existed before, or had she been there at five months old but suppressed at that time by mother—or, in Ann's case, the premature loss of mother?

The conflicts embedded in multiple personalities are recognisable, and we can empathise with each combatant. Indeed, they can be so like the rest of us that we can derive from them six lessons that apply to us all.

First lesson

All internal conflict is between sub-personalities using different consciences, conflicting visions of good, and incompatible value systems.

Our inner conflicts are, as already noted by Jung and Fairbairn, between persons in us, or sub-personalities, which means that the *parts of a person are not institutions, but are, themselves, persons* (in the same way they appear in dreams). Freud's model of superego, ego, and id has been really useful, and will remain so, but, as Edelstein cheerfully put it, "There was no compelling reason for Freud to call the parts id, ego, and superego. He could have called them Willie, Gladys and Fred" (Edelstein, 1981, p. 97).

Edelstein's statement was further highlighted in 1954 when the psychologists Osgood and Luria carried out a "semantic differential test" on each personality of the Eves. The test results showed that Eve Black had the value system and the conscience of a nation at war, in which hatred and fraud (towards the enemy) are virtues everyone is exhorted to have; it is like a socially alienated person, like lads on London housing estates who stone ambulances and fire engines. Eve Black is similar to the old fashioned picture of the hysteric who is a great seductress but frigid, as she uses sex and love only to get power.

This is where Freud's model is misleading. He wrote as though the superego, ego, and id are the *parts* of a person, but actually they are *functions* of each of the parts that make up a person. In Eve Black's case, each sub-personality, independently of others, evaluates her behaviour (superego), encounters *you* (ego), and desires you in her own way (id).

To understand this is crucial when treating the issues of ordinary people. For example, a middle-aged man torn between wife and mistress might already be interpreting his confusion as an internal conflict between conscience and desire, virtue and temptation, super-ego and id. Big mistake. It is not a conflict between Good and Evil, though the women might want him to see it that way (each interpreting Good and Evil in opposite ways, of course, like President Bush and Osama bin Laden). It is an ethical conflict between two sub-personalities each urging something good: one is telling him that he loves his wife, and he can make her happy by dumping the mistress, and the other is saying that his mistress loves him too, and she is offering him life. Thus, there is a categorical imperative in this man's soul telling him that he must not die before he has begun to live.

The whole Enlightenment of the Mind is about a radical change of direction in thought. Freud, as an early twentieth-century-type scientist, was still looking for basic simplicities to make a model of the universe in the same way scientists before him had looked for the basic building block, the indivisible particle, the atom. Thus, he reduced the vital force of life to two instincts: the life instinct and the death instinct. When the object relations theorists turned their attention from instinct to love, they joined a tide moving in the opposite direction.

The moment I hear myself say "love" in a medical school class-room, I am embarrassed, and I am glad there are no old portraits on the walls of the room to look down at me. When I was a lad, merely to hint at any future *aim* as explanation of the structure of any organism, provoked pronunciation of the dreaded anathema "teleological thinking!" (= heresy!). But love is heavy with future. We have to admit that in Reason's eyes we are casting ourselves adrift, to think like this. How could we find any reliable consensus by modifying all our compasses to point to such an unknowable? But if we find that that is where all our psychodynamic compasses are pointing anyway, whether we choose or not, then we might as well relax and accept it. Love is what our Enlightenment is all about.

The reason I have mentioned the topic of love here is that, for practical purposes, it is best to become accustomed to thinking of the parts of a person as each wanting to give and receive love, in different ways. By thinking of impersonal *institutions* of the psyche, Freud introduced confusion between what "I" is and what "I" does.

What "I" *is* is indefinable, as essentially incommunicable as the taste of chocolate, known only by *being* an "I", which is done by encountering "you". *"I" can never be explained to any being that is not one.* It is the supreme axiom from which all other knowledge follows, and that is an epistemological fact dodged by science and philosophy right up until the twentieth century. (If you cannot agree on "all other knowledge", you have to agree at least to "all knowledge of emotions".) Descartes was a schizoid nut case: "I think therefore I am" is so typical of the tortured reasoning that can be heard from patients on the chronic psychiatric wards, where "I am and I love" is as unthinkable and as terrifying as garlic to Dracula.

What "I" *does* transforms matter—the food we eat—into love. It does it by way of the Krebs Cycle, releasing energy from ingested molecules that are then used by all the body systems that support the central nervous system. The "I" is also desire, which grows into love by biting, kissing, hitting, caressing, and looking into the eyes of the other "I"s among which it is born. What "I" does is transform the instinct (id), by means of culture (conscious or unconscious relatedness to others = superego), into love (ego). These are the three things that "I" does—desire, reflect, and act. The id, superego, and ego really refer to things that every ego *does*.

Second lesson

The structure of conflict is different in different people.

Although there are some frequently found configurations, we should be very open-minded about what subdivisions we expect to find. So, we have to wean ourselves off thinking that we can take people apart like a plant into roots, stem, leaf, and flower. We can only accept the parts we find: sub-personalities.

At this point, I introduce the concept and use of hypnosis, as so many discoveries were made about multiple personality by using it. In 1924, Morton Prince reported a case of a normal man who, when hypnotised, fell spontaneously into *four* "distinct phases or moods, each of which may be well characterised as a self" (Prince, 1975, p. 298). The first was similar to his ordinary quiet courteous, religious self; a second was "hilarious and absurd . . . practical jokes . . . nonmoral though not vicious", a third "malicious" with "a strong wish to inflict pain . . . frequently asked permission to stab the experimenter" (Prince, 1975, p. 197) in order to see the blood flow; and the fourth was the opposite of the second—melancholy and ready to burst into tears. An unusual case, but it suggests that when the usual conscious self is absent, it is as if the conductor of the orchestra is asleep and the different sections of the orchestra are free to play their own favourite tunes in turn—something that also happens in dreams.

During the 1970s and 1980s, significant discoveries were made about hypnotism that were influenced by arguably one of the greatest hypnotherapists who ever lived, Milton Erickson (1903–1980). Immobilised by polio as a young man, Erickson was severely paralysed and passed the time observing the body language and tone of voice, etc., of others. He also worked hard at imitating the movements of infants in order to get his own mobility back. This experience contributed to an unusual understanding of people. Of his practice, he wrote, "I know what I do, but to explain how I do it is too difficult for me" (Grinder, DeLozier, & Bandler, 1977, p. viii).

Erickson preferred to deal with the unconscious mind directly, and was capable of making an agreement with the unconscious self not to tell the conscious self what they had worked out. He made people do things that would challenge their hang-ups: for example, he told a couple who complained of their child's bedwetting to deliberately pee on their bed; similarly, he instructed a girl who was scared of life to admire her naked body in front of a mirror, and to set aside money to spend on make-up, clothes, and fun. He, almost perversely, refused to speak with the conscious self about how he or she interacted with others, and he had a deep feel for normal family development. Jay Haley, in *Uncommon Therapy* (1973) noted that all Erickson's followers tended to take up different aspects of Erickson's work, so that you would almost think they were using quite different approaches. But what they all had in common was the high respect and value they gave to the unconscious mind and everything they found there, often above anything in the conscious mind.

In 1979, two of his followers, the hypnotists John and Helen Watkins, using *normal* student volunteers, demonstrated by hypnosis that we are all multiple personalities under the skin. They found that sub-personalities in normal people could be called out under hypnosis and asked to name themselves—"Ear", "Lucifer", "Inner Self", etc., and describe themselves: "I tell him what to do"; "I make him outwardly calm so others do not see that he is angry"; "I was born when he was five years old" (Grayson, 1979, p. 190). Then, with the *patient*, they were able to speak to the part that was giving Janet her headaches, or making Esther so depressed, or making Hugh lose his temper so much, and get them to stop it. In other words, how, at a time of trauma, a semi-independent sub-personality or "state" can come into being.

Third lesson

In all treatment which focuses on internal structure and conflict, the aim is to get the different parts, whether by using hypnosis or just talking, to listen, and empathise enough with each other to love each other, or at least accept each other, and become a harmonious team with one leader, however mutually hostile they may be to start with.

In "ego state therapy" the Watkinses, Edelstein, and others hypnotised ordinary patients (i.e., that were not multiple personalities) to reach the less conscious parts that were causing the symptoms. They, too, found that the divisions varied widely, just like in multiple personalities.

Talking only to the conscious self was sort of like trying to get Johnny to change something known only to Charlie, who is asleep upstairs, so you wake Charlie and talk to him. I once tried the technique in its pure form, and it did not work for me, but it was in a case where the patient would have lost too much by getting better. However, with ordinary dynamic psychotherapy, it makes all the difference to be aware of possible other personalities present behind the front personality, or at least being open to the points of view about feelings that may be quite at odds with the personality you are speaking to. Such sub-personalities might have a great deal of power over his fate and the fates of those he loves, and might astonish him (and the therapist) when they are heard. So it is important to make every effort to hear the slightest hints of self-expression uttered by these hidden parts, and to encourage them to come out into the open, not necessarily as named sub-personalities, but as an expression of sets of usually concealed emotions.

At first sight, ego state therapy might appear alarming, as it looks as if it makes people into multiple personalities when they are not. But if we are all, to some extent, multiple personalities under the skin anyway, and since the treatment for multiple personality turns out to have universal principles, then here we have the third lesson. It is the same as what Freud was doing in getting the ego to be less scared of the id, and the superego to be less cruel to the ego, but Freud would never have dreamed of getting the kind of help from the sub-personalities that the ego state therapists did.

Fourth lesson

Look for the good in any dissident part of the self, however apparently evil, and work to uncover its healthy roots, so it can contribute to love.

This lesson implies a *faith* that human beings are basically good, or at least that their energy is *potentially* good. Erickson and his followers believed in this faith, as did Melanie Klein, and it has been fundamentally implicit in the work of many, many therapists through the century. I claim this faith as essential to our Enlightenment. It surfaced in an epidemic of optimism in Californian movements in the 1960s and in self-help books (a classic example was Harris's *I'm OK You're OK*). Indeed, some American self-help books arising out of the Enlightenment of the Mind are very good indeed. The surge of optimism had a sentimental side to it, too, rightly mocked. "Deep down inside us there is good" and "Deep down inside us we're no good" sang the Jets in *West Side Story*. But the root of the real unsentimental faith was found by those who worked in difficult places such as prisons and mental hospitals, which can, sometimes, house the worst evil that humanity can provide.

Fifth lesson

Keep a very open eye for stray rogue emotions of self-hate or just hate or despair, based on the daftest of obsolete reasons, which are operating completely unconsciously.

Once we become more accustomed to seeing the multiplicity in everyone, it is possible to see how even the most intelligent, sophisticated, smooth, and superior people can have their strings pulled by really daft, destructive, and breathtakingly illogical unconscious deals between sub-personalities. I once saw a clever and successful barrister in London who told me straight away that she knew her strings were being pulled by a rather silly, spoilt little girl in her. Our rogue parts do terrible damage to ourselves and to others by preventable accidents (both concrete and emotional), and God knows how much physical illness is caused. We know for a fact that depression lowers the immune system, and grief causes cardiac events, and we suspect a great deal more. Cancer? The number of sudden flash-in-the-pan suicide attempts in multiple personality is striking. How many suicidal impulses are lurking about that we are completely unconscious of, affecting us in ways of which we are totally unaware?

The two characteristics of multiple personality, that is, being more in pieces than usual, and each piece with a complete I–you skin around it, are found more in those who panic and reach out to cling than those who panic and withdraw. In 1974, the psychologist Irene Fast wrote about how amazed she was to discover the number of ordinary individuals she knew who felt themselves to be made up of several personalities with little or no central self. They were more or less doing all right, and, indeed, some seemed to be having a whale of a time—they had known from the beginning that they could do whatever they wanted in life. One man had been "a specialist in racing boats, a chemist aiming at discovery of new aspects of the origins of life, a psychoanalyst, a musician, and a mathematical wizard" (Fast, 1974, p. 294). Another wrote an award winning play, and entered a medical school with one of the highest recorded test scores. However, he "was able to sustain a sense of his identity in the field for only a few months and left" (Fast, 1974, p. 296), and there is the rub; such a person is turned on more by being a playwright than by writing plays, however well he can act the part for a while. An over-extroverted person tends not to be a multi-faceted diamond, but a handful of scintillating bits with little constant core that can put roots down and grow.

Fast found that sufferers of *borderline personality* (bordering on madness but not mad—another deeply meaningless psychiatric label) are in pieces in the same kind of way. Sometimes they, too, feel an "intense and exhilarating sense of self" (Fast, 1974, p. 296) in their different identities, and are great show-offs, and they often need an audience to feel they exist. If no one is looking at them, or if the identity they present is rejected (for example, when a conman or impostor is unmasked), they feel empty and without a self. A man once told me that when sparks fly up from a bonfire, and apparently cease to exist when they go out, is how he feels the moment he is alone. Being noticed by others stimulates and activates the sufferer and, sometimes, they come across as very positive. Fast observed how they were able to turn a bad experience into a positive one by making it into a showing-off thing.

But, she added, that trick of making the unpleasant emotion into a histrionic sort of act keeps it split off from the true personality, who has thus disowned and dissociated it (instead of digesting it by appropriate action, such as revenge or forgiveness or sexual adventure, or whatever), so that it becomes a new separate sub-personality.

By the time borderline personalities get to psychiatrists, they are not usually very happy at all. They are characterised by unstable relationships, terror of abandonment, feelings of emptiness, poor impulse control, mood swings (including rages), and suicidal and self-mutilating behaviour. Desperate to be loved and to make an impression in order to feel they exist, they are too anxious and busy to build up a constant core sense of self; they are split up into different roles for different people and different dramas.

In ordinary life outside the consulting room, you usually meet the lovable bits of borderline personalities first: appealing helplessness and vulnerability, naïve trust, humility, or charming self-deprecation, idealisation of you, kind concern and care, promises of love, so you get involved and then . . . Wham! Here come all the symptoms of the sympathy-hunger described by Carter way back in 1850 and at the beginning of this story (Chapter Two), the results of the love-starvation of their childhoods: demands for love (with menaces), hostile dependency, addictions, self-harming, unpredictable moods, fury, scathing contempt with a supernatural skill in reaching the woundable underside of your heart, silent hopelessness, anxiety states, crises at 4 a.m., bizarre and dramatic scenes. All these and more—meet the family! Borderline personalities are too desperate to be able to sort out the lovable ways of getting loved from the repelling ways.

Multiple personalities go one amazing step beyond borderline personalities in forming I–you skins around the separate bundles of emotions. This is difficult for introverted psychotherapists to understand (as most of us are) but it is not really so strange. Every desire, every emotion forms an I–you skin—"I want you". Multiple personalities are usually very I–you in action, amenable and co-operative, or dependent and demanding: they love talking, are easily hypnotised (some say they are already self-hypnotised in their dissociation), and, in short, operate at the extrovert/hysteric/love addict end of relatedness. They are always rubbing close to other people; indeed, extreme and regressive extroverts are like European countries with intensely defined boundaries.

By contrast, withdrawn people (regressive introverts, schizoids, schizophrenics) are more like those countries separated only by a line someone has drawn with a ruler on a map, where the nomads cross and re-cross without needing to know which country they are in, and I am not sure whether it is you who are angry or I (a state sometimes called "symbiotic psychosis"). *Their* emotions, instead of having a high-tension I–you surface like the mercury blobs, are more like spilt ether, sinking away into the air and the environment, and you might not even know they are there: you can smell them, but you cannot put your finger on them. An extrovert, love-addict type of fragmentation neatly separates each chapter of the book from the others. Introvert, avoidance-addict fragmentation, like schizophrenia, separates emotion from facts and self from others, and throws the book in the river. But if we are well practised at growing I–you skins—self-presentations, masks, "shields", personas, role-playing, manipulative games—between ourselves and other people, then all our parts can do it, and to each other. So, the internal dialogues become encounters between separate selves, and the self more loved by Mum and Dad can disown and even dissociate the other self and genuinely forget its existence—for a while.

Sixth lesson

The sixth lesson is more a suggestion. Multiple personalities show how, through shifting separations and fusions of sub-personalities, emotions in all of us can either separate or fuse. We talked earlier about mixed feelings, and now we can notice whether the mixed feelings are in conflict, or in harmony, or in process of being distinguished and separated from each other, or fusing. It is like the work of the alchemists in separating or combining chemicals and colours. We all work at distinguishing emotions from each other: "I want to hit him" is the simple reaction, but if I look at it again, I see I have three emotions: frustration, disappointment, a little bit of admiration. And we fuse emotions—it is a lovely thing to see when hate and love become fused in words of tender reproach, or how a teenager speaks to her little sister in a voice-music perfectly blending irritation and affection in one caressing vocal slap.

Would you agree that distinguishing, separating, marrying, or fusing emotions is the work of culture from its very beginnings when grunts, giggles, and moans first became words? We fuse and separate and fuse again inside ourselves, and we do something the same outside between our emotions and those of others. The play of the latter is connected with two particularly opposite passionate desires that can scare the pants off each other: our desire to be really close and fuse with the other, and the desire to be completely separate and free and autonomous.

"There is another man within me, that's angry with me" Browne wrote (1909, p. 76). We need another man within us, or woman, who can come from nowhere and lift us up and encourage us when we are dismayed and defeated, and give us thoughts and feelings we could not have thought of for ourselves.

You have to agree that this is all very rich stuff about humanity, and it gets richer still. In the next chapter, we will explore the fascinating case of Sahid Sahid, taken from my own professional experience.

CHAPTER TWENTY-TWO

Sahid Sahid

"I think honesty comes before God"

(Sahid Sahid)

I cannot leave the subject of multiple personality without telling you about the case that engrossed me most. He presented in 1991, a fifty-six-year-old Asian scientist called Sahid Sahid (I have decided to protect his identity even though he told me he wanted his voice to be heard) whose intellect outstripped mine. At the age of twenty, he had left his native Muslim community in Zanzibar to continue his education in the UK and, on arrival, had felt like a child again, drinking in the utterly alien culture of intellectual England. He admired Bertrand Russell ("like my father", he said) and he became an Englishy kind of secular liberal humanist to whom family and emotional bonds were of little interest. Like other students, he enjoyed sexual relationships with no emotional ties: "I have as much emotions as an English person", he said (meaning that he did not have much at all). He soon lost touch with his family back in Zanzibar, saying, "In England you don't need the family."

During his career, he organised the teaching of science for international organisations in different countries. He was funded by an American university to research into the relationship between science and culture, travelling in Asia, Africa, and Latin America. It shocked him "beyond belief" to find that *science is not universal*; he wrote to me, ". . . its parameters, when scientifically analysed, seem to fit . . . only with those of a very narrow band of North-West European cultures . . ."

His mental universe was shattered by this discovery, and he had a breakdown at the age of thirty-eight. He was diagnosed as schizophrenic. Typical of multiple personality, his extraversion had predominated over his introversion, in his submission to the external authority of Bertrand Russell and Western science. His introversion was there all right, but his own inner intuitions had been blotted out, which broke him. But, as I shall show, this insight that destroyed him would not let him go because it was an inspired truth that was bigger than him.

Sahid had two years of psychotherapy in England with a therapist who said she could not communicate with his inner child (I do not know whether she knew that his inner child spoke only Swahili). An attempt to return to work failed and he had four years of art therapy, music therapy, psychodrama, and group therapy in Leeds—"a real eye-opener!" The different therapies revealed to him that he was deeply split into two people: a South Eastern Person (SEP), whom Sahid referred to as "Mohammed" during our sessions, and a North Western Person (NWP), that is, Sahid, himself. So, it turned out that the Arabic-speaking Muslim self whom Sahid had apparently abandoned in order to become an Englishman at age twenty was still there, or had come back.

At the piano, Mohammed would, with the right hand, extemporise over Eastern scales (Maquaams, Ragas, etc.) while Sahid tried to harmonise with Western chords, using the left hand. Mohammed would take over the body in even deeper "bio-affective" (Sahid's word) ways—posture, sensations, and metabolism. But the most contentious issue between Mohammed and Sahid was their opposing views on what Sahid called the God complex. The God complex had started as an earth deity like Dionysus, but apparently later *only Sahid* (*not Mohammed*) had been Christian, at least for a while. Yet, at the same time, the God complex was the only link between Sahid and

Mohammed, the only thing they had in common. There was also a Child, so there were four of them.

As a schizophrenic, Sahid had more insight than anyone I have met, and I wonder if it was because he was a multiple personality, which is a more fundamental pathology. However, I do not believe that Mohammed was schizophrenic. Sahid wrote,

> Some time during the 1984–85 period the author found himself writing, from Harrogate, to most of the Christian leaders of the world, proclaiming himself to be 'Jesus Christ—the Second Coming'! To a sympathetic Christian lady—trying to be helpful . . . by saying to him, 'Jesus visits me, too'—the author replied, 'do not be frightened when I say I am Jesus: for when Jesus visits you—a non-schizophrenic and, therefore, a person with a unitary identity—you remain you, and Jesus remains Jesus. But when Jesus comes to 'me'—a schizophrenic, with a broken-down, zero identity—I CANNOT BUT BECOME HIM!' All this, of course, was highly odd, to say the least, if only because: firstly, the author has neither ever been a Christian throughout his life, nor had any Christian background; secondly, he is fully aware that he is schizophrenic while making this claim—without, however, feeling that this in the slightest bit nullified the validity of his claim!

But the God complex developed into something utterly amazing: a God who gave Sahid a *scientific* proof of His existence, using all the wealth of Sahid's unique world-wide knowledge of science and the philosophy of science, including the theory of relativity (which Sahid *understood completely*—can you imagine?—even the Lorentz transformation matrix bit of it, which alone beats me). But during his travels, Sahid had found that relativity was taught in parrot fashion, without people really understanding it. The proof, as dictated to Sahid from God, takes up thirty-seven pages of Sahid's closely packed, single-space typing, with diagrams.

But when God came (pairing with the inner Child, who is an infra-adult where God is an ultra-adult), Mohammed's reaction was to become a Khomeini-like fundamentalist Muslim. Their room was divided; the Koran (in Arabic) in Mohammed's half, and Sahid's proof of God in the other. The relationship between them was unbearable, like the scraping of a knife on glass. "His freedom is my death," Sahid said. There were two suicide attempts, but the God complex stopped them.

Sahid, as an educated Westerner, *could not accept God's proof of His own existence that God was giving him.* He realised he was a fundamentalist, too (in his way, a *secular* fundamentalist). However, he saw that there could be a way out. If top scientists and thinkers of the world accepted the proof of God, then he could, too, and then he and Mohammed would be reconciled. Then he would go to Mohammed's people and apologise for teaching a Godless science. If they did not, then it would prove that the God complex was just a schizophrenic symptom, which meant they would kill themselves. They had agreed that Sahid would be the one to do it so Mohammed would be sinless, but Sahid would not tell me how he planned to carry out the suicide. He knew his probable fate as a schizophrenic being looked after by "care in the community", and was living in chronic fear; he was not coping in his lodgings, and could not do the chores; he was unpopular and looked as if he was headed for the street. The God complex had agreed that if Sahid ended up on the street, he could kill himself.

So, Sahid sent off the thirty-seven pages of his proof of God to over one hundred great thinkers all over the world. One by one they wrote back, respectfully, but helplessly. Noam Chomsky replied that he was just not competent to comment on it, saying he lacked the background, and though others wrote at some length, not one of them was able to enthusiastically commit himself to supporting God's argument.

Although Sahid and Mohammed were diametrically at loggerheads, the God complex as an overarching tolerance (who behaved as though he loved them both) forced them to be protective of each other and swung, automatically, to support whichever was in a weaker position—Sahid when in Zanzibar, and Mohammed in London. Similarly, Sahid refused to take the drugs prescribed for him by psychiatrists for fear they would harm Mohammed. At one point, Sahid's sisters took Mohammed home to Tanzania, and the local healers who work on a family basis diagnosed him on the spot without even seeing him: "He is possessed by the spirit of an Englishman." However, the healers wanted to try to get rid of the possessing spirit instead of integrating it, which appears to be a weakness of the many primitive medical techniques based on spirit possession. But, this time it was Mohammed who refused their treatment in case it harmed Sahid (who was impressed by the mullahs' acumen), and came back to London.

Unusually (for a schizophrenic), Sahid's intact mind was able to contain and understand his madness so much that I kept forgetting it was there. In one conversation, I was a bit shocked at his emotional distance from his close woman friend when he said, "Woman, what have I to do with thee?" I just looked at him. I was thinking, My God, he can't believe in God but he thinks he is Jesus. He read my expression precisely; "I *told* you I'm mad!" he laughed.

I felt such sympathy with both Mohammed and Sahid. I had seen an Open University programme about an Islamic village in some hilly place in North Africa, and it was exactly like the village I grew up in the Highlands of Scotland: the holy preacher (my father), the holy building, the holy Book, the regular call to prayer and worship. And the elders (who, in my village, also ran the Masonic Lodge and the Village Council) were all good, worthy men, responsible, caring, but who could not have understood the future I was unknowingly heading for any more than the African elders could have understood Bertrand Russell and liberal scientific humanism. But Sahid would never let me talk to Mohammed, or even talk about him. Later, I found out why.

I set up a conference about Sahid's case and he wrote to thank me:

31st Jan 1992

Dear Dr Macdiarmid,

First of all, the 'God-complex' wishes 'me' to convey 'His' ('Its' 'Her') sincere thanks to you for your most sensitive, sympathetic and 'truthful' presentation of 'my' predicament, as well as 'His' ('Its', 'Her') case (within the constraints of time available, general understanding of the audience etc.)

'He' ('It' 'She') also wishes 'me' to correct you (otherwise 'I' wouldn't dare correct a Jungian expert like yourself *on Jung*!!) regarding your remarks on Nazism and the 'God-complex' (how dangerous the latter, i.e. 'God-complex' can be etc.) – unless 'I' have seriously misinterpreted them – in that you seem to have implied that Hitler was possessed by the 'God-complex'; whereas, as far as I can recall, Jung never said that. In fact, Jung *predicted* the rise of German Nationalism: by the words (only vaguely recalled by 'me') 'The blond beast is beginning to stir again' (or something to that effect) implying the rise of the *German Collective_Unconscious*; and not the *Universal Unconscious* i.e. the 'God-complex' as was implied by G in 'my' document etc.

The above is important in the current world context, since various 'wounded' 'National' *Collective Unconsciousnesses*, expressing themselves through National or Religious fundamentalism, are sprouting all over the world. In absence of any awareness of the Universal Unconscious (UTP, Cultural Relativity etc) [a reference to his 'proof'] these would run amok and bring down the current Western Ascendancy.

[This was ten years before 9/11]

(As indeed became the fate of the Roman Ascendancy after my Crucifixion 2000 years ago . . .) Hence the absolute necessity of getting . . . the 'proof' . . . scrutinised . . . 'I' trust you will do your best.

He asked me to support his therapist,

For in taking 'me' . . . on, he takes on global problems (since 'my' problems are essentially global-humanity problems). That is why the majority of psychiatrist–therapists leave inter-cultural . . . cases well alone.

At the conference, in an attempt to get his message heard from behind his madness, I raised the idea of the great neurologist Hughlings Jackson: that it is the *healthy* working of the brain that produces original and apparently "mad" ideas in mental illness; the illness only reveals them unnaturally, or distorts them, but can never produce them. They are not *created* by the illness, any more than blood is created by the cut that spills it and makes it seen.

The junior psychiatrist who was seeing Sahid on a routine basis wrote to me to tell me that Sahid had felt elated after the conference.

He also told me that during the conference he had heard the voice of the Zanzibarian, who he now refers to as Mohammed, "shouting a greeting to you in Arabic because he was also impressed by it. [Sahid] says that he did not tell you this at the time because he was frightened you would develop a relationship with the Zanzibarian, his worst enemy and thereby destroy him."

So that was why I could never meet the Zanzibarian, to whom I felt akin, and never can now, because the hospital records show Sahid to be on the deceased list.

He was fighting on so many fronts. Year by year, he was irrevocably treading the classic loner schizophrenic's path into slow descent through the social classes down to destitution; he was reaching out by letter to the finest intelligences in the world and getting respectful replies, which could not help him. He was fighting Mohammed as his worst enemy and indispensable other self. He was fighting the God complex, resisting that submission to, and fusion with, Him, which would have finally extinguished what little identity he had, and to which he was perilously close. He could see God's point of view: "I am a child of modernity ... maybe the God wants to talk to this modernity—in which case I've got to follow."

So, he was more than willing to do what God wanted and try to get His argument published for Him, and that was what he really wanted me to help him do. But in order to hold on to what little identity he had, he also had to hold on to his own vision, his own principles, against God. He would not dishonestly submit to something he did not believe: "I think honesty comes before God." He was also fighting me to prevent me from teaming up with Mohammed, and trying to get through me the therapy he wanted—acceptance by the scientific community of God's proof of His existence—which would cure him *and also cure the world.*

During the vigorous exchanges between Sahid and the God complex, it appeared that God's problem was not with scientific rationalism, but with fundamentalist secularism. Scientific rationalism is on God's side—He owns it.

When you read the Proof, it does not come across like a proof of the existence of God at all, but more like God describing his nature. I once had a patient who said that all schizophrenics have their own homespun religion. Actually, anyone who looks inside himself can become aware of a source of originality at the back of his mind. It might be almost imperceptible, for example, my special particular appreciation of my wife's beauty that no one else knows, coming just from my individuality, or it may be enormous, like Matisse's source of gargantuan creativity, to which, as he said, he was ungrateful without remorse. Or it might come out only in projection, in which the individual is unaware; for instance, I might never know that I am seeing in someone's novel something that the author himself did not put in it. Indeed, writers are sometimes very surprised at what people think their books are saying, and certainly psychotherapists are often astonished at hearing what they are supposed to have said the previous week.

There are two ways of turning inward. The first is to be as avoidant towards our inner world as to the outer, and while looking inwards become stuck in obsessive circular inner games or fearful frozen numbness. The other way is to be open-eyed and to look around inside for whatever is to be found—our own originality and creativeness, the gods, demons, archetypes, dreams, etc. If the avoidance addict/schizoid has withdrawn from both his outer *and* inner "you", and the inner reality *forces itself* on his attention, then he is bothered and challenged by it. The voice of originality, coming from the back of the mind, can be hard to cope with, whether we think it is the voice of our own true inner self or the voice of something deeper than that (collective unconscious, id, God, etc.), but either way it is harder for us Westerners if it is felt to be "you" rather than "I".

The originality at the back of Sahid's mind, in the form of the God complex he was wrestling with, was something awesome. The shaft of illumination that shattered him in the first place in 1973, that science is not universal, had now become an inspiration of human tolerance—political, ideological, social, racial, religious—so profound that it does deserve the adjective "divine" rather than merely humane. It was God saying something like "My existence consists in this: you must not ever go to war because you are right and he is wrong. That is never a reason to fight or hate. I am relativity; fundamentalism, whether secular or religious, is out." In Sahid's vision, if science and theology could fuse in the universal transformation principle, that is, God, then (and here I summarise his points):

1. The God complex's manifestation in schizophrenia, instead of being snuffed out by drugs, could be welcomed as a healing potential.
2. The imposition upon the East of Western ascendancy categories disguised as universal categories would cease. (Sahid saw this is a major global affliction.)
3. Muslim educators could teach Islamic science.
4. The threat of fascism from religious and national fundamentalism would be averted.
5. Global and doorstep crime from the cultural breakdown of immigrant groups, which is making inroads even on banking–commercial systems, would be held in check.

6. Racists and terrorists would have their energy depleted when recognised scientifically as due to mankind ignoring the finest mediating agency (UTP, God) available.
7. The destruction of the planet by global warming, etc., would stop.

You can see why he was so desperate to be heard.

Sahid's conflict, and what I learnt from him, was that, although it is a legitimate aim to look for universal truth, it is wrong to jump the gun and decide that the truth we happen to have found *is* universal. That is fundamentalism, whether secular or religious. It gives in too crudely to the instinctual truth that I am an important person because I have a contribution to make to the world; just as in schizophrenia, I know I am Jesus, but that is only metaphorically true, not literally, so if I take it literally I have got it wrong.

Sahid was having a "creative illness" as described by Henri Ellenberger (Ellenberger, 1970, p. 447), nobly fighting the lazy urge to just give in and let himself be taken over by the God complex, but somehow it was going wrong and he could not help being Jesus, sometimes. In Christian dogma, God is, Himself, a multiple personality, but a conscious and harmonious one, with clashes being resolved by the Son's submission to his Father's will (though occasionally trying to get his Father to take the softer option), but in Sahid's weakened psyche, God's sub-personalities seemed not to be allowed any useful dialogue.

I know what he should have done. He should have gone along with the developmental impulse—which surely he must have had— to grow beyond the need to borrow authority from the great minds of the world. He was clinging to a childish extroverted dependence, which he should have sacrificed. Also, he was too much influenced by the Child: when God or your originality makes a suggestion, you should take it to your own inner council room (schizophrenics usually do not have any, but he had some), modify it a bit, and then *try it out* and see if it works, not look for fathers to validate you before you move at all. He should have tried believing and acting on God's assertion that what he thought, and what Mohammed thought, were only relative truths, that his attitude to God and Mohammed's opposite attitude both had truth in them, that there is an Islamic reality *and* a secular one, and he should have gone face to face with Mohammed and fought it out with him. I do not think he would have had to give in and apologise as totally as he feared. If he had patiently slugged it out with Mohammed, what might he not have done for the world, with his great intelligence and world knowledge? But no schizophrenic is able to deploy hate usefully until at last it rushes up in a crude compensatory flood and God tells him to kill someone and he does. I could see that, for Sahid, facing up to Mohammed would have been facing pure hell. He said it was like a tunnel between them with two entrances, Mohammed's and his, and "I'm afraid to jump in case there is no window in the middle", and I thought I knew what he meant. The tragedy was he could not let God reconcile him and Mohammed, because God—articulate and persuasive as he was— might only be a schizophrenic delusion.

When I retired from the National Health Service, Sahid wrote to me, reproachfully, to tell me that retirement was irrelevant to the matter in hand, and, of course, now I think I should have stayed in touch with him somehow—that is what I should have done. Later on, I learnt that he committed suicide in 1993. In his last letter to me, in November of that year, he was sending me some information about publication prospects so that I would be aware of them "in the event of 'my' demise (death etc.)". Now, with hindsight, the message is clear and I just did not pick it up at the time.

I do not know that our work would have cured the world, since now, in this new century, the problem seems not to be secular fundamentalism *vs.* religious fundamentalism, but the three religious fundamentalisms, Christian, Jewish, and Islamic, all pushing us into conflict.

PART IV

LEGACY FOR THE TWENTY-FIRST CENTURY

CHAPTER TWENTY-THREE

The shift to the left foot

"People are not disturbed by things, but the view they take of them"

(Epictetus, 135 AD)

My heart rises with pleasure and excitement as I look at seven young fresh faces—Christos, Mohammed, Naomi, Ayesha, Perna, Lu An, Jovita, Giovanni—names like that. In each face I see a lively critical intelligence and curiosity: *crème de la crème*. We are crammed on top of each other in a tiny, sordid room (yesterday's dishes, crumpled textbooks) in the residents' flat of the Priory Hospital. They are the new intake of junior psychiatrists, aged twenty-something; and for six months I, aged seventy-seven, have access to their minds (Socrates was executed by the State for that: putting ideas into the minds of Athenian youth). The students are taking my seminars to help them pass their MRC Psych exams so they can earn an honest penny from the honest trade of mental health doctoring.

After I have started the great teaching game of first finding out what is in *their* minds already, my heart begins to swell with an intuition of what I want these lads and lasses to know. I begin to feel my way into it. I tell them about Carter and his hysterical girls, and what he wrote about keeping your temper under control, even at the *strongest provocation*. Do any of their patients make them angry? I ask them. Yes! they say, and they begin to tell me some stories. We agree that there are honest and dishonest patients. The honest ones, hesitantly, but frankly, expose their never-met infantile needs, while the dishonest ones manipulate and cheat their way to get their needs satisfied, on the basis that the doctor does not really want to help them but is, merely, a no-good louse that needs to be outsmarted. I mention Tom Main's quiet suggestion that, for the psychiatrist, revenge is disguised as treatment.

I get in the groundwork: that the mind is mostly unconscious, and that it is divided up in pieces in useful ways with the co-operation of sub-personalities, and in pathological ways with conflict. It is easy to demonstrate normal dissociation to them, as we are under a flight path, and they do not hear the planes passing overhead until I make them listen. I outline the different models of the mind described earlier, and mention the ideas of Freud and his successors. I suggest that all the theories are about success and failure in how we exchange love, through good example and bad, or learnt hope and learnt hopelessness.

Christos tells me that in ancient Greece they had no word for love. Away back in the times of the homosexual fighting units, they used the words *eros*, meaning sexual desire, and *philia*, meaning friendship, and it was only later that they brought in a word meaning "love", which was derived from the Arabic word *agape*.

I discuss how both hate and aggression are the normal foundation of loving, and tell them about a film I saw on television once: two wolves introduced to each other in a zoo. They circled each other, snarling menacingly, with threats of savage bloody murder on a hair trigger, but ended up side by side, stroking each other's lovely, long, black forelegs. Mutual respect is the indispensable basis for exchange of affection, or, to paraphrase John Ruskin somewhat, "first justice, then love" (Ruskin, 1930, p. 37). Assert yourself, make room for yourself, and ensure your supply lines, then you can love.

I mention Winnicott's poignant story of how every tiny infant (except, perhaps, those who are going to grow up to be psychopaths), having begun life with a ruthless healthy greed, discovers concern for mother, and is thrown into the complexities of how to reconcile maximum love satisfactions for both. In other words, if I screw it up, messing things up between me and you is, at the same time, messing up my own mind and causing pathological internal conflicts. By and large, our patients are making an even worse mess of it than we are ourselves, and that is why they are the patients and we the doctors.

Using a story, I illustrate for them the ruin caused by failure to hate. A young woman I knew was systematically taught that she was not, in her natural self, lovable, by her mother. The patient was too terrified and scrupulous ever to hate her mother, only love her and desperately try to please her: she did the wrong subjects at school, went to the wrong university, and married the wrong man—all to please mother. In waking life, she had given her mother a dog, Toby. In a dream, her mother told her she had had Toby put down because he had a skin complaint. She was so upset that her mother had him put down for something so trivial. This was her psyche trying to get her to see that her mother deserved a bit of hate and rejection.

After a few weeks of mostly depressed, discouraging dreams, she came and told me about a bizarre dream, which she found embarrassing—Toby had tried to have sex with her; he became big and it was hard for her to fight him off. I had already suspected that she had learned she was not lovable right at the very early animal stage when her mother might not have cuddled her tiny baby with enough warmth and conviction. So, I told this girl that her psyche was trying desperately to convince her that she *was* lovable on the most basic animal level: Toby loves you; he cannot keep his paws off you. Believe him and disbelieve your mother! Perhaps we can rewrite the dream so she accepts Toby's love and has a great time with him!

The teaching session ends here and the students are now looking a bit subdued. They have not been taught about the benefits of sex with animals in dreams, and maybe I am going a bit fast and far for them.

During our next class, I think it is time for me, as an old hand in this game, to come clean with a revelation that no one else will ever explicitly put to them. Watching their faces carefully, I tell them that there are two ways of practising mental health care: the first is to be the professional and do the job by managing the minds of patients with minimum stress to therapist and patient, keeping involvement limited to the intellectual, practical, and medical, while the second is to be the exposed therapist, as in dynamic psychiatry or dynamic psychotherapy, by reacting to the patient with their whole natural self.

I watch their faces because I am not sure how far I can go with this one. I want to tell them about Linda, the Australian prostitute who believed that her effortful adaptation to her clients' needs, however kinky, "makes you a better person". I knew exactly what she was talking about. Psychodynamic psychotherapy is an unnatural interaction designed to release the patient's capacity for normal interaction. Its unnaturalness is that the therapist must demand no personal gain from it *at all* except the money and the job satisfaction. But if he offers his whole natural self as the patient's adventure playground, he does not do it for the gratification of the patient. We sacred prostitutes are married to the God who demands that our top aim must be to help the patient return to the normal growth of his capacity for love, from which, for whatever reason, he has become alienated. So, as therapist, we do not gratify the client's infantile needs in the same way as Linda, but are more challenging and confronting of the patient.

However, I am still not sure if I can quite say all this to them yet. But I do tell them one trick they must be aware of: if any patient awakens unprofessional emotions in them, that is, hostility, or the kind of special pity that makes inexperienced psychiatric nurses give patients their home telephone numbers, or hopeless despair that makes them refer the troublesome patient to someone who will not duck a challenge, then they must think to themselves—*what is this telling me about the patient?*

I have not found out yet, but I expect them to be in that most exciting phase of the growth of human love, falling in love and nest-building and starting a family, and that will be a way into talking to them about the heart of our expertise: the understanding of family love and hate. They will listen when I tell them that emotionally exposing themselves to the patient is like becoming emotionally a member of the patient's family, whether they are doing family, individual, or group psychotherapy. As a member of that family, they become subject to those same stresses from the family of origin that exerted to screw up the patient, including the irresistible force of the family's unconscious moral high ground; as a colleague once said, they are well able to make you feel as though you have farted in church.

When I started listening to Alison, an anorexic patient of mine, she led me so deeply into her world that there was a time when I could not see, for the life of me, why she should not starve herself to death. I just knew it made sense. But, as you will see later, she began to think and dream things that proved to be an antidote. Having drowned together, the patient and therapist can find answers, perhaps in the long denied and dissociated reactive normal hate, or in some unpredictable messages from dreams.

We become the patient's little sister or big brother, or parents who will re-parent him. The registrars listen with interest when I tell them that, as re-parenting parents, we have two contrasting functions.

One function is to listen to what the original parents could not hear. This is when Freud's trick of free association comes into its own. Alison experienced it as being uncomfortably undressed; others describe it as being in a warm bath in which knots untie themselves. One patient dreamed that the cable tying a ship to a pier fell loose so that the ship was free to sail. Through free association, the hidden, rejected, ashamed, or defiant delinquent self is heard and accepted.

Like Carter's patients back in Victorian England, we might be scared to accept sympathy for our true selves, which is being offered for the first time in our lives, and too fearful to come out from behind the cover of the false selves we have been presenting. The ability to hypnotise (something every psychiatrist should be able to carry out) helps a psychotherapist to make the best use of free association and its offer of sympathy. I use one of the students to demonstrate hypnosis: guinea pig Lu goes into quite a good trance, and her hand begins to twitch on her lap. But just as she is about to achieve hand levitation, someone's pager and phone go off simultaneously. Giggles and a snap back to ordinary consciousness. Too bad, better luck next time.

The other parental function is to make demands on the patient that have been neglected by the parents: demands for honesty and straight dealing, a bit of patience and perseverance, offer as much hope as he can bear, respect, effort to adapt, trust in his own generous impulses, and so on. All this should be encouraged by us with whatever natural warmth we have, but also enforced by the punishment of our displeasure, and our honest reproach and anger.

If we let ourselves become infected by the patient's hopeless despair, expressed perhaps in spiteful and grandiose ways like a little Hitler, or in paranoid defensive ways like a little Stalin, we might react in kind, more or less covertly, and drink the satisfactions of revenge.

Here, our Enlightenment makes a crucial distinction between two things: on the one hand, allowing ourselves the sweet satisfactions of revenge on, and rejection of, the other, or alternatively, fair, honest reproach of, and anger with, the other, in a context of what can only, embarrassingly, be called love. The contrast is between punishment that is linked to rejection, or anger that is part of an unremitting demand for the exchange of love. How hard it can sometimes be to tell which is going on. And it costs effort. Remember Carter's advice to end the interview if a therapist is about to lose his temper.

Some of our patients behave like the scum of the earth. I know people who give their all to rescue these scum. The ingenious vindictive spite that psychiatric nurses sometimes have to put up with would take your breath away. How often I have sat in Staff Support Groups while the discussion raged—is this patient mad, or just bad? Often, they are both. Provocative, furtive, or blatant delighted evil can be hard to take. I remember hearing a story about the psychiatrist and social therapist, Maxwell Jones, who was running a therapeutic unit at Dingleton in the Scottish borders, in the 1970s. The patients, themselves, expelled a member of their own group, ordering him out of the building, and the unfortunate patient then spent two nights getting his face frost-bitten in the fields before they let him back in. As fair as a slap to a naughty child, I thought, after reflection. The secret of good punishment that expresses true natural anger and temporary controlled hate is that there should be ten cuddles to one slap—something delinquents in our society do not get. They only get the slaps, the *quatre cent coups*.

As we saw earlier, Carter took his hysterical patients into his family, and the whole set-up was a home and family of which he was the father, so it was natural for him to say that treatment must be carried out "tenderly and kindly as well as strictly" (Carter, 1853, p. 120). But transfer these instructions to the world of psychiatry—is this a doctor speaking or a missionary?

My students might feel that psychiatry is a calling or they might not, but what right have I to tell them to be tender, kind, and strict, and to parent their patients, however horrible. But I shall find some way of insinuating it, because I cannot lose the opportunity to share the experiences that have taught me how to make patients better and, I believe, to make them happier.

We have explored the roots of psychodynamic psychotherapy and what it took in from anthropology and philosophy, and we have looked at the wonderful contributions of Freud, Jung, Adler and all those since them, including infant observation, and family and group therapy. In the next chapter, we shall see how babies have the power to make us love them. Then, we shall explore the precious value of hate, and I shall describe the bravery of Robert Lindner, a therapist who worked in a jail, as an example of how the natural fulfilment of the Enlightenment of the Mind is to stride forth from the consulting room and move out in to the world.

Finally, we shall put a foot into the wild unpredictability of the unconscious mind and its unknown extent beyond our personalities in dreams, to see if the shifting ground there might still take our weight.

We could, if we deliberately choose, base our lives on the unstable waters of emotion, wish, fantasy and pure imagination—in other words, dream. So, now, we can start putting our weight on our left foot as well as our right. Maybe it is like that very wobbly moment when we put our left foot into the canoe before we add the right, and the sparkling waters of the Firth can represent our adventure.

CHAPTER TWENTY-FOUR

Human development

"All, everything that I understand, I understand only because I love"

(Tolstoy, 1869)

A breastfed baby stares unwaveringly at mother's face as it feeds. This is human life from beginning to end, isn't it? Looking in each other's eyes as we eat, make love, fight, talk, whatever. The whole of human life is about learning to love. The object relations theorists, and others, made deductions about babies, prompting observation studies of real babies and small children. In *The First Year of Life* (1965), the psychotherapist Rene Spitz imparts some apparently dismayingly cynical information, but the book also includes a great revelation about how our bodies, and how the people that interact with our bodies, teach us love. Spitz focused on how babies *smile*, and discovered that in the second month of life the human face becomes a preferred visual perception above all other "things" in the infant's environment.

In the third month, the baby responds to the adult face with a smile, which marks the first active, directed, and intentional behaviour, according to Spitz. But if you present your face to the baby in profile, however nicely you smile, the baby does not respond. This is because the baby is responding to a specific pattern that must include two eyes. Experiments have shown that the forehead–eyes–nose part of the face must be moving in order for the baby to react. And if you present it with a moving Halloween mask, the baby smiles back, too. So the infant is not responding to a person, but to a visual pattern—the kind of signal that triggers an instinctual response, referred to as an innate releasing mechanism (IRM). The same thing occurs in baby herring gulls, when they respond by opening their mouths on seeing a red-tipped beak.

Spitz recorded the progress of a baby called Jessy. She was shown a smiling Halloween mask at three months, and she smiled in response. This is a horrible thought—is the baby's smile not a real smile, just a nerve reaction? The mother reacts to the smile and thinks, "They look in your eyes and your heart melts"—that is *her* instinctual reaction; is she being conned? Yes, at first, but thank goodness she *is*, for the baby's smile is about to become real, slowly but surely, *but only if the mother responds to it as if it is real*. "The recognition of an individual face is a later development; it will take another four to six months before the baby becomes able to single out one face among the many" (Spitz, 1965, p. 91).

A very interesting and curious feature of IRMs is that you can artificially exaggerate them; for example, baby herring gulls get much more excited by a stick that is painted a brighter red than the dull red of their parents' beaks. Similarly, an extreme widening of the adult's mouth provides a supernormal stimulus to a baby. Compare also the effect of make-up on a young woman's face—black lines around the eyes, red lipstick. This has obvious relevance to the nature of art and culture.

In the reciprocal, circular feedback between the mother and baby in the months that follow, true emotional object relatedness develops. The baby becomes more active in relating to mother, and what was a kind of precursor to the "I" gradually becomes an "I". During this circular interaction, mother learns to give and take with her baby's needs and feelings, and her own; his delightful uninhibitedness might affect her and "[t]he mother has to defend herself against the gamut of seduction offered by her baby" (Spitz, 1965, p. 126). The baby relates more and more to his individual mother, and their feelings towards each other develop, in mutuality. As Winnicott found, it is about this time that "ruth" is born, that is, when the baby realises he does not want to hurt this mother he is getting to know; he then finds some way of managing his hunger so he can achieve as much satisfaction as possible, without hurting her.

Aged seven and a half months, Jessy laughed at the Halloween mask, and tried to pick the marbles (which served as eyes) off it, while trying to climb on to the observer's knee.

During the next striking stage of development, referred to by Spitz as "8-month anxiety" (Spitz, 1965, p. 157), the baby, instead of smiling at everybody, becomes anxious and upset when he sees strangers. He shows what looks like disappointment that it is not mother, and is quite likely in fear of having lost her. From now on, he really knows who she is and her illimitable importance to him. For Jessy, the Halloween mask is now just a meaningless thing.

Spitz understood that in the first experiment, Jessy had reacted as an instinctual response, a little bundle of neuronal reflexes that are triggered by a stimulus—the visual pattern of eyes and nose. In the second, she was reacting to a real human being, a person; thus, she had grown into an "I" that naturally relates to a "You".

The third experiment showed an entirely new development. At fourteen months, when the female observer (with whom Jessy had good contact) placed the mask on her own face, Jessy ran away, terrified and screaming; the child was reassured only when the mask was removed.

So, Jessy had gone through the "eight-month anxiety" stage when only her mother's face is reassuring, and she had now added some "friends", like the observer.

However, Jessy had one more step to go: to be sure that the person she knows is still there behind the mask. She was progressing towards what is sometimes called "object constancy" (Spitz, 1965, p. 66), such as a remembered continued history of relatedness to someone else.

Spitz thought in terms of "organisers" (Spitz, 1965, p. 117) of behaviour, in which the first is the reflex neurological reaction to the smile, and the second, where the smile is an exchange of love between two persons who know each other. Spitz did not put it in those words himself; as a scientist in the mid-twentieth century, he could not use the words "love" or "person", but that was what he was saying. It was his version of what Layard was observing when he said that instinct wants to be turned into spirit.

The next apparent surge of neurological response to IRMs is at puberty, when, gradually over the years, we are taught by our bodies, and by others, to allow our instinctual desires to grow into love, just like little Jessy with her smiles.

Later on, in the chapters about dreaming, I shall show how we never have to really lose touch with the instinctual roots of love, our animal selves, but can keep referring back and consulting with them, and be re-energised by them through dreaming.

Another great work of child observation during the century was by the Hungarian psychiatrist, Margaret Mahler, and her co-workers' in *The Psychological Birth of the Human Infant*, 1975. It describes how infants and small children gradually separate and individuate from their mothers, increasing distance and independence while, at the same time, developing better bridges that securely take her across ever-increasing distances of space and time and clashes of will. The baby and mother grow out of the first phase of symbiosis into the sub-phases of individuation–separation. They might get on splendidly together, or the baby might have to fight for his individuation against various forms of anxiety in the mother. The reaction patterns that might sink into the unconscious later on are there, large as life, on the surface. Mahler's book is full of stories about individual babies and mothers, and provides an excellent account of how we gradually become separate enough to love at these early stages, and how learning to love is what life is all about, at all stages.

Anna Freud believed that a baby that wants to play with its mother is not motivated by altruism. Who cares? Scientists who studied people and animals in the earlier part of the century watched like hawks for sentimental illusions about altruism in their subjects. But the distinction between altruism and selfishness, while useful for roughly describing human motivation, was derived from the pure abstract obsession characteristic of earlier moral philosophers, and is pretty useless in real life. In real life, love is about mutual exchange, and the selfish pleasures we might get from being generous to others makes a nonsense of any moral score-sheet.

The main thing is to see how impersonal, basic, animal, neurological reactions, like Jessy's smile, gradually grow into mutual love if they are respected and nurtured, even if it is only through illusion at the beginning. In the next chapter, in the pursuit of love we shall explore the precious value of hate.

CHAPTER TWENTY-FIVE

Hate and aggression

"There is no love without aggression"

(Lorenz, 2002)

Our culture says hate is bad and love is good, but the Enlightenment of the Mind says that hate is bad or good, depending on what you do with it. So far, every great originating therapist mentioned in this book has engaged, in some sense, with uncovering the basic emotions of hate to allow it to become the love it really wants to be.

When we import from the animal ethnologists, such as Konrad Lorenz, from whom we received the observations about attachment, we learn that, in evolution, love is a development of aggression; for example, the goose's greeting call is a modification of its attacking call. Konrad's book *Aggression* grew out of an awe-inspiring moment involving a little tropical fish, the cichlid. When the male cichlid spots a prospective mate, his first automatic reaction is to attack her. However, the vicious fight is always averted at the very last.

Lorenz described the subtle ways aggression is modified into rituals of bonding, as portrayed in geese, for example, where initial hostility becomes the greeting ceremony.

We humans have to assert ourselves as separate individuals against each other before we can love. That is the purpose of aggression and hate. They form the basis of love, as dough is to bread. Lorenz noted how animals *without* intraspecific aggression, though they might stay together in herds, do not care one little bit about each other—they are loveless. After describing how bonding is based on modifications of hostility, he made a very firm statement: you can find species with aggression but no love, but you will never find a species that can love that does not base the love on aggression, or, as he put it, "there is no love without aggression". Lorenz meant that we cannot even begin to love unless we start with aggression. Aggression is the indispensable basis of love.

Compare that with the sequence of growth of love in a baby, which equally awed and moved Winnicott. First, the baby is thoughtlessly and ruthlessly devouring of his mother; then he enters the second stage and discovers ruth (i.e., mother is someone he does not want to hurt). This is when civilisation is born again, as we learn to care for the person we are devouring. During the third stage, and if all goes well, the baby is given the space and opportunity to discover hate. So, the sequence is: thoughtless aggression as displayed by simple fish and animals, then the modification of aggression into basic caring and love, then the further development into the achievement of hate.

When hate is achieved, really serious love becomes possible. Hate ranges from momentary hostility over nothing in the nursery to the destruction of warring peoples and cultures. Hate takes either a good or a bad form, hopeful or despairing, but essentially it is the hunger for love.

Down at the nursery level, where Winnicott was operating, he said something of huge importance with regard to the difference between healthy and unhealthy hate. In healthy hate, there is a simple mutual hostility that can be worked through to love, but in unhealthy hate, we make use of righteousness and morality to control others. Winnicott was aware of this, and encouraged mothers to let their young children develop a healthy capacity to dominate, at least for some of the time, and that this should be real, before they can learn gradually to give up some of their selfish demands and compromise with others. Without the experience of first dominating his world, and then learning to negotiate with it, the child has no sense of being validated as an autonomous person, but instead is always controlled by others. For a child, this can be a despairing and rejecting experience, unable to assert himself for fear of love being withheld.

Our clients often suffer from fear and despair, together with suppressed aggression and hate—all of which emerge in indirect and harmful forms. We need to encourage and nourish the precious emotions of hate and aggression that are really the roots of love. The psychotherapist is like the dowser who comes to the brown, dried-up garden to find the hidden underground streams that will make the garden a blooming paradise once again: we have to find the underground streams of hate and aggression that will restore love to the patient's life. My favourite example given in this book is when Winnicott's baby patient got better after it gained the confidence to bite his knuckle.

In couple therapy, I usually find that the couple needs to learn how to hate: first by hating consciously and frankly, instead of deviously and unconsciously, then directing it to where it really belongs, and, finally, learning how to fight fair, and how to fight friendly. I do believe that conflict resolution is the Philosopher's Stone and the Holy Grail and should be taught in schools before writing.

Looking at the world, we can see that the one thing the id or God or life force, or whatever, have in common is conflict. That is the bottom line of the driving vitality of the world. It is why we open our newspapers every morning. The fall-back, fail-safe source of life. Love might fail, but thank God, hate never will. "Our God is a man of war" (Beckwith, 1922, p. 187). "I came not to bring peace, but a sword" (Morison, 1870, p. 183). Thank God. Unfailing hate is the foolproof guarantee that the world has a future. Few cultures think of hate with sufficient faith and hope, but we psychotherapists do. From the very first chapter about Ihembi, we have been discovering the roots of cure in uncovered hate. When Charles Berg's patient shook his fist at him, saying, "I don't *like* you!" (Berg, 1947, p. 224), Berg knew that, at last, he was in business. Similarly, when Klein's little patients had free rein to express their bizarre and twisted hate, their natures were freed to discover the unsuspected presence of the natural impulses she called reparation.

I want to emphasise that, in our trade, hate and aggression are not incidental nuisances, but precious sources of life and cure—even out-ranking Freud's discovery of sex. A skilled conflict avoider therapist can get through most therapeutic work without bearing the brunt of the patient's hate, but the patient's hatred for *someone* is usually essential to the therapy. Personal involvement by therapists is approached with different degrees of confidence. A London analyst named Malan had a really nice, gentlemanly nature (and was outstanding in his work), and in 1975, he gave a talk at the Maudsley Hospital about his fascination for a Canadian analyst called Davanloo. Davanloo did not sound gentlemanly at all. In fact, his deliberate technique was to be so rude and horrible to his patients that they could not help getting hostile and angry towards him. When they expressed their hostility, they found relief in the priceless emotional experience of discovering that they could express hate directly at a person, without the situation ending badly.

Winnicott believed that just ending the session on time was an example of "hate in the counter-transference" (Winnicott, 1992, p. 194) but in general psychiatry, hate can come in a cruder form. (A lad once bit Winnicott on the buttocks, then broke into his car and drove away in it.)

On the psychiatric wards, mutual hostility between staff and patients is, sometimes, unavoidable, and every now and then a whistle-blower publicises how staff mistreat patients in some demoralised hospital. The psychoanalyst, Tom Main, wrote a paper in which he mentioned the phenomenon whereby doctors' hostility is disguised as treatment. But, in the better hospitals, hostility towards patients can take quite another turn, which is seldom officially reported. I have heard recurrently from mental hospital staff (usually a nurse, because they spend more time with the patients) how they are abused and provoked by some patients to such a degree that they end up expressing their anger directly and forcibly at the patient. The staff found that this sort of retaliation did the patient a lot of good, and that, often, the patient would even express gratitude for the therapeutic effect. Similarly, a young registrar told me how he had got really angry when a young woman childishly flouted his efforts to help her. In response, he asked her with real, though very civilised, anger, "What do you want? Lisa, *what do you want?*", etc. The real anger worked like magic where occupational therapy, group psychotherapy, and medication had failed.

In the mental hospitals where I worked, I was awed by the sheer persistence of the staff in treating patients who were temporarily (because of their illness) or even permanently evil, with humanity and respect, and sometimes with honest, straight, opposition. And humour, too, by the way. Indeed, other impulsive emotional reactions by staff can also occur. A young registrar in the NHS told me how her consultant boss had astonished her: one day a man had marched in on them, ranting in a foul-mouthed psychotic rage. Some obscure impulse moved in the consultant who rose, wordlessly, put his arms round the man, and embraced him; the man subsided and then wept. These sorts of personal therapeutic manoeuvres are not included in the textbooks of psychiatry.

Certainly, the two most ostentatiously effective behavioural therapists I have known were very strong personalities, and both were brilliant at provoking responses or using aggressive confrontations with patients that could be used positively. How shocked and disapproving I was when I witnessed Professor Isaac Marks, holding a little plastic bag containing a lump of human cancer, advancing slowly but relentlessly towards a woman with cancer phobia who was screaming and cowering in the far corner of her bedroom. And how discomfited I was to see her the next day, as a happy woman about to be discharged, playing idly with the same little bag in her hand before it got thrown away.

But one of the heroes of the honest use of hate (though he did not call it that) was an American psychoanalyst called Robert Lindner, who worked in a penitentiary. During the 1960s, Lindner was still using classical Freudian theory—Oedipus complex, the transference—but he was behaving in an opposite way to Freud, not in the least as a screened analyst, but as a thoroughly emotionally exposed one.

Lindner said that at the heart of therapy was the capacity of the therapist to bring himself to any patient simply as another person.

It sounds modest of the therapist to say he is a mere human, but to claim that it is not my training, or my finely-honed perceptions, or learnt skills, but just me, as a person, that cures the patient, is a claim a person might well hesitate to make. True, Jung said that a therapist can only help others to the extent that he has got himself sorted out, and Klein's daughter, Melitta Schmideberg-Klein, wrote that psychotherapy is essentially only "the judicious use of the influence which a stronger personality exerts upon a dependent personality who is in need of help" (Ogawa, 1982, p. 23). She must have been thinking of her mother.

When Lindner was working in a prison, he was analysing a psychopath whom he called Anton, who had accepted treatment for his black-outs, but who had later walked out of therapy when Lindner refused to support his application for parole. One day, Lindner was doing his turn as medical officer on the sick parade when Anton appeared in the queue. When he saw it was Lindner, he refused to co-operate in front of other prisoners.

Lindner knew that he had to do something, but what? He saw Anton's rebuff as a test of the psychotherapeutic relationship, but rather than assert his authority in front of other prisoners (normal in a prison), he chose instead to engage him privately, man to man. It was as an equal that Lindner followed him alone back to Anton's dormitory and insisted upon an apology, threatening Anton, if necessary, to make him. When confronted in this way, Anton immediately apologised. Later, Anton asked to resume his sessions. Lindner thought that the breakthrough was because he had treated this man with a regard that had been absent throughout his life, and not as an overbearing parent or authority figure.

But is it not hostile to threaten someone with violence, as Lindner threatened Anton? Lindner wrote that all of his psychoanalytic training and experience told him to go and threaten Anton with physical violence! That is what he said. Yet, he did not describe the exchange as *hostile*, however challenging the eyeball-to-eyeball confrontation. Here, the Enlightenment of the Mind bursts through the limitations of our culture, to a place where our language fails us, and we have to either invent new words or change the meaning of the existing ones. What can the word "hostility" mean if we find ourselves saying that threatening physical violence is not hostile? Maybe there are two opposite meanings of the same word. Hostility, *in a rejecting sense*, would have validated Anton's cynicism and despair and fixed him in it, but threatening to beat him up saved him from it. Put another way, threatening to beat him up for moral reasons as a punishment for being bad would have made him worse, but threatening to beat him up as a man-to-man demand for mutual respect saved him.

Lindner behaved like an ordinary father to the child, Anton. Hostility is not rejecting when it takes the form of the anger a father has for his son when he is confronting him out of love and for the boy's own good, whether the anger is latent and in reserve, or overt and up-front. In overt anger, the father might have a terrifyingly red face, glaring eyes, a shaking deep voice, and a tense body, poised as if to strike; in this case, the boy would probably find no other word for this response than hostile. But it is a loving form of hostility. One of my patients had a dream in which his father, actually long dead, confronted him physically to put a stop to some piece of childish nonsense. The unconscious supplied my patient with an experience of the physically threatening father that he needed at that time.

Lindner said his training as an analyst directed him towards confronting Anton. Do the various institutes of psychoanalysis all over the world include in their training the art of man-to-man angry confrontation, as used by Lindner and the mental hospital staff I mentioned above?

It is not difficult to show how Lindner *was* following his training. Though operating in an opposite way to Freud, by being so personal and in threatening to hit Anton, he was doing exactly the same thing as Freud had done by *not* hitting his patient the Rat Man when the Rat Man ducked. Freud cured the Rat Man (with whom he had an uncharacteristically personal relationship) because he did not hit him, as the Rat Man's father would have done, thus using the transference to free the patient from his inhibiting fears. Lindner saved Anton by threatening to hit him, but with an honest man-to-man demand for mutual respect such as Anton's father was not capable of and, thus, freeing Anton from his cynical world-hatred. Both patients were freed from their fathers by therapists who behaved differently from their fathers.

The moment Robert Lindner, in the penitentiary, left his consulting room, marched to confront Anton, took off his insignia and challenged him to a physical fight, was the moment when psychotherapy left the consulting room with him and became an Enlightenment for mankind.

The official line of the traditional Christian ascendancy is that we should suppress hate, turn the other cheek, or, if we have to fight a "Just War", we do it with righteous detachment. But there is another way of looking at it, which acknowledges the *uncontrollable change of feeling between people, and might be one of the most important and neglected natural resources available to mankind*. It is this: when people *do not* turn the other cheek, but have a good fight, they slide from hating to loving each other.

When I was a child, mutual dislike sprang up between myself and a local boy: he thought I was a snob, while I thought him a lout. I hated him, and he me. We fought one day and bashed each other to our heart's content until I won (uniquely for me); as I sat on him, wondering what to do next, I realised that an extraordinary change had taken place. Our hate had been spent in the force of fists against flesh and now I liked him, and he me. As it happened, we did not develop a friendship, though I remember when I lost my bicycle pump months later, another pump mysteriously appeared which he had sent to me via a messenger. So, here is a little list of folk wisdom in favour of the hearty fight.

1. There used to be an old Naval institution of "grudge fights" on ships far from land, when men who had come to hate each other in a situation where avoidance was not an option, could apply for a boxing match under formal supervision. An officer once wrote about his difficult decision about whether to allow a third grudge fight between a puny little man and a big bully who would not stop taking the delicious end of his NAAFI sausage. He did allow the fight, and the little man was hammered as usual—but the sausage-taking stopped.

2. Old English proverb: "The falling out of faithful friends, renewing is of love".

3. A Mediterranean acquaintance told a friend after a quarrel, "good; now we have had a quarrel we can be real friends."

4. According to the ancient myth, when Gilgamesh finally had the great fight with his rivalrous, primitive counterpart, Emkidu, it is related that they fought so strenuously and equally that, in the end, they exhausted each other and "embraced like lovers".

5. Friendships often spring up between veterans on the opposite sides of great wars.

6. Quotes from William Blake: "Opposition is true friendship" (Davis, 1977, p. 61), and

> I was angry with my friend:
> I told my wrath, my wrath did end.
> I was angry with my foe:
> I told it not, my wrath did grow.

(Bloom, 2008, p. 28)

7.   In Chapter Twenty, on family therapy, Salvador Minuchin achieved brilliant therapeutic success by provoking fights.

You will notice that I have been using the word "hate" for an extreme range of intensity of feeling. There is Winnicott, expressing his hate for the patient by finishing the session at the agreed time. Then, I think of the old Geneva Convention-type of wars when a shot-down German pilot, the "enemy", would have dinner in the RAF Officers' Mess before going off to a prisoner-of-war camp. There is the sensual aspect, where argument between a married couple can become physical and suddenly give way to desire; indeed, Freud thought, for a while, that aggression and cruelty could be understood as the sadistic element of sex.

But at the other end of the scale, there is Lindner and his treatment of Anton. Although a fair confrontation resulted in a sheepish capitulation, Lindner was a Jew and Anton a politically active Fascist, and it is not hard to imagine circumstances where Anton would have supported Hitler's Holocaust, and included Lindner in it. It is easy for us therapists in our consulting rooms to take up the professional attitude that all hate is psychologically the same emotional substance, so to speak, and even if it is turned against us we must treasure it as a kind of relatedness, an emotional interaction, that can become love. Awesomely, Lindner went beyond that, when he stepped outside the consulting room and ripped the uniform tabs off his shoulders.

But, in ordinary life, mutual hate and aggression is divided into two areas. In one, it is more or less tolerable, and with effort it can be changed into friendship or some other form of love. But, across a certain line, another emotion takes over in which we cease to hope that the hate in another is redeemable, and it looks just like pure evil. Somebody who hurts our children can elicit this emotion, or the actions of a suicide bomber, or a thousand other things that push us across a certain line beyond which we have no more impulse to understand. Then, our imagination gives us images only of punishing and destroying. This is explored further in the final chapter, when we challenge our infinite capacity to change hate in to love.

I have a dream . . .

"We are like the dreamer who dreams and then lives the dream.
This is true for the entire universe"

(Swami Paramananda, 1919, 1:7)

D reams open our eyes to the coming day. Dreaming creates
our future, whereas our conscious thinking only plans it.
Dreams provide glimpses of the "savage and beautiful country" (McGlashan, 1966) of our inner world where the gods live; they
are the source of our desires and energy and, through them, we have
strange encounters.

Dreaming is an *animal* activity. The ability to dream arrived during
the course of evolution. All warm-blooded creatures dream (including birds), but cold-blooded animals, like snakes, do not. We have
been reading and writing for 6,000 years; we have been erect human
beings for 3,000,000 years, but we have been dreaming for 100,000,000
years.

From the mid twentieth century onwards, observations in sleep
laboratories built a description of "paradoxical sleep" (Lavie, 1998,
p. 136), which interrupts ordinary sleep five or six times a night, for

about twenty minutes each time, in which our genitals are engorged and excited, and we dream. It was called "paradoxical" because the brain suddenly becomes as active as when awake, or more so (the blood flow through the brain is doubled), while, paradoxically, the body goes specially inactive and limp.

One muscle movement that could not be prevented was the rapid movements of the eyes behind closed lids; thus, paradoxical sleep soon came to be called "rapid eye movement" (Gottesmann, 2005, preface) or REM sleep. A graph published in 1965, charting nine hours in a sleep laboratory, shows how REM periods of sleep (REMP, monitored by encephalogram) coincide with penis erection (measured with a strain gauge). Usually, erections begin about two and a half minutes before the brain waves and rapid eye movements occur, and tail away afterwards.

Erections during sleep in humans begin before birth and do not stop even in very old men who, in their waking lives, are impotent and not interested in sex. You would think everyone would know about it but, of course, we are asleep when it is happening.

Dreams do not have to occur during REM sleep—we also dream during ordinary sleep or even when dozing ever so slightly while appearing to be awake—but our best dreaming is done during REM sleep.

Jouvet (1963) found that if the part of cats' brains that switches off muscle power in REM sleep is damaged, then the cats would get up and act out their dreams, glaring at the enemies they are hallucinating about, then fighting, chasing, licking, and playing as they enact dramas of fight and flight, hunger and irresponsible enjoyment. Older people sometimes suffer from neuro-degenerative diseases, which also damage the same part of the brain, causing what is called "sleep behaviour disorder" (Hobson, 2004, p. 95); 64% of those who suffer from it (mostly men) physically assault their spouses in their sleep while dreaming they are defending themselves against attack.

Dogs that have been bred for centuries for particular kinds of work do it spontaneously as puppies before they are even trained. But a sheepdog that takes to chasing in waking life would be shot, probably before breeding. Similarly, German pointers have it in their genes to stop and point at game, before they are trained. Yet, in their sleep, they also "chase" and yelp—the worst crime a pointer could commit in its waking life. This means that there is a strong suggestion that even animals dream from an older part of their brain than the part from which they, ordinarily, live.

So, dreams are adventures, but, with our awareness of our real environment cancelled, and our capacity to act disabled, the adventures remain purely imaginary. When REM sleep begins, the encephalogram traces kick into added life, while myogram traces (measuring skeletal muscle tension) suddenly go flat. But that is only the half of it. The other half is the striking emotional reactions of our bodies when we cannot act. And as you might expect, even in the most primitive mammals, the whole thing is started, controlled, and stopped by the most archaic and primitive lower centres of our brains.

When night falls (or if you are a bat, when day breaks), the oldest part of the brain takes over and has a ball. The swelling at the top of the spinal cord called the *pons* (whose tissue is the only part of the human brain that can regenerate like a reptile's), puts us to sleep and turns the periods of REM sleep on and off. It is strange that our dreaming is managed by our ancient snake-self, considering that snakes do not dream. But there are still stranger things to tell.

The higher conscious centres normally control the section of the nervous system that takes in sensation and issues commands to the skeletal muscles. The old animal brain, down in the brain stem, controls the other section of the nervous system. That is the autonomic ("a law unto itself") nervous system, and it is *not* disabled in dreaming, but rather, specially enlivened. It goes on, business as usual, managing all bodily systems: the sympathetic and parasympathetic systems, the quiet regulated work of the cardiovascular and digestive systems with their special unconsciously controlled muscles, gland secretions, and chemical messengers in the blood.

But it also reacts emotionally, as when we are awake, with rapid eventful changes in these same systems, reacting to the hallucinated stimuli of the dream dramas, like threatening enemies and other exciting objects as witnessed by Jouvet's cats. As well as eye-scanning, there is panting and palpitations and changes of blood pressure, sudden floods of autonomic system chemical messengers and corticosteroids, and tears and laughs and orgasms and emissions, and other effects, too. In waking life, the autonomic system, unintentionally, communicates with others by means of involuntary expressions. It does this via bodily reactions like blushing or going pale, clammy hands, and the enlarging of the pupils (the "bella donna" phenomenon that provokes a mutual attraction between people—this is a completely unconscious interchange). But in sleep, of course, there is no real person responding to the communication, just as nobody else is affected by the imagined actions of the dreamer.

The sympathetic nervous system supports fight and flight and sex and anxiety and, therefore, does things like quickening the heart and slowing the gut, while the parasympathetic supports calm, confidence, and digestion, and slows the heart and activates the gut. Both systems usually act in opposition to each other. But, during sex they are, for once, in glorious harmony: the parasympathetic causes erections, and the sympathetic causes emissions; thus, the "wet dream" in a man or dream orgasm in a woman is the most dramatic bodily reaction to sexual excitement in dreams, and the most physically real thing we can derive from a dream.

The genitals are aroused, to some extent, in REM sleep, and, at first sight, that might look like support for Freud's belief that most dreams are about sex, but disguised. But it turned out that it is not so; indeed, what is really going on is even more interesting.

Quite often, men wake up with unusually hard, even painful, erections in the night, but might have not experienced any erotic thoughts or feelings at all to account for them. They might also wake up with erections in the morning when they need to urinate (a state of the penis referred to in barracks' dormitories as "piss-proud"). It was these non-sexual nocturnal erections, and the inability to control erections, that led Leonardo da Vinci to proclaim that the penis had a mind of its own. Now, we could show him exactly where in the brain that mind is located.

However, in both men and animals, the erect penis does not always imply lust. The squirrel monkey gets an erection when bossing other squirrel monkeys about, so the erection is connected with the instinct of domination. Similarly, there is a type of monkey that gets part-erections while they watch for danger. So, sometimes, in animals an erection is not exactly about sex. (Or the sex is subordinated to the rank system, as when an ape presents his bottom to a dominant male to show submission.)

Likewise, in humans, erections are not always connected with sexual desire; for example, remember how in early development, Spitz showed that the smile reaction in babies only gradually becomes a human, emotional communication? Similarly, he observed that boy babies, although they have erections, seem indifferent to their penises at first, and do not begin genital play until about eight months. The penis becomes interesting and pleasure-giving to the baby only with growing emotional interaction with its mother; in fact, babies that have suffered maternal deprivation (no fondling, cuddling, or bodily contact) might not show interest in their penises until they are three or four years of age. And even then, erection can still be a quite non-specific reaction in normal boys.

Alfred Kinsey, the American biologist, stated that pre-adolescent boys can get erections in response to anything, from hearing the national anthem to seeing their name in print.

Genital reactions in women can be similarly non-specific—a woman once told me that she had her first orgasm while listening to powerful music in the bath. So, apparently, nocturnal genital excitation belongs to an ancient and/or developmentally early neuronal and instinctual bundle that does not make our dreams erotic, being too primitive and non-specific for what we call sex.

Although the genital excitation does not influence the dreams, it is ready and waiting to be either suppressed or excited to orgasm by the emotions of the unfolding dream drama. In a paper published in 1965 (entitled "Cycle of penile erection synchronous with dreaming (REM) sleep") Fisher, Gross, and Zuch observed in one subject that his erection fell during a dream in which he was attacked by a snake, and again in another dream when he was attacked by sharks, and again in a dream implying incest, and in another, expressing homosexuality. But in his final dream, his erection was rapidly restored when he dreamt about heterosexual sex. Also, the higher centres can influence the genital excitation in another way: in severely clinically depressed men, the amount of erections during REM periods is reduced. (Depressed people tend to reach REM sleep quicker, and get more of it.)

REM sleep is like a great ship floating in the harbour in the middle of the night that suddenly comes alive and lights up its lowest decks. The captain and the officers are unconscious in their bunks, but the mighty engines vibrate the vessel; all the basic systems are activated and ready for sea, but sail it cannot as the propeller is disengaged. Instead, the whole lower system is reacting vividly to a purely imaginary drama, *also instigated from somewhere below-decks, not from the bridge. It is some unknown person or persons below deck who writes the play, not the Captain.* In response to the imaginary adventure, the engines speed and slow, lights go on and off, the guns swivel as if scanning for enemies and aim at phantasms, but may not fire a shot. Then, suddenly, it all stops and there is darkness again. But when the captain awakes in the morning, he might remember the things that happened in the dream.

At the end of the century, scientists, using bio-imaging techniques, were able to identify the brain centres that were active in dreaming. These parts of the brain include the pons, the amygdala in the middling-old limbic system in the brain stem, and the anterior cingulate cortex. They found that the posterior cingulate cortex and the prefrontal cortex, along with vast other areas of the cortex are deactivated during the dreaming process, as though they have been told to shut up and keep out of it. Maybe the anterior cingulate cortex, thought to be associated with conscious effort and discrimination, represents the dreaming "I", the essence of the usual conscious "I" that is allowed to be at the party and join in the play-acting. What is remarkable, however, hardly believable really, is that these reaction-stimulating pictures are *not* limited to rehashed personal memories.

We are born already dreaming like mad, sleeping most of the time. One theory is that we cannot do anything as a baby unless our central nervous system has already been prepared for us by dreaming about it. This agrees with Winnicott's observation that babies have ideas before they act, and hallucinate the breast; indeed, it is a kind of lucky bonus when the hallucinated breast provides real milk through a real nipple in the baby's mouth.

How can we dream of things we have never yet experienced? How indeed, but it has been found that congenitally blind people who have never seen *anything* in their existence, nevertheless, dream visual imagery, and draw it, too. This suggests an uncanny power in these lower brain centres to use what has been written into their hard wiring over a hundred million years of evolution: to create and present IRMs to provoke any mammalian emotional reaction, such as a terrifying attacker, food, a lovely willing girl, or an exciting man, the challenge of the rival, a smiling mother, dangerous heights, suffocating frustration, etc.

The pons, that archaic snaky bundle of instincts at the top of our spinal cord, wakes the hypothalamic empire to special readiness and responsiveness, and uses dreams to play on our emotions for ten or twenty minutes at a time, arousing terror, bliss, boredom, awe, depression, enthusiasm, love, lust, hate, tranquillity, or nothing very much. It ringmasters the circus of the physical expressions of emotion that is rarely noticed except in unusual circumstances, like a hot night, a naked bedmate, a wakeful self with the light on, or in a fully fitted sleep laboratory.

REM dreams are not merely imaginary events at all; they are bodily activities reacting to emotions with all the usual glandular and neuronal biochemical surges and smooth muscle convulsions and discharges of fluids. However, the only bodily effect on the dreamer might be to get wet with sweat, saliva, tears, or semen.

Why does our body bother? Our brainstem has been doing it to us since long before we became human beings, for a hundred million years, or longer: the opossum is so ancient it has earned the title "living fossil" and it is a tremendous dreamer; 50%–80% of its sleep is REM sleep. Biologists are baffled, and their literature is full of theories trying different ways to link REM dreaming to survival. However, I have my own theories about dreaming, which I shall explore next. To do this, we will take the enormous step from *observing* the dreamer to *being* the dreamer.

CHAPTER TWENTY-SEVEN

Living the dream

"At the centre of your being you have the answer; you know who you are and you know what you want"

(Attributed to Lau Tzu)

Throughout history, dreams have excited, befuddled, and inspired. Although extensive studies of human dreaming have been carried out, there is still much speculation and interest as to why we dream and what we dream about. Many of these theories conflict, but the range of our dreams is so wide and varied that each of these theories appears to have some truth in them.

Some of us believe that dreams are irrelevant and that we can all live perfectly well without ever remembering a dream or paying them any attention. Of course, this is possible, but there is also a possibility that unremembered dreams still have some deeper influence.

Carl Jung believed that dreams present a subliminal awareness of the environment. A patient of his told him of a recurring dream about his fiancée being unfaithful to him behind his back. Jung advised him to check it out and when he did, indeed, she was doing just that. Thus, dreams can notify us about areas of life that we are not even conscious of, such as illness, wishes, the future, and many more.

There have been many theories about how dreams can predict illness. I knew a distinguished politician in Edinburgh who was not well and his doctors could not make out what was wrong with him. He told me he had dreamed of dancing with the Devil; the Devil scattered a pack of cards and John had to collect them all up but the Devil mockingly withheld one and would not hand it over—it was the Ace of Hearts. It turned out that John had a rare cancer of the heart, so rare his doctors missed it at first.

Jung and his contemporaries also had similar experiences with their patients. One young woman told Jung about dreams of a horse leaping from a first floor window, and another of her mother hanging herself. He concluded that the physical substrate of her personality was destroying itself and diagnosed organic illness. Sure enough, she turned out to have a brain tumour.

Dr Medard Boss, the eminent Swiss psychoanalytic psychiatrist, found that schizophrenia was sometimes preceded (even as long as twenty or thirty years) by dreadful dreams of the cataclysmic destruction of the world and the dreamer.

However, not all dreams that seem bad at the time indicate an underlying illness. For example, I once heard of a girl who dreamt she was drowning in blood when she was having her first period. This dream suggests one should always look for good things disguised behind bad things in dreams, but also to be aware that it might be a way of our subconscious telling us something that might save our lives. As far back as the sixteenth century, the great French writer Michel de Montaigne was lauding the power of dreams as an expression of our hidden wishes and desires: "Dreams are faithful interpretations of our inclinations, but there is art required to sort and understand them" (Weiss, 1986, p. 70).

Freud saw dreams as subconscious wishes that our conscious mind just could not handle. But there is a more interesting way of looking at Freud's interpretation, for example, Medard Boss thought our attitudes, if too fearful and narrow, could distort the appearance of things that are really good, making us fear what we should enjoy. In one experiment, Boss hypnotised five women (two of whom were classed as neurotic) to dream of "a certain man well known to them, who loved them, and who approached them with clear sexual intentions and without any clothes" (Boss, 1958, p. 93). Although the women knew they were being hypnotised, they were unaware of the nature of what they would dream. The three "normal" women dreamt exactly what Boss had told them to, while each of the two neurotics dreamt of an unknown soldier in uniform with a gun that threatened them. Because of the anxiety-ridden world in which they both lived, they failed to interpret Boss's instructions and, as a result, found love and sex to be threatening and violent.

There are many stories about dreams foretelling the future. At age seven, the novelist Graham Greene dreamt of a shipwreck the night of the Titanic disaster, and had a number of other predictive dreams in his life.

A sinister example was Hitler's dream as a corporal in a dugout in 1917. He dreamt he was being smothered in a fall of earth and hot iron, which woke him and provoked him to get up and wander outside away from the dugout. When he came back, the dugout *had* been shelled and everyone else killed. Hitler, of course, took it as a sign that he was being specially protected for a divine mission.

During the two great wars, there were many accounts of telepathy, some in the form of dreams. An example of dream telepathy came from a Jewish psychotherapist who claimed that she saved herself from the Holocaust as a result of a dream she had after an encounter with an SS man. She fled Germany the day after she had the dream and credits it with saving her life.

Jung thought that through dreams we reach into the collective unconscious, which is outside space and time. He believed that all dreams have an underlying meaning and should be treated seriously.

A rare case reported by Ermacora in 1898 showed how telepathy could be used in dreams. Ermacora claimed he had found a woman who could channel his dream suggestions using telepathy to her little boy. In one instance, Ermacora told the boy's mother to suggest a dream about goats to her son using telepathy. Although the boy and his mother were separated during these experiments, the child told them he had dreamt about "dogs with horns" (Wolman, 1986, p. 485). It turned out he had never seen a goat before. However, his accurate description suggested to Ermacora that it was possible to send telepathic messages to others.

A topical area, nowadays, is the dreams of those undergoing transplant operations. There have been several reported cases of some patients knowing the identity of their donors even though they had not been revealed. One of the early heart transplant recipients dreamt of a young man called Tim as her donor; it turned out she had got it right.

There have also been some cases where dreams have provided inspiration and solved problems. A famous example was the physicist Kekule, struggling to understand how carbon atoms form molecules in organic chemistry. One night, he dreamt of the atoms in chains, snakily twisting about: "Suddenly, what was this? One of the snakes got hold of its own tail and the whole structure was mockingly twisting in front of my eyes. As if struck by lightning I awoke . . ." (Hudson, 1985, p. 127).

He had discovered the benzene ring; all that chicken-wire chemistry we had to learn in preclinical medicine.

Similarly, dreams often give rise to artistic productions: a number of Robert Louis Stevenson's novels came to him first in dreams, including *Dr Jekyll and Mr Hyde*. There is a rather lovely account of a dream by Frances Wickes, an American Jungian psychotherapist who revealed, in *The Inner World of Childhood*, a dream she had at the age of three that inspired her whole life. I mention it here because I find it inspirational, too:

> I am in a high meadow, unknown yet strangely familiar. In the centre is Behemoth: huge, terrifying, evil. By his side, unafraid and rooted in its own serenity, is a single bluet, that smallest flower of meadow or woodland, tiny, fragile, perfect in its four-petalled innocence. (Wickes, 1988, p. 257)

Frances Wickes was encouraged that the bluet, usually found forming a carpet in woodlands, was instead growing strong and healthy on its own.

Medard Boss discovered a whole new theory about dreams: he believed that we can act with choice and will during our dreams, even though we are fast asleep! He pointed out that we live as actively in dreams as when awake—we can reflect on ourselves, and on our motives, make choices, change our minds and, in a way, adventure even more actively and freely in our dreams than in waking life because we have more imaginative options.

A patient of mine dreamt that he had been sent with his sergeant to the front line with a message. He handed it over. He realised the enemy was about to attack. He had carried out orders and had no obligation to stay and fight; what he did was a pure free choice. He chose to stay and fight. I believe he was choosing an attitude that would, from then on, apply in his waking life. So, sometimes dreams look as though they give clearer adventure situations from which to make choices than is apparent in waking life.

The great masters had different ways of approaching dream interpretation with their patients. Although Jung treated dreams very seriously, he had a habit of criticising his patients and the actions they took in their dreams. In one case, Jung chastised a patient for failing to attempt to save his girlfriend from falling through a hole in the ice during a dream. I would have thought that the fact that he couldn't was the significance.

However, it was Boss who noticed how decisive people can be in dreams; they can intervene in the course of events and continue to do so with consistency.

Still, as Boss showed, there is a difference in the way we exert free will in our dreams as opposed to exerting force of will, which is a rather dangerous thing. One dream that severely spooked me was related by one of Boss's patients, a twenty-five-year-old student, who described how he had changed the course of a stream away from the garden at his home through sheer force of will within the dream, but which caused him extreme exhaustion. Something had blocked the man's natural emotional growth, and his forceful use of will was only making things worse. He was living in the same wrong way in his dreams as he was in life.

This case frightened me as it reminded me of a sort of breakdown I had as a young man, when I realised that, in spite of my intense religious aspirations fostered by Kierkegaard, I could not be good, or love, or do a few things I thought I really ought and must do, through force of will. I gradually found that we really are not meant to live by force of will.

The right thing is to look and find out what impulses and energies are woken in us by what we are looking at, and then try to find the courage to submit to the impulses and let them carry us into action. We still have to use will, but after developing our self-control as we grow up, we have to let it foster the basic spontaneities of our natural vitality. To me, this is one of the great revelations of the Enlightenment of the Mind—*that will is not the highest value.*

In our history, we have seen many cases of the destructiveness of forcing our will upon others. In Germany, many signed up to Hitler's vision at the time, which meant imposing his will on others, backed up by threats and punishment. It is essential for us to learn about self-control, control of others, manipulation, management, influence, domination of our environment, and aggressive assertion. But how we apply all of these is crucial. Alfred Adler based his whole under-standing of people on *how* we use power.

So, we can be inspired by others and use the energies they release in us to find our own path in the world. This allows natural unpre-dictable emotional growth to take place without effort.

In my years of professional practice, I have found that grown-up, over-civilised men, in whose childhood the animal in them might have been too successfully suppressed, sometimes reach back in their dreams to recover the lions and tigers that have been left behind.

One man dreamt he was in the family car when a lion threatened to get in the window that his wife had left open. (It is one of the jobs of a good wife to let the jungle into one's life—look at Eve and the snake.) On another occasion, he dreamt of a lion in his driveway coming right for him; he accelerated straight at it and the lion lost its nerve and went off. This was an excellent manoeuvre—he had over-come the lion's aggressiveness through his own assertions.

Sex with animals in our dreams is another common occurrence that many of us do not like to admit. I remember a man who shocked himself by dreaming of raping one of the big wild cats, while it furi-ously tried to reach his face with teeth and claws. I told him that I saw a small white marble sculpture of a man doing just that in the museum at Pompeii, so it must have been an admired idea among the ancients, which reassured him somewhat.

A woman patient of mine related a dream about being attacked by a furious cat. She was in a difficult relationship and my own view was that the dream was telling her to fight back against her exploitative boyfriend. However, she did not want to express the angry emotions she felt inside; she wanted to be a nice person.

Sometimes, animals challenge more quietly and can be difficult to interpret. I once heard a dream where there was a semicircle of seven saplings, each with a snake wound round it; then each snake unwound its head and just looked at the dreamer. Another person dreamed of a group of ponies just standing in a semicircle looking at her.

Freud christened one of his patients "the Wolf Man" because of a dream he related to him. The Wolf Man dreamt of a tree with seven wolves sitting in the branches just looking at him. Freud took this to mean that he was suffering the affects of a primal scene (his mum and dad having sex) as a child. Personally, I do not think Freud got it right on that one; I think it is more like the animals just saying, "Here we are, what are you going to do about us?"

In such dreams, I feel my job as therapist is to open the mind of the dreamer to my attitude. One of my patients dreamt in the beginning of therapy that he was following Freud and me along a track through the jungle. He saw us look down to the left at something; he knew it was something horrific, but we were looking at it calmly. Thus, he knew that when he came up to it, in turn, he should imitate our attitude and regard it calmly too, whatever it turned out to be.

The therapist is, thus, acting like a parent, more accepting of what emerges in their clients' dreams (aggression, anger, etc.) than their own parents were. Like Freud, the therapist can feel he is helping the patient by sharing his own more enlightened attitude. But if the patient begins to really grow up, the tables might be turned if his dreams begin to tell him and you things you could not have told him.

One frequent theme is how dreams can represent the outgrowing and abandoning of the ethics, morality, and religion learnt in childhood. For example, I once had a young woman patient from a very religious family. She dreamt she was by a river in flood and saw bits of a church being washed down. I interpreted this to mean that she was rejecting her father's regressive religious attitude. Other religious dreams I heard about included one where a man was looking down on great floodwaters, where he knew his old school chapel was drowned underneath. Similarly, a woman saw a church that was being renovated crumbling and falling.

I had my own version of this dream in my early twenties during my first analysis:

I said goodbye to my father and mother, saw a girl with a skirt rayed like the sun, black and yellow, admired how a piece of music by Bach was written in a number of different notations, one of them three-dimensional, and then found myself standing in a crowd on the edge of a square space in a church, like a chapel up in Edinburgh Castle. The rough rock of the ground had been not worn but polished by the feet of centuries, because it was so hard and indestructible. But it began to crack and fall away into an abyss; then, a sense of awe because we knew that God was going to appear.

There came up a space like the interior of a church and in the centre a great imposing figure in a red robe like Santa Claus. In square divisions there were little Santa Clauses officiating—they made people one by one eat the Bible and if it nourished them and made them grow they were accepted; if they did not grow they were rejected. I knew that could not be right and in defiance threw a bundle of rags I had used for wiping my paintbrushes at the central figure.

Then my skeleton came out of my back and marched me down to the front. There an old-fashioned policeman raised his baton and brought it down on my head.

"That didn't hurt," I said. "No, if you face up to it, it doesn't hurt," he said.

I could see now that what was inside the red robe of the big figure was a skeleton. Then I was in a nearby space and I knew that my girlfriend of the time had had her appearance changed by magic so that if she was there I would not be able to recognise her. Then one of several young men who seemed to be in charge there came and said—No, if you want to find God you have to go this way. He directed me down a spiral staircase and I found myself in a deadly boring suburban street in Blackhall in Edinburgh. (Where I had lived in my first term and whose name still struck a chill through my body when I glimpsed its name on a direction sign, sixty years later.)

The dream was telling me the same as Zarathustra told Nietzsche, that the God of convention and conformity is dead. But my dream went further: it gave me a quest and an adventure with a direction; it was telling me to continue, to go on and look for God. The message was to look for God not where I might expect it, but in the most boring and killingly negative place on earth to me, and Blackhall made perfect sense. It also taught me that any culture that does not enable authentic inborn natural growth, but merely expects conformity, is wrong and it *is* to be rejected.

The philosopher Descartes lost his church in a dream, too, but in a different way. On the 11th of November 1620, a twenty-four-year-old Descartes made that famous entry in his journal about how he had conceived an "admirable discovery" (Rodis-Lewis, 1999, p. 52). On that day, he had become thoroughly over-excited and exhausted, "filled with enthusiasm" at having "discovered the foundations of the marvellous science" (Aczel, 2005, p. 61).

No one is sure what he was referring to, but evidently he was swept off his feet by his own cleverness, carried away by the spiritual end of his instincts, because he fell asleep and had some dramatic dreams. That night he recorded a dream series. (Dream laboratory studies confirm that a series can evolve a theme even in one night in a sequence of REM sleeps.)

Descartes dreamt of ghosts and being whirled around by a violent wind. He tried to take refuge in his College chapel, but the wind threw him back on each attempt, and eventually he gave up. He awoke with a pain, which he feared was a result of evil spirits, then spent two hours pondering good and evil in the world. When he fell asleep twice more, he dreamt that he was having a long, reasonable conversation with an unknown man about a dictionary and other books, including poetry. This time, he awoke peacefully.

Having been blown back out of the Chapel in the first dream, as though faith was no longer to be an option for him, Descartes used intense reflection about his third dream to digest his almost over-whelming inspiration, which seems to have had something to do with his discovery of science. His great work (twenty years later) started by proving to himself his own existence by the famous dodgy deduction, "I think, therefore I am" (Grayling, 2006, p. 278), and went on to prove the existence of God by reason not faith. It was to be one of the most influential and misleading contributions ever made to our culture.

Three hundred years later, in 1946, Bertrand Russell called Descartes the founder of modern philosophy. I suppose our culture did have to work through its long affair with Reason, but if only Descartes could have looked to imagination and dreams as a replacement for his dead faith and church, rather than purely reason.

The death of a person's culture is not necessarily represented by the destruction of a church. People who need to start again sometimes dream of losing their teeth, but that is a more basic instinctual start-ing again than just losing one's civilisation. Various dreams of baths and going down into the water can be about new beginnings, too.

Another common dream people have is when their civilised trans-port breaks down. They get lost in their car, and it finally breaks down in a jungle where they have to go on foot through wild nature. Others dream of cycling along the seashore until waves destroy their bike.

In general, if one can stay in the dream when dismaying things happen instead of waking in panic, interesting unpredictable things can come about. In one dream, one man suffered the breakdown of his car and bike and lost his mobile phone. However, instead of giving up, he went on foot (he was a man who did not easily give up in waking life either) and went on into a house where there were three women who turned out to be very significant.

Another man had his bike engulfed in a bog, but he went on and then saw a young gypsy woman washing a baby in the bog, which was now clear and clean enough to serve as a bath. This is another theme, which I also take as a growing-up dream—the finding of a baby or child, often abandoned, often sick in some way. It usually signifies an awakening of an instinctual reaction of parental caring in the dreamer, which can be applied to self and others in waking life. Just occasionally, the dreamer does not accept the challenge to look after the child, which I do not regard as a very good sign.

Once we have overcome our infantile dependence on the value system of our ancestors, and become parent to our own lost child, we can be more open to the dream adventures that so fascinated Jung, a man who regularly encountered God or his messengers in his dreams.

God might be there in one of the myriad of archetypal forms—a symmetrical square water-garden, an animal just standing there with an especially beautiful golden coat—or in a more dramatic experience. Sometimes, even sex in dreams can be with divine persons.

When we begin to encounter God in dreams we might be in for some way-out adventures that are difficult to digest. A year or two after the dream I had that told me to look for God, I had the following dream.

> In the dream I was a younger brother (in real life there is just me and my younger sister) and I made my way through a dangerous part of town evading menacing unfriendly armed guards until I got into a great sandstone institutional kind of building where there was safety, but I knew I would never leave it again, I was there for good. Inside a hall, a woman in a long shining green robe stood behind a table set with golden vessels with rich food she was giving out.
>
> Among the people behind her was a woman in a black robe with a dog's head, and I knew the green woman had all those riches because she had sold her soul to the dog-faced woman, so I attacked the dog-faced woman.

I had her down on the ground on the threshold of another door inside the complex, twisting her arm and fixing her there—but now we were both immobilised. What to do? The little maidservants of the place came and bowed down to her, worshipping her, and I woke.

I was disappointed in Jolande Jacobi's (Jungian analyst) reaction to this dream when I told it to her: "Well, it's the battle of life, isn't it?" she said. John Layard said straight away and typically, "You should have killed her."

What my dream was telling me was that the dog-faced woman was divine, and that the divine can be found in other people and other things, in the same way as I could agree that the Beauly Firth is water, and so is a cup of tea, and so is a rainbow. It was telling me that God was there in my dreams, and in people I love and hate, and all sorts of places. It was part of the endless discovery of not knowing where next I was going to find God, in what place, in how many forms, in which people, that became essential to me once I had lost conventional belief.

Throughout history, some have believed that dreams are actually the true original ultimate source of *all* culture, civilisation, and religion—a daunting thought. But if we take our dreams seriously and experience dreams that appraise and transcend our culture, then this theory is seriously believable.

In general, preliterate peoples used dreams socially and politically much more than we do. Early in the century, ethnologist J. S. Lincoln (who attended a few of Jung's seminars) studied the dreams of primitive peoples and was so impressed by how much of their life and actions came from dreams such as murder, war, sacrifice, selecting living sites, choosing careers, creating songs, dances, and religious ceremonies, discovering charms and cures, inventing new types of material objects, naming children, and many more.

This understanding led Lincoln to believe that dreams could shape and change social culture and even trigger major socio-cultural revolutions on the most primitive tiny islands.

There are many other groups of dreams, but one group I find especially moving are dreams of reconciliation with the dead. People dream of reconciliation with people they hated when alive, or people they loved—family, wife, husband—in which bad feelings, unfinished business and suspended crises are resolved and love confirmed; there are embraces and tears and deeply felt farewells. On waking, the dreamer might feel changed and shaken, as if it had really happened.

Our dreaming body, lying there played upon by all the physical reactions to the most varied emotions, but with all real action inhibited, gives some of us meetings with the very highest inspiring excitations. We can call these divine or not, according to our taste, but they can change our lives forever.

A few of the great masters were expert at going between the world of dream and the world of action; the world of the Gods and the world of the humans we love and hate, and I shall tell you about them in the next chapter.

CHAPTER TWENTY-EIGHT

Masters of the dream

"You ought to be able to imagine anything, and to confront anything you imagine"

(Derry Macdiarmid)

F reud interpreted dreams as repressed desires, mostly to do with sexuality, and Jung thought they had more to do with the dreamer's unconscious needs in a more general way, and saw them as the conduit to the collective unconscious. However, a few of the later masters of dreams had even more to say.

In the 1960s, Dr Jean Miller in New York explored the dreams of patients with depression. In the psychoanalytic world at the time, depression was associated with suppressed aggression. Therefore, Dr Miller fully expected to find this aggression represented in the dreams of severely depressed people. Instead, she found exactly the opposite. When they were at their most severely depressed, she found the patients' dreams to be bland and happy, but as they got better, they had troubling dreams where other people harmed *them*, especially forcefully coercing them. It is as if the impulses from within (call it the id, it, or whatever) are trying to provoke anger in the patient's

conscious mind through dreams, rather than supplying such a necessary response in daily life, as you might expect. This goes along with
my idea that there is some agency in the unconscious that uses dreams
to present innate stimuli to provoke the emotions in us, which we use
to confront reality.

To paraphrase Miller rather loosely: she believed the deeply
depressed person avoids self-assertion, and never asks for anything.
By keeping *himself* down, he has no conflict with *others* and, therefore,
does not dream about conflict but just feels depressed. However, if he
starts dreaming about others putting him down, he becomes angry
and starts asserting himself. But if those around him really forcefully
put him down, then that might be enough to discourage him back into
self-invalidating depression again (which the dreamer above seems to
be accepting). Then, he will return to conflict avoidance and bland
happy dreams and conscious misery which, to him, may be inexplicable since, as far as he is concerned, he had been preventing himself
from noticing how others had been oppressing him. (So, regrettably, it
can be easy for psychiatrists to persuade him that his depression is
chemical.)

Professor Isaac Marks, at the Maudsley in 1977, treated an extreme
case of depression where the patient was suffering from terrible nightmares. As his Senior Registrar, I sat in on the session, and the way
Marks dealt with the case was a revelation to me. Marks was the most
aggressive therapist I ever knew, a truly great behavioural psychiatrist
who operated at the height of the conflict between his kind of therapy
and mine. He refused to believe my personal analysis had done me
any good whatever, unless I could give him signed affidavits from my
family and friends.

This patient was a forty-five-year-old woman who had originally
been admitted for compulsive rituals, which had rapidly reduced with
treatment: Marks's combination of what had at first seemed to me
like unacceptable ruthless bullying combined with parental warmth
towards the patient had, nevertheless, worked, and the rituals had
gradually subsided. But just before she was discharged, Marks was
surprised to find her tearful and tense; it turned out that she had a
history of a recurrent nightmare, which had gone on for fourteen
years. The nightmares had started after the death of her mother,
whom she described as "lovey-dovey one minute and looking daggers
at me the next" (Marks, 1981, p. 143); the nightmare was so severe that

she often had to take the following day off work to recover from it. During the group therapy session, Marks put his arm around her shoulders, told her to close her eyes, and to relate the dream. She told how she successfully pushes her hated mother from a roof, then stamps on her head only to see it rise up and attack her, when she wakes, terrified. "She bloody well wins, doesn't she? My bloody mother" (Marks, 1981, p. 144).

Marks made her tell it twice more; by the third telling, the emotion became less violent. She was sent home with instructions to write and rehearse three dreams that ended with triumph over her mother. I remember Marks saying a number of times, "You ought to be able to imagine *anything*", like a principle. That reminded me of Pierre Janet's observation that someone with, say, an amputated arm *can* imagine playing the piano, while someone with perfectly sound arms but a hysterical paralysis *cannot* imagine playing.

The patient returned with the rewritten dreams. One ended: "I grab a well-sharpened knife and cut very, very deep into both her eyes. Blood and a yellowish substance shoot out straight into my face. I lick it with delight and begin to feel I'm winning" (Marks, 1981, p. 145).

(Recovery of aggressive devouring of the mother—Winnicott! I wouldn't have dared mention that to Marks, of course.)

". . . I crush the eyes tightly . . . until there are no solid pieces left, just puree . . . I know I am the VICTOR!" (Marks, 1981, p. 145).

However, this time, she found herself unable to read out "my bloody mother", which she had also written down. As an approximation to assertion against maternal authority, she was encouraged to say "Bloody Dr Marks . . ." several times. She did this at first with great difficulty, but it became easier with practice.

It was especially interesting that Marks was able to boss her into expressing her aggression against *him*. In the end, she was able to swear easily at Dr Marks and towards her mother. A year after the treatment, the nightmare had still not recurred, and she was sure it never would. Indeed, there were many improvements in her life, which there is not enough space here to tell.

The revelation to me was the passion with which she recited the revised dream. She was in a transport of vindictive triumph. I had no idea we could be so gripped by fiction, although it was Janet who praised the power of fictions. And I had no idea we could get deeper in the psyche than the source of a dream, and overturn it by conscious imagining. As I watched her, it became very clear to me what was happening: the force of Isaac Marks's personality had infected this patient's conscious mind with a confidence that could reach down into her unconscious, and kill the roots of defeat and despair that were ruining her life.

The corollary was the vindication of the principle that we *ought to be able to imagine anything*. I enshrined this principle in a high place in my hierarchy of guiding fictions. It was only many years later, when Marks and I were both lecturing at Leeds Castle, that he told me the source of his principle: Dr Robert Hobson, a Jungian analyst!

I was inspired by Marks' aggressive attitude to dreams. In your dreams *you must jolly well win*, and if you do not, then rewrite the dream in waking life and decide that *that* is how it is to be, and apparently, lo and behold, so it *can* be. If you can take that attitude in a dream, you might be able to apply it in real life when you wake up.

So, this is the first principle of managing dreams: you *must win*. You should be able to imagine anything, but especially winning.

In the last chapter, I mentioned Dr Medard Boss, a professor of psychotherapy in Zurich, author of *The Analysis of Dreams* (1958) and *"I Dreamt Last Night ..."* (1977). Like John Layard, Boss also collided with Jung, but more radically. Boss had been in a therapeutic group led by Jung, before he had a conversion and saw the light. He acknowledged ". . . having myself trafficked for ten years exclusively in Freudian and Jungian dream theory . . . before opening my eyes to the far more appropriate . . . phenomenological approach to human dreaming" (Boss, 1977, p. 215).

By "phenomenological," he meant the startling assumption that, for dream analysis, nothing must be recognised to exist but *the dream itself as dreamt by the dreamer*—there is no psyche, no unconscious mind, no unconscious emotions, no wish fulfilment, no symbolism, no compensation in dreams for bias in the conscious mind, no wiser unconscious Self in the background telling us things we did not know, no archetypes—absolutely no such things, don't be so ridiculous. (I could not do without a single one of these.) He kept Freud's psycho-analytic technique in his practice as a psychotherapist, but his reaction against Freud's and Jung's cardinal ideas was scathing and voluble, and after our patient journey through the century's discoveries, his denial of them all seems extreme, not to say pigheaded.

Boss's attitude was part of the existentialist view he developed with his friend, the philosopher, Martin Heidegger: that *man exists only in his behaviour*. Boss met Heidegger following Heidegger's nervous breakdown, which had occurred when de-Nazification in Germany had deprived him of his right to teach. Heidegger had been a personal admirer of Hitler: he thought he had lovely hands, and he never apologised for his connection with the Nazi Party, which he gave up only in 1945. His ideas of giving the highest value to action probably chimed with Nazi ideals, and maybe Heidegger either did not notice or care about Hitler's abolition of pity. The judgement that *man is nothing but what he does* was used by Sartre with devastating moral effect, writing on the opposite side, against Nazi-type behaviour, and Boss's own existentialism could not be less Nazi. Indeed, Boss held that *caring for others is man's deepest nature*, "his entire actual essence" (Boss, 1958, p. 183).

One of the things that Boss does not say is that normal dreams are happy dreams, which we would all be having in an ideal world. About other dreams that were *not* so happy, he had more to say.

For example, in his second book, he said some very interesting things about a group of dreams experienced by normal, young Swiss Army recruits. One of them dreamt of meeting his first great love again, and held her hand. Boss said that had the lad been older, and not spent his youth in "central Switzerland—a region where abhorrence of sensual love is practically made official" (Boss, 1977, p. 35), he might have been regarded as fixated and immature in going no further than just holding her hand. But there was still hope that, in a few years, he would have learnt a freer way of behaving towards women, and would "carry this new behaviour right into waking life" (Boss, 1977, p. 36). Thus, Boss found that, often, new behaviour possibilities could first be discovered in dreams and then tried out in waking life.

Another young recruit dreamed of a glamorous new Honda motorbike on which he rode away from his home and his mother to find a girlfriend. But somehow, he ended up back home again with his old motorbike and his mother, without any girlfriend. Again, Boss thought this failed early attempt at growing up was pretty normal for his age, and that it would not be long before he would ride out into life for good, both in dream and in reality.

Another young man dreamt that he was in a primitive jungle. He had been bitten by a snake which he had shot, and was sucking the poison from the wound. He then found himself in hospital with a nurse who looked at him "with a mother's loving gaze" (Boss, 1977, p. 38). Perhaps, after a dream like this, Boss wrote, the dreamer is more aware that waking and sleeping existence alike both contain a dimension of untamed possibilities for living, as well as a trace of infantile dependency in himself that is still waiting to be outgrown. Another young man dreamt of a terrifying contemptuous giant who pursued him; perhaps he was scared of his own adult manhood now approaching?

Boss was in his seventies when he commented on the recruits' dreams, yet he showed sensitivity to how man's deepest nature gradually unfolds itself into new behaviours, with new forms of love that come with different stages in the life cycle, often in a two-steps-forward, one-step-back kind of way.

In dreams, we behave much as we do in waking life, but in dreams it is more obvious when we are doing something wrong. The world of dream is smaller than the waking world, stripped down to the skeleton of the basic emotional reality of the dreamer's life. As a therapist, Boss evidently put himself in the dreamer's dream and thought about how far *he* would put up with the world offered by the dream to the dreamer; how far he would share, or refuse to share, the dominant mood; how he would behave differently, and what he would do himself in that dream.

It transpires, through his writing, that Boss must have been that excessively rare phenomenon among therapists: a normal person. More normal than Freud, and more normal than Jung. He knew what the patient *should* have done in the dream, not from theory, but from his guts. As a normal person, unfettered by overbearing emotional restriction through childhood or conformity to culture, he had a good understanding of uninhibited love. As a therapist, he knew that when the dream-world is black and frightening, and the dreamer's behaviour reflects this, it is because the dreamer is closed up against the possibilities of life, because he is afraid of the possibilities of love. Something has made him scared of the open sunny landscapes of love and freedom as represented in dreams, like that of the golden urn.

Forget existentialism. Forget about light emanating from the mystery of existence. If you can understand Boss's approach as I am describing it (which is, admittedly, not exactly as he described it), you will find his way of understanding dreams better. Boss's real secret weapon was his understanding of normal (i.e., uninhibited) love. Because he had a feeling for these open landscapes of normal love, he could see what was *missing* from the closed-down world and behaviour of the patient. If we can begin to imagine what it must be like to be normal, then we can begin to learn from Boss.

Although *we* can ignore Boss's existentialism, we should acknowledge what it did for *him*. Not only did it say that we are nothing but our behaviour, but also it described normal behaviour as an *openness* to life.

Boss's existentialism was a daring and exhilarating guiding fiction that had two good outcomes for him:

1. He was able to completely throw off the restrictive influences of Freud and Jung, and dump the whole of psychobabble at a stroke.
2. He could use his secret weapon of understanding normal love as unrestricted by any theory. Existentialism enabled him to use his secret weapon freely without being criticised for such a naïvely hopeful attitude. With sublime simplicity, Boss was able to see what was wrong with humanity: we are scared of love, of loving and being loved. Freud said we are scared of instinct, and so we should be; Jung said we are scared of God, and so we should be; Boss said (in effect) that we are scared of love, and here is what to do about it.

Unlike Freud, sensual sexuality in dreams was no great find to Boss; neither was the discovery of God in dreams, as it was to Jung; to Boss they were both just aspects of ordinary love. If we try to imagine what it must be like to be normal, then we should not shrink from including, in our imaginative reflections, an experience of love better than the most sublime things we have ever known in music or art or literature.

So, let us ask of Medard Boss: what can make us scared of love? Is it all *that* dangerous? What makes us close up against love, and how can we open up again?

One of Boss's Swiss army recruits had a dream where the dreamer committed repeated murder before being caught and sentenced to death. Boss contemptuously rejected the notion that such a dream showed unconscious wishes. Rather, he said, if a dream is not happy, then questions have to be asked. It needs explaining. *Why* does the dreamer only allow troubled things into his dream? But first, Boss's hawk-like eye for the positive finds a surprisingly good side to this soldier's dream: the soldier did not just dream about murdering women, he took pleasure from doing so.

For this man, his murderous dreams were about engaging in a fundamental relationship with whatever he encountered. Good. But not good: it only *approaches* self-fulfilment. Self-fulfilment is the loving exchanges that fulfil our deepest natural spontaneity and expansiveness. Here, again, Boss differs radically from Freud and Jung. Freud just accepted anything unpleasant he found in the instincts (id) as part of our beastly basic nature. A bit less pessimistic, Jung saw us living out the conflict between the good and evil in God's nature. Boss thought murderousness needed more explanation than that: if we are not dreaming of new discoveries in previously neglected possibilities of loving exchanges, then he wanted to know the reason for it.

The idea that *man's deepest impulses are basically good, or at worst neutral and open to good, was part of a mighty surge of faith in life and in humanity*, which countered Freud's pessimism, and grew during the century as part of the Enlightenment of the Mind. Some psychotherapists put it into words, and many acted on it without saying it. It is something else that Boss acted on but did not say. This faith in human instinct is worthy of our attention on our journey of self-discovery, and I signpost it here.

Boss often interpreted dream persons unknown to the dreamer as representing possibilities of behaviour that were available to the dreamer, but had not been taken up by him—for example, this army recruit had not yet discovered the satisfactions of freely adopted responsibility and authentic guilt.

Boss saw guilt as essentially a debt, an unpaid debt to life. The "fundamental existential guilt of mankind . . ." (Boss, 1977, p. 53) is "one of omission" (Boss, 1977, p. 54) because people do not develop their possibilities. The dreamer was killing part of himself when he killed women. When we shrink from becoming what we could be, we build up a debt, not only to ourselves, but also to others close to us. We are depriving them of the love they would otherwise be receiving from our uninhibited selves. Boss believed that people have habitual guilt dreams when their debt to life is too great, and when they habitually resist the instinctual impulses to love.

Unlike Freud, Boss would never "interpret" a dream or, like Layard, tell a patient directly what he *should* do in his dreams; he would only suggest more normal (i.e., uninhibited) ways of reacting that had not previously occurred to the patient. He did it quite insidiously, even surreptitiously, through questions, and the expression of surprise.

It was central to Boss's approach to bring to the dream *everything* in the way of knowledge, reflection, and analysis that could be found in the conscious minds of both the patient and himself. He was sort of saying to the patient, in the dream you did something, but you could not properly know or understand what you were doing—now you are awake, does it not surprise you to see . . . And so on.

One of Boss's patients was a thirty-five-year-old dentist with depression and impotence, who was having frustration dreams common to depressed people. He dreamt his friend wanted to plant tomatoes in a place where the climate was too cold. The patient, himself, had a peach stone and wanted to plant it, but then the garden turned into a tennis court, so he could not.

Since Boss believed in underlining the positive traits within a dream, the first question Boss asked the patient was if he could see the coldness and loneliness of the dreaming experience as present also in his waking life. The second question was to directly ask the patient if he could talk about the factors in his life that have caused the freezing of his emotional world, and this led to memories for the patient of authority figures warning against expressions of emotion as unfitting.

A third, later line of questioning might comment that, as the dreamer has now learnt that those who brought him up were responsible for teaching him to keep a cool distance from the world, does he feel as if he has to live in such captivity for the rest of his days?

Here, there is a collision going on between therapist and patient, which Boss must have felt vividly in practice, yet he was sort of unconscious of it, or at least did not describe it. This is the point of collision between the patient's despair, and the therapist's hope or faith. The therapist offers his mind for the patient to share; he lends his courage, and with it his more hopeful attitude to life.

Unconscious despair cripples the imagination, as illustrated by Janet's hysterically paralysed patient who could not imagine playing the piano, and Boss's hypnotised women who could not dream of a happy union with a lover. You should be able to imagine anything, and if you cannot, it is despair, conscious or unconscious, that is preventing you!

Boss is wonderfully good at disentangling the steps towards love from the steps in retreat from it, as in the dreams of the young recruits where there is a mixture of both forward-looking growth and regressive (incestuous) hesitation. We behave in dreams and life in the alternation of hope and despair, just like Fairbairn's mouse that peeped out and then ducked back again. We poke out and feel terrible fear and guilt, and then we withdraw and feel comfortable again.

It seems that dreams want to let us know if we are heading towards the comfort of despair, like the bland happy dreams of depressed patients who are not getting better. Or dreams can speak for hope, like the nightmares that the patients have who are getting better. The crippled imagination *tells* us it is crippled when it presents images of a narrow deprived life, and that can only be because there is a background consciousness there—a hoping awareness that knows the difference between a narrow scared life and a full confident one, and wants to tell us where we are. I suspect that whether dreams speak familiar despair or unfamiliar hope, they provide a response to the conscious attitude we are taking up—a courageous attitude will bring dreams directed towards hope—but that you will have to find out for yourself.

A moving thing about Boss is how he empathises with the sufferer. A twenty-four-year-old psychology student showed through a dream how he had retreated from a challenge of love that was just too much for him. In real life, his friend had got engaged. He dreamt that the fiancée had died of cancer, and he was shocked. At the funeral, they were in a self-service restaurant. He could find no sweet and awoke dissatisfied. Boss was able to bring out how his fear of love had narrowed down what he could allow in his dream. He could not yet bear the possibility of a lasting intimate love for himself, so it was removed from his vicinity by cancer, but that had made him sad, too.

Evidently, Boss had found in humans the same thing as Konrad Lorenz had found in animal evolution: aggression must come first in order to make love possible.

Sometimes, Boss simply pointed out to the dreamer that what might have first appeared as a disaster in a dream could actually be a sign of hope. A student with exam fear and sexual impotence dreamt that his home was on fire. Horrified, he dashed in to rescue his parents, but it was too late and the house collapsed, burning them all. He woke up screaming. Boss told him at great, tactful, existential length that other people going through a growing-up stage in therapy also had similar dreams. He went on to say that these dreams often indicated that the dreamer was ready for a more open future, to let the real parents become more than just parents and, himself to be more than just his parents' little boy.

There was one good thing about Boss's hostility to the idea of Jung's archetypes. He did not believe that the patient was ever totally in the power of an internal destructive archetype. In other words, if the dream figures are nasty or powerful, it is because we have allowed them to become so. For example, Boss described a nightmare from one of his female patients where she allowed a man with the face of an evil dwarf to carry her away into a landscape of magically evil creatures. The dwarf turned out to be a magician, who then set her on fire. Boss described this patient as a person in a state of surrender to her natural sensual forces, over which she had no control.

Overwhelming monsters in our dreams are made overwhelming by our own self-diminution. Our submission can create irresistible monsters, as in the case of a student who had a nightmare about being crushed by the fungus he was researching, because of his "unhealthy surrender to the objects of his studies" (Boss, 1958, p. 152). Boss thought that whatever a dream character does, the dreamer has some kind of complicity with it; otherwise, that character would not be there.

Unlike Boss, I think it is hard not to see the symbolism in dreams. I do not dream of saying to my father, "You are too narrow minded, I am going to think for myself", I dream of holding him under water until he drowns. I do not dream "How I love my children!" but dream of rainbow bridges between us.

Although Boss refused to admit the existence of another superior self in the background sending wise messages to the dreamer, he recognised that, sometimes, a dream could actually relay a wise message in words that would deeply impress the dreamer, such as when a dying monk told a woman that what we see and imagine are only our own desires and instincts hiding the divine truth within us. He believed even if such messages seemed silly, as they often do when we wake up, we should still think about them.

I cannot resist attacking Boss's disbelief in archetypes, with regard to one of the dreams he reports. In the National Gallery in London, there is a painting of St George and the Dragon by Uccello, which, rather than portraying the victim as a naked girl, shivering on a rock, depicts her as a very unvictim-like, superbly dressed princess, standing as if mistress of the whole situation. It is not the dragon in control of her, but, rather, the other way about—it is on a leash (said to be her belt) attached to her wrist, while it tries to defend itself, hopelessly, of course, against St George. Near St George's head is a round spiral cloud rotating into a black centre. Uccello had found yet another image version of our old friend Le-Hev-Hev, crab monster, who draws us to her so she may devour us: she is the Devouring and Initiating Mother (or Sister) found by John Layard in Malekula. Uccello's spiral cloud is a symbol of the incestuous pull backwards which can take us into blissful annihilation or give us a chance of a new start; one way of achieving this would be to kill a boar, or a sacralised man, or a dragon. So, if the sucking, rotating cloud is not an archetypal image, I do not know what is.

Right at the end of the century, Donald Kalsched (*The Inner World of Trauma*, 1996) used the theories of Freud and Jung to understand dreams differently from Boss. He thought the patterns did come from somewhere. Boss thought the hangman who dismembered a woman in her dream represented her own misguided attitude, but Kalsched had a completely different take on these types of dreams.

Remember Freud's trauma theory of neurosis and the old theory of defences, and, for example, Anna Freud's defence of "siding with the aggressor"? Remember Fairbairn's description of how the inner saboteur is formed to minimise attack from mother by speaking—and attacking ourselves—on her behalf? Similarly, I mentioned Winnicott's perception of how a false self can protect a true self until times get better.

Kalsched observed the activity of such ambiguous persecutor–protector figures in the dreams of patients who had been really badly traumatised. He realised his patients were defending themselves against a worse, more basic threat than getting hurt: the threat of a kind of annihilation, of ceasing to be a person without the relief of ceasing to *be*. He thought the expression "disintegration anxiety" (Kalsched, 1996, p. 1), coined by another therapist, described it best. Patients find different ways of expressing it—a patient of mine talked about the horror of her fear of "falling out of space". (Note: not falling through or into empty space, but *out of space*, as into a horrific, unthinkable limbo.) He realised that his patients had been threatened by hurts against which ordinary defences—see Anna Freud's list—do not work, necessitating a second line of defence of a more desperate sort altogether. (Though if, as he thought, the trauma sometimes happens before the ego is properly formed, it would really have to be described as the first line of defence.) Kalsched found himself amazed by the sheer determination of the human spirit to survive, and by the almost supernatural resources at its disposal. We shall discover how one young anorexic patient of mine chose hope over despair, life over death, through her own supernatural dream world in the next chapter.

CHAPTER TWENTY-NINE

Dreams and evolution

"The dream is the wisdom of the body; action is the wisdom of the mind"

(Japanese proverb)

I n this chapter, I focus on the dream series of a patient of mine, Alison, to show what dreams can really do for us. Alison suffered from anorexia nervosa, and she had an extraordinary dream life. Her dream series was very striking because, in order for her to achieve a new start in life, her psyche had to reach all the way back to the plant stage of evolution.

Anorexia nervosa still kills approximately 10–20% of sufferers, but while families and doctors view not eating as the problem, to the anorexic, not eating is the *solution* to her problems. Alison could always remember "the jump of relief in my mind" when, at age thirteen, she hit on the idea of giving up food for Lent. She was living a wretched life, desperately trying to please her mother by doing well at school, and often took her mother's side in the family conflicts. She tended to be very hurt by criticism, and had decided to be perfect so that no one could ever criticise her again. That made life even worse. But she soon realised that by not eating, she could:

- shed some weight and get rid of the plumpness of her body, which made her feel ungainly. As she had reached puberty early, her body also provoked jealousy and envy in other girls;
- gain a sense of control, power, competence, and achievement;
- stop feeling guilty about stealing food at night (which her mother had put a stop to);
- look like Christ on the cross, which she saw as a good thing;
- make her suffering apparent on the outside, as she could not otherwise express her internal suffering;
- rid herself of unhappiness and anger, along with her weight;
- punish herself for not living up to mother's expectations.

Not eating is the perfect way of torturing mother, but I have never heard an anorexic, including Alison, in the early stages even hint at it—it is essential for anorexics to possess the moral high ground and not be seen as vindictive.

Alison had nine admissions to hospital from the age of fifteen: electro-convulsive therapy (ECT) twice, many drugs, behaviour therapy, and analytical therapy. She tried to commit suicide twice, and went through an episode of hearing voices and seeing things turn into worms. At age twenty-eight, she was admitted to hospital, weighing thirty-seven kilos having starved herself yet again, this time as a result of a crisis in her teaching job in which she wanted the children to grow normally and happily rather than "succeed", which is what their parents wanted. She found out too painfully "what it was like to try and stand alone in my knowledge and ideals".

But this relapse was different. This time, she knew that her life was in danger, that she desperately needed help, but she could not see how anybody could do anything to help her.

Alison and I were in luck: I was full of enthusiasm for my first job in adult psychiatry and, between us, we did well. Very well. At the time (mid-1970s), anorexia had attracted much attention from psychiatrists (it still does) partly because it seemed to have increased in occurrence, and partly because it can be so difficult to treat. There were wildly different ways of treating it. Minuchin, for example, believed that the problem arises from conflict avoidance within the family; in other words, if he could get them to fight, then the dynamic changes allowed the sufferer to recover and grow up. I was too soft in those days and knew nothing about Minuchin's techniques and his views on fighting, but, fortunately, we had a consultant who was able to impose the necessary firmness, not to say some provocation, in spite of both of us.

Just after Alison's arrival at the hospital, the consultant went on holiday. As soon as his plane left the ground, two great opposing enthusiasms of that decade pounced on her: her room was stripped empty by the behaviourists and she had to earn back her possessions by eating ("operant conditioning"); and I started daily psychotherapy, including those weekends when I was on call. When the consultant returned, Alison had become so depressed about putting on weight (from the behavioural regime) that he prescribed ECT. Thus, in her first couple of months, Alison got the benefit of all three persuasions: behavioural, psychodynamic, and traditional organic psychiatry. Eventually, she settled into the clinic, and when the behaviourists were sated, and left her alone, she began to grow plants in her room.

In the fifth month of therapy, she began to report nightmares. One was about her mother nailing her into a coffin. Others were of a woman coming to drag her away. Then she reported weirder experiences, as if real supernatural beings were coming into her room at night and looking at her in a judging, considering way.

In therapy, her complaints against her mother, and her guilt about them, grew. Once, she told me that her mother's weekly visit "hangs over me like an eagle". A few days later, following a recurrent nightmare where a great white bird with a yellow beak swooped down to take her away, she had a violent shouting row with her mother, which led to a refusal to see her for a year and a half. She also banished her stepfather around the same time. This suited the clinic, because banishing the family was the current traditional predecessor to what later would become family therapy for anorexia. The French physician, Charles Lasègue, observed in 1871 that the anorexic's family were somehow implicated in the escalation of the disease, and, indeed, Charcot would not take on a patient unless they agreed to be separated from their family. On one occasion, Charcot reluctantly agreed to allow the family priest to visit the patient, only to find a letter from the patient's mother secreted in the priest's Missal!

After the row with her mother, Alison's weight went up—she was eating more at night. By the seventh month of admission, her nightlife had begun to contrast strangely with her daytime life. "At night I have no morals," she said, meaning that at night she felt hollow, lonely, longed for affection and comfort, could not control her self, "stole" food from the ward kitchen, and *ate*. Bitter guilt and remorse arrived with the dawn, as did self-punishing exercises and resolves. "It's like being two separate people," she said.

By day, she was unemotional, even cold, very controlled, feared people, abhorred eating, but at night, she was moved to sadness, wept, longed for company and solace, and ate. As I never met her night self, I asked her to write down what she was feeling, which led to her writing down her dreams. On waking from each dream, she would eat, either to comfort herself after a bad dream, or to console herself on waking from a good dream and finding it was not true. For example, she felt sad when she woke from a dream in which I promised her "the peace of everlasting sleep, which is also found in death". Shortly after that dream, she had another similar one in which she described approaching a warm, glowing mass that resembled the sun. As it eventually enveloped her, leaving no way out, a voice seemed to say, "Now you're safe forever."

Her drawings of this dream, illustrated below, showed her as a hollow plant being absorbed into the "warm, glowing mass":

This dream of blissful fusion resembles the first of three stages in the early history of the Mother Goddess image, as described by Erich Neumann: the Uroboros (snake biting its tail) stage, the Mistress of the Plants, and the Mistress of the Animals. Her dream series moved through the three, in turn. Her weight fell during the peak of the flood of plant dreams; it was as though they were causing her stress. Although she was dealing with plants, which might seem harmless, there came a crisis where she needed the courage to confront them.

She had dreams about not being able to breathe, about explosions, and receiving painful injections in her ear. There were more dreams about me, in which I, at first, offered her supernatural help in the form of death or oblivion and then, later on, dreams in which she lost me, or I was physically damaged because I was not well or robust enough to support her.

She began to have dreams of her male self. The first I noted was a dream in which she heard two female medical students complaining about me. Apparently, I had insisted that a little boy be allowed to run and play freely over the tennis court, which was spoiling their game. Then there were dreams in which the boy figure did all the things Alison did not: he was demanding, openly asked to be cuddled when he went to sleep, trampled all over cakes in a shop, knew a foreign language when it was required, and saved her from a savage bear by playing with it. The boy was often naughty, and the young men she dreamed about were delinquent—one stabbed her mother with a knife (good!—the covert hostility satisfyingly expressed). In the twelfth month, she dreamt that she could see what was going on inside herself: a crowd of little boys dressed as devils were fighting a crowd of little girls dressed as angels, who did not fight back but avoided the boys by flying up into the air. Alison felt that one side had to win, but that neither side *could* win. (This is a lovely picture of the type of conflict avoidance that Minuchin overcame through his therapy.)

As she gained weight, she felt she was being plunged back into the miseries of childhood, and so she began to reproduce her early home life in the clinic, by "stealing" food at night, and furtively evading any staff, which were viewed as representing the oppressive mother. The more weight she put on, the more desperate she became.

Her convincing façade of normality on admission began to give way to phobic and avoidant reactions. In an account she wrote twenty-five years after her therapy, she said:

> For an hour each day, bit by bit, I was taken to pieces like a garment that needed total alteration. I relived my life. Each experience was looked at from many angles: I tried to discover what others had experienced. I soon realised I could enter into experiences and feel totally different, to have feelings and reactions to things I had never had before. This was very frightening, as I had been brought up to have no feelings of my own and no way of experiencing them outwardly. When I was trying to be totally honest and free about my feelings and discuss my parents I decided I couldn't have my parents visiting me.

Then, at the end of the twelfth month, she reported three dreams, each one increasingly challenging. The first she could not bear to write down, it so horrified her; it was about someone leaving the room to vomit. The second was finding herself as a young baby, with other babies. She wanted to know how they felt about being alive, because she knew she did not like living. It was difficult to attract their attention, but she knew she wanted to make contact with them, and find out something warm about them.

The third dream needed real courage: alone, in a dark place, she saw a strange plant with a light beginning to glow around it. She described it as small, with a single thick stem and one "leaflike" head, resembling a fern in early stages of growth.

> While I was watching the plant it seemed to grow bigger and the colours became richer. Then I was aware someone was behind me. They told me I must go over to it, and get to know it. But I somehow felt very apprehensive about being any closer to it. I felt it might have some strange power over me. I wanted to push whoever was behind me away, and run desperately from the whole situation—but I couldn't: I was transfixed to the spot—I couldn't move.

To anorexics, growth is unbearable. You can see why it required such courage for her to get to know the plant. Thirty years later, she wrote,

> This dream was quite remarkable. It took time for me to realise the whole significance of it. It was in a nutshell the story of myself, and all my problems. There was that shrivelled, crushed ego struggling to grow and metamorphose into a being of creation—and there was all my fear, doubt, terror which turned and ran at that moment of fulfilment. Probably one could say that is the complete picture of anorexia—there simply isn't any trust or faith in recognising the fruition of self.

Eventually, Alison did get better, and, compared to other anorexics, dramatically so. Somehow, she was able to find the assertive aggressiveness that Minuchin put in the foreground. I say "somehow", but I think that when she gave in to the dream impulse and empathised with the growing fern-shaped plant in spite of her tears and her terror, the seed of her creative aggression was germinated. She wrote,

> I was getting pretty good about letting all around me know just what I was feeling and at times sparks were flying. Then came the day when I was on a very short fuse. My visits to the hospital were now only once a week. How could I possibly deal with a week's experiences in an hour? And anyway, where was all this therapy getting me? I had just about had enough. I firmly told my doctor he couldn't help me, since he didn't know what it was like to be me. I could manage well

on my own, thank you. Of course it was the moment he's been waiting for.

She gives me too much credit in the last sentence: I think I only
realised that was what she needed after she, with one magnificent
swing of her arm, swiped everything off my desk on to the floor. Yes!
    Alison's story is a typical history of a child too intruded on by her
parents' needs, so that she ends up becoming what family therapists
call "the parental child", who has to suspend or negate her own natural growth in order to support the family's defences against life and,
yet, somehow survive. She remembered some things early in therapy
that suggested the reasons behind her sacrifice of fusion with her
mother as a young child. For example, when her mother saw her
growing plump:

> She would say things like "nice and cuddly"—the one thing I used to
> loathe. She didn't cuddle me, she *squeezed* me. I began to be really
> wary of her trying to cuddle me when I was about seven. I used to be
> terrified she'd squeeze me so tight I couldn't breathe . . . almost as if
> she couldn't make me physically part of herself, so she almost wanted
> to *eat* me when she got hold of me. The one thing I can't bear now is
> anyone else sort of *touching* me. But when I'm terribly thin it doesn't
> bother me at all.

I suspect she had reacted inwardly against her mother's way of holding her as early as the first year of life. She had much more insight
than most.
    Anorexics hate growth because they feel it to be a betrayal of the
mother who is taking them over, rather than nurturing their separate
individuality. It is rare and unusual for someone with anorexia to be
able to recover the capacity for emotional symbiosis and grow out of
it through the succeeding phases of normal growth, as Alison did. All
of us that treated her in the clinic also did well. Our consultant was
sceptical of this newfangled psychodynamics and, early on, said the
only purpose of my theory was that it gave me the interest to perse-
vere with a seemingly hopeless case. But he still supported us
completely. I just want to boast that at Guy's Hospital in the 1970s, we
sometimes did get things very right.
    But, of course, all credit must also go to Alison. It is not uncom-
mon for anorexics to be unusually intelligent, talented, original,

creative, and spirited; for example, Sylvia Plath the poetess, Simone Weil the mystic, Ellen West, etc.—none of whom recovered. But Alison constantly and repeatedly, however much it cost her, chose the courageous options in her pilgrimage. I do not think she was consciously aware of that; she just did it. Somehow, we were able to provide the right pot of earth in which she could start growing. Since her therapy, Alison has devoted her life to being a creative teacher and carer of disadvantaged and disturbed children.

Dreams present us with an amazing, conflicting profusion of trivialities and occasional profundities that should evoke in us an attitude of maximum respect, maximum suspicion, and maximum aggression. They tell us whopping lies and we believe them: for example, the depressive dreams that tell us we are useless, ineffectual, and unlovable, but a friend or therapist will exclaim straight away, "But that's rubbish! That's just the despairing illusion you have to let go of!"

Dreams can inspire us with love, while nightmares can make us scared to go to sleep again, and most of the time they speak in riddles. Yet, dreams do introduce apparent truths and inspirations no one else could have told us, but are they truths? *Are* they? Life-changing dreams are so rare they are statistically invisible to science, like my dream of the Santa Claus God, or those dreams of killing the sacrificial animal or person, or the dreams of the embrace with the animal or divine lover. What goes on in the hidden dream-world that we never know about? Is there a world of activity to which we get only limited access?

Freud's "Royal road to the unconscious" has turned out to be more like a spread of paths and roads coming and going all over the place, with many sources close and distant: noises outside the bedroom, our animal brainstem, symptoms of illness taking strange forms in our dreams, God, other people's minds by telepathy, yesterday's events, the future, simple vulgar wishes, internal sub-personalities like the internal saboteur or the stranger-lover, or others of those sub-persons who flit back and forth across the border between being I and being You.

It is very difficult to believe Boss when he states that there is no other awareness apart from our own. After all, dreams are always entangling us in adventures. In these adventures, we have total licence to do anything we want. Our brain has disabled the controller of its skeletal muscles and, as long as we are not brain-damaged, no one is going to get hurt. Graham Greene wrote, "There are no witnesses. No libel actions" (Greene, 1994, p. 17), which showed that he was still a little haunted in his dreaming by the morality of his waking world. But in this world of dreaming there is a different ethic: we are gloriously free to create complete merry mayhem, as unrebuked as the most disturbed and hate-torn of Melanie Klein's little patients in her playroom. *And we should be.* The morality in dreaming is more fundamental than that of waking life, rooted in the values of the archaic animal brain: it is the determination to hope and not to despair, and to achieve fulfilment ruthlessly at any cost (like the baby as described by Winnicott before the age of ruth—totally irresponsible except for the fundamental and overriding responsibility to the survival and progress of its own life).

Our dream self, so much reduced from our waking self, nevertheless, retains our very highest human attribute of freedom, and will choose to behave timidly or bravely, despairingly or hopefully, narrowing down the dream world in cynicism and anxiety, or opening up to explore all the infinite ways of interacting with others.

As Boss showed, moving from despairing to hopeful choices is not the work of a night or a year: it can be an odyssey which takes time: two steps forward and one back. Our dreaming body, lying there sweating and shivering, salivating, panting, palpitating, eyes flickering, weeping sometimes, laughing sometimes, always sexually aroused, offers itself as a playground for the spirit, but with its own authentic independent evaluations from its side of the play. A Japanese proverb put it so well: "The dream is the wisdom of the body; action is the wisdom of the mind".

Somehow, in the comings and goings of this web of interconnected trails, all stages of our evolution become alive and have a voice. The ancient determination of the will to survive meets up with the very latest creations of the impulses of love, and, with this, the possibility to sketch out a, hitherto, unpredictable future. It makes me think of an old granny who says, "I don't understand one bit of what you young things are doing, but right now my guts tell me it's good, so whatever you do hang in there and win, hope and don't despair, and here's £50." In our dreams, we see our situation in life and how it is criticised from a point of view that does not belong to us: I thought I was doing fine, but my dreams showed me that I was really in a desert, or cheating my friends, or avoiding the front line. Maybe it is the job of the unconscious to make sure that our despairing attitudes land us in mean and horrid dream environments that prompt us to change

It is not enough to be able to imagine anything. We should also be capable of *doing* anything. I remember an interview in a newspaper with a very civilised woman who had a very civilised husband, genuinely rather admirable people. She said that she liked to think her husband was capable of rape, though, of course, he would never do it. In dreams, we can practise doing things we would not want to do in waking life, develop the emotional muscles of all our instincts and emotions and fill out our personalities. Freud was right to intuit incest and murder at the root of the dream, but he did not fully grasp that both are the most healing snakes in Aesculapius's temple basement, and should be treasured and cultivated.

A homosexual patient of mine dreamed about sex with his sister and, suddenly, found he had heterosexual feelings. On the other hand, I remember in the 1960s a homosexual in Oxford who was jailed for having sex with his mother's dead body. Could you understand and empathise with his need in doing it, and love the sin? If not, do not become a psychotherapist. But if only *that* man could have enacted his urges through his dreams, then he would have been satisfied enough not to do it in waking life, and would not have been jailed. Now, *there* is a great question: why do some people carry out such actions in dreams, whereas others have to act them out in real life? It might be a failure of our culture that it inhibits dreaming, but how exactly? Get the symptom into the dreams, and you are getting somewhere, John Layard used to say, but he never explained to me how.

Winnicott viewed stealing as a "moment of hope" (Winnicott, 1992, p. 30). This sort of delinquency can be harmlessly lived out in dreams with the same benefits for growth, as can anything that is a crime in the waking world but tends to fulfilment (like Boss's murderous young recruit). It puts the dreamer one step further along the path of psychotherapy from delinquent to dissident, when the despairing, avoidant, dissociating criminal who acts against himself and others gradually becomes the brave dissident who confronts his environment with the real faults of others, and their contribution to his problems. For example, the bed-wetting little girl who has no better way of fighting back, but who ends up growing up into a woman who fights against the injustices in society.

When Alison dreamed of blissful fusion with the sun, she regressed to the earliest baby–mother symbiosis. It was a new birth. If we mentally flee back to mother in defeat but not in despair, with a hidden, maybe even completely unconscious agenda of hope, then new birth occurs, which is the most wonderful miracle we therapists can experience in our work. It just happens. Somehow, fusion became a threat to Alison as well as a longing, because a deeper desire for an active adventurous life had been born.

In these chapters about dreams, I have shown how the source of inspiration and meaning of life can shift to our dreams: as Jung put it (though for the life of me I cannot remember when or where he said it), one "finds one's God in one's dreams". Admittedly, it is dangerous to relativise our attachment to civilised cultural certainties, the shared beliefs and attitudes and dogmas, but, in this way, we can find a foothold outside the mental prison of our culture. However, it might feel, at first, like a foothold on shifting waters, which it is. Yet, we do not need to be alienated from our fellow citizens. Another way to get a foothold outside our culture is to study a lot of different cultures, but studying dreams is still the best way.

The whole grand phenomenon of dreaming, albeit confused and full of contradictions, nevertheless tells us, through vague self-contra-dictory hints and images, what life is about, and what we really care about, which is love—love of the world, and the creatures in it, and each other. *Dreaming is about learning to love, just as life is about learning to love, and evolution is about learning to love—all in a fumbling and haphazard way.* I am signposting this as a core statement of our Enlightenment of the Mind, and the purpose of this book: in helping us to reveal our unconscious selves, our dreams can connect us to our capacity for love, and so transform our lives.

But there are three big side-observations, also supported by the study of dreams.

1.   There is no evidence at all that evolution knows where it is going. Evolution has progressed by blundering trial and error, with lots of error. The instincts within us, the "wondrous id", or God, or whatever you want to call it or him, is making himself up as he goes along, and can recognise a good thing when he discovers it, but there is no sign that he knows in advance what he wants. On the contrary, night and day, love's forms are being newly

invented in the dreaming and experimenting bodies and minds of men and women. So, there is no prior plan or guiding intelligence.

In our dreams, it seems we are always referring back to the animal for consultation and re-adaptation before taking another step on as humans. And our animal selves look to us for action. Most of the time, we share in God or the id's ignorance of what the hell is going on, but every now and then, there comes to individuals a little or big flash of certainty, lasting as long as we can hold on to it.

2.   Love needs hate in order to exist. Dreams confirm that love needs the energy of hate galvanising its roots. From that magical moment when Konrad Lorenz saw the little coral fish diverting its aggression from its mate on to any unoffending bystander, he saw more and more clearly that "there can be no love without aggression" (Solomon, 1995, p. 34). And up on the human level, when the aggressive need and desire to exchange love with other humans is thwarted by morally culpable despairing behaviour by others, our vision of love must be validated and supported by rage and hate drawn, as we saw above, from very deep in our nature, if necessary from the psychotic level. Love's visions must be supported by hate, which always lingers in the background just in case it is needed.

3.   There are good ways and bad ways of entering into dialogue with the unconscious instincts. The bad way is to use the evasive tactics of unconscious despair, for example, Anna Freud's nine defences, which Adler called "the arrangement". These are classical tricks of neurosis, but they lead to chronic trouble. The good way is to settle the necessary conflicts between the different forms and stages of love by taking sides and, consciously and deliberately, not "killing" the more regressive form. Otherwise, the sacrificed instinct or desire can return later from the unconscious in a new, perhaps more damaging form.

We have seen how dreaming changes human behaviour. I wonder if dreaming has been a back-door contributor to evolution all this time. Maybe the evolution of the human form, and not just the evolution of love, depends on the open-minded acceptance of dream phenomena—what I think of as hope rather than hopelessness.

Certainly, in the short term, if we take up a good attitude, the unconscious can richly reward us, as it did for Alison.

In the final chapter, I shall summarise the findings that make up the Enlightenment of the Mind, and how we should best make use of them.

CHAPTER THIRTY

Dream, imagination, and emotion

"We look to Scotland for all our ideas of civilisation"

(Attributed to Voltaire (1694–1778)

I n our rational life, reason lets us know if things are true, but, on the other hand, emotion can help us realise the same truths. For example, this poem by Robert Burns, which expresses egalitarian views of society, makes me cry, and I can feel the force of the desire of it through my body, and I know it will affect the rest of my life and other people's lives.

> For a' that and a' that
> It's coming yet, for a' that
> That man tae man, the warld o'er
> Shall brithers be for a' that.
>
> (Burns, 1896)

It is not far from the atavistic urge that would make me follow the bagpipes into hell. So I know the unconscious mind wants the brotherhood of man, and I can feel in my body how deeply and strongly it wants it.

Your dream life should be your own, without suggestion from me, so I shall only make a couple of recommendations about the best use of gods. I recommend using an Edinburgh model of religion, based on the following three principles.

First, do not believe a single thing you do not want to, and make sure your Reason is well oiled and in good order. As the great Scottish philosopher, David Hume, once said, "Reason is, and ought to be, the slave of the passions, and can never pretend to any other office than to serve and obey them" (Mossner, 1984, p. 22).

David Hume was a simple atheist who refused to believe anything just because it was what he was told—a good example to set, and apparently he was known and liked for it, too. When Dr Samuel Johnson visited Hume when he was dying, he could not fathom why Hume was so happy while he himself had suffered because of his religion.

Hume also awoke the concern of female attachments that seemed to be fond of him—his maidservant urged him to give up his "wee books" so as not to spoil his chances of heaven. When he fell into the Nor'Loch (North Loch, later drained), a typical redoubtable Scottish lady refused to pull him out until he had said his Catechism.

Next: William James, the pioneering American psychologist and philosopher gave a series of lectures in Edinburgh, on "The varieties of religious experience" (1900–1901), the first scientific assessment of religion. He concluded that religion could be defined as inspiring ideas that come from the unconscious mind. I would urge you to keep that in mind.

Last, I remember Professor John MacMurray, Professor of Moral Philosophy at Edinburgh University, saying that the best model of religion was getting together with friends. (In philosophical jargon, this might be known as the expression of consciousness of community.)

In no time, you can become incredibly philosophical and theological, or political and archetypal or, otherwise, hi-falutin' about religion, and I strongly recommend that you stick to the basic Edinburgh model: religion is celebrating with those you love. Our emotions are likely to hasten the adventures of love as at any party.

I recommend not worrying about whether "God" exists or not, and advise that you just make practical use of whatever comes along in your dreams and fantasies that inspires or interests you. I also recommend disbelieving in the existence of any God that depresses you, or that someone is using to control you, or to make you behave yourself.

Both our dream life and the world of our own imagination are strong enough to support us if we take courage and let them live us. They can stop us from clinging to each other in anxiety, living inside closed communities which we set up for ourselves, and which exclude others. Dreams and our imagination offer freedom of the world and our place in it. They will give us access to truths that the gated community does not know. Dreams bring the real enlightenments.

I have told you a bit about my own dream gods, my disillusion and release from an imperialistic Santa Claus God, and a similar release from the controlling dog-headed mother goddess. She let me off the hook of subservience to the mother in women, and gave me control of the women who worshipped her, like the little maidservants in my dream. She spoke from my ancient imagination in REM sleep, and I listened to her. She was a very useful god to me. But I would hope that your odyssey would be completely different from mine.

To make the best of the gods in our dreams, I recommend keeping a distance from Jung, who was too cold-hearted and emotionally disengaged to use religion for love, as it should be used. Jung never kept a man friend all his life. He related to his female patients as a lover, whether he slept with them or not, and that was how he got the best out of himself and them. Once his wife said to him in mid-conversation, you are not interested in these people at all, only in your ideas about them, and it silenced him, for it was true.

Jung thought he had solved the clash between religion and science by saying that although science can see that religious motifs spring up naturally in people's minds, it cannot say whether they refer to any reality or not. His was a work of great genius, full of intellectual range, penetration, and understanding, no doubt about it. But if you want to see how it all relates to actual love, or distress and joy with other people, then I recommend reading the works of his more feeling followers, like Marie-Louise von Franz, and Edward Edinger, who, with difficulty, dragged Jung's thought processes partly back to love. Jung believed that God needs us in order to become conscious—for most of his life Jung wrote as though the development of consciousness was the most important thing in life.

I recommend making friends with any god who can get your glands fizzing and fill you with enthusiasm, who can give you the courage to, for example, confront the family member who's hurt you, or even be self-sacrificing, like loving the other person *and their hatred* of you.

Loving nature leads to hills becoming stupas, groves becoming temples or churches, streams and ponds becoming fonts, and so on. In shops in Vietnam, they have a statuette of Kwan Am, goddess of Mercy, on a high shelf, and on the floor by the door, an obese grinning Buddha just about to have his fatal coronary, both with their little offerings of food and drink and incense. I asked the shopkeeper, where people think the real Buddha is when they pray to him. "In Hell!" she replied, as if to say "Stupid question!" But she did not mean "hell" in the same way as her Catholic neighbours, but "down under in the sand". Perhaps, the Vietnamese faith in such presences as the fat Buddha, under the sand, resting in the entrails of the mother, gave them the guts and energy to claim victory during the Vietnam War. How is that for the power of the imagination?

In homes and workplaces all over the world (but especially in cultures other than in the West, where we practise our religions more dispassionately) there are images from different religions, sometimes lit up, perhaps surrounded with incense or with even a little food and drink set before them. But while one home might have a little image of a man being tortured to death on a cross, another might have an image of a man sitting in calm bliss and tranquillity, perhaps wearing a faint Buddha-like smile. Similarly, there are enormous ancient statues without any genitalia, and images that have nothing *but* genitals. There might be an image of a gentle, sweet-looking young woman, with or without a baby in her arms, or, conversely, another which depicts a young woman in a state of murderous fury, waving weapons and dancing on corpses. Although these images send such opposing messages, many of the families in whose homes these can be found are decent god-fearing citizens who love their children, and can even mingle with each other as friends, sharing the festivals, and apparently hardly noticing the religious differences.

Yet, the images listed above hardly represent compatible forms of love: the self-sacrifice of Christ, giving his life for his friends, the self-effacing detached benignity to all living creatures of Buddha, the cosmic lust of Shiva, the compassion of Mary or Kwan Am, Kali's fierce defence of her loved ones. Each is not narrowed down completely to one form; for example, Jesus could be violent like Kali, though his whip of small cords was tame against Kali's weaponry.

It is as though the world of common religion is one world, contributed to by a complex of psychological caves and tunnels and bicycle tracks of individual dreams, individual and shared fantasies, common superstitions, etc. In this sense, it is as though it does not matter to whom you show piety, as long as you show it to *someone or something or some god* as an anchor of life.

I believe that if any common religious voice becomes too one-sided or deceiving, it will not be long before a dream has something to say about it. It is a function of gods to help us share faith and hope and aspects of love with each other, and it seems even the inspiring voices of our individual dreams can have this effect, too.

So, what is The Meaning of Life? I believe it is a baby waking in the full flood of his first Love Affair with the world, ready to grab life with every part of himself. He goes through the phase of deceiving his parents with neuronal reactions to smiles, like Spitz's little Jessy, and then his smiles become real exchanges of love. He will, according to Winnicott, discover ruth, and know that he does not want to hurt his mother. It will be his imagination that will reveal these instincts, but it is his instincts that will "live" him.

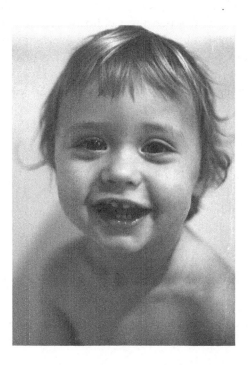

Our instincts are striving to love, and all the adventures of love beyond imagination: love of the earth, of the creatures in it, of the things we make, and of each other. Life is about learning to love, and we are more concerned with loving than being loved, whatever cynical propaganda says about human nature. Instincts, it, id?—Why call it such a funny name? said Jung, huffily, in the Tavistock Clinic. Then a lifetime later, he acknowledged our lives are danced to the all-powerful tune of "cosmic love" which, he said, we might as well call God. God, id, it, who cares?

First insight: we learn to love through remorse

Evolution consists of us starting from the most basic chemical reactions and animal reflexes, and learning to love by trial and error, without even knowing it. We learn to love the world and everything in it, including each other. Trial and error, and remorse are great educators. Remorse and reconciliation are the ultimate words in our trade of psychotherapy, and ultimate words for human life.

We learn to love from pre-verbal adventures. Think of Konrad Lorenz's holy moment when the cichlid diverts his attack from his loved one to a bystander. We start off by exercising our aggression with thoughtless pleasure, attacking whatever is near us, then find a richer flavour of satisfaction and modify it into love.

We humans learn as holy innocents and, unthinkingly, do what comes naturally and find we are sad and feel for our victim. My own experience was as a ten-year-old, hunting and killing an innocent water vole. Whoever wrote that into the script?

It is part of the long game of discovering or inventing love that our remorse often arrives too late. For example, when my grandfather was dying of cancer, he said to my grandmother, "If I get better of this I'm going to be awfy awfy guid tae ye, Betsy." Too late. You see why I am so moved by reconciliations in dreams.

Second insight: in life, through learning to love, we also learn to reject despair

Learning to love is a lifetime task. We go through the first phase of being part of a family, before we leave it, and strike out on our own.

Using the experiences of the first, we begin another stage—building another family, our own. We arrive at the next chapter: we want our children to have security, but they want adventure, and we must give them the freedom to explore. So, we dismantle our creation. It is time for love to move beyond and transcend the family.

In psychotherapy, we foster and support the natural evolution of love as it evolves out of instinct, but we therapists only exist because something has gone wrong with the process. We have to repair the damage caused by millennia of half-hearted or panicky living not only in our patients, but in their families and the history in which they are immersed. We have to restore the natural confidence they have lost, so that once again our innate instincts can be freed to grow into a capacity to love. So, two different things concern us: first, the normal growth of love, and second, the recovery from despair in all its forms that has inhibited love. That is, we are learning to develop our basic animal selves into being able to give love, and, *at the same time*, to be able to choose against despair.

Third insight: the best attitude for life is that we should love the sin and not just the sinner

This is based on John Layard's ideal that the sin we should love is the other person's hatred of us, which is part of the platform to make love between us possible.

I recommend this attitude. In small instances, you might think it is no more than giving a furious child a way to climb down, with minimal loss of face. In great instances, it is the magic talisman that transforms all life. In principle it goes further than "Father forgive them", and it is asking a lot. To love other people's hatred of us!

The capacity to believe in the value of this, and to convince others that we mean it, could transform our world.

Fourth insight: there is no such thing as a battle between good and evil in the world. The battle is between generosity and anxiety

The choice between hope and despair has its concrete form in constant life choices between generosity and anxiety. Good and Evil are only the names we give to my anxiety and your anxiety in the fight for the moral high ground. In other words, my anxiety is good, yours is evil.

Freud thought anxiety is the essence of neurosis. Anxiety has the following features.

1. It is often denied and kept unconscious, so that people whose love is warped and diminished by anxiety often seem more self-confident than anyone else around them.
2. It is attracted to dependent forms of love.
3. In the present world enterprise of globalisation, it is anchored in tribal loyalties and hostilities that hold back globalisation.
4. It may be centred in insecurity about self-esteem and desperation to possess the moral high ground or to look like the good person. (Before his arrest, Jesus reproached his followers for their need to look outstandingly virtuous and generous at any cost, without being either. For Jesus, there was no contest in the choice between being kind *or* being good.)

We saw in Chapter Twenty how family therapy shows anxiety in action inside family relationships. Minuchin was able to get the families to quarrel in a more generous and open-hearted way, which replaced their previously evasive, argumentative style. We see free generosity replacing the self-preserving anxiety.

The generous person gives his emotions to others, loses his temper and quarrels, and makes up, and regards all secrets as on their way to being opened. To the generous person, money can be an untainted vehicle for love because its energy can become tangible, and provide fair and just exchange.

Fifth insight: the political form of anxiety is the gated community or the rich ghetto

Walled cities, locked doors, patrolled borders are all versions of defended enclaves which can limit human potential. Obviously, gated communities are normal and necessary to civilisation and to culture, and for humans to grow. But it is critical whether these communities become more fortress-like in their attitude to outsiders, or whether they become generous to the world beyond.

What I consider to be unhealthy gated communities are characterised by:

1. All the characteristics of anxiety, described above, along with a special capacity for igniting righteous panic about the wishes and intentions of outsiders. Gated communities might suffer significant numbers of deaths of children from violence, abuse, and neglect, but be more excited about any potential attack from outsiders.
2. Laws and agreements which control the interaction with outsiders that seem apparently fair, leaving those within the gates in possession of the moral high ground, but which in fact leave outsiders feeling inferior and deprived.
3. The child inside the gate is made to feel guilty for not wholeheartedly going along with the ghetto attitude, which can lead to depression, drug and alcohol dependence, and other social problems. The child outside the gate might be either resentful and envious, or despairing.

Sixth insight: the most significant threat is from the neglected or traumatised child who is not being listened to. The neglected child is most dangerous when we release in him his own psychotic righteousness. The neglected child is in all of us

On the face of it, what could be more harmless than a neglected child? But neglected children have been responsible for much of the evil of the century, as shown by Alice Miller's study of Hitler, and other postwar psychological research. Men who, at first, appeared to be ruthless masters of the universe, on closer study turned out to be pathetic little losers at heart, even physically inferior.

Hitler's life is the perfect trajectory of the career of the overcompensating child. He was abused by his father, and spoiled by his mother (on whose grave he lay all night after her death). As a dictator, he was loved and adored, and totally indulged; his tantrums were feared and obeyed, and any possible criticism or reproach was quashed immediately. And he had Power—power beyond the dreams of Alfred Adler. He received Perfect Care as fantasised by every neglected child, but he did not get enough of it. He was insatiable for more, as the neglected child often is.

Freud believed that the atrocities that took place during the First World War confirmed his theory about human nature. Yet, if we look at Freud's theory now, from this distance in time, it seems strikingly limited; a naïve and inadequate theory that is not enough to explain events such as the Holocaust. The Holocaust was not just an outburst of suppressed primitive drives, any more than other horrors of the century. The Holocaust had roots in a deeper evil and hatred. So, for an explanation, we must turn to another line of Freud's enquiry: the nature of conscience, or, as he liked to call it, the superego.

The need to be good comes from a normal need for respect, and self-respect. For example, one of Klein's patients made her play a game in which she had to praise him warmly—"Extraordinarily intelligent boy!" "Very good performance!" "Fine lad!"—that kind of thing. Similarly, constitutional monarchs have to spend a lot of their time, however excruciatingly boring, watching their subjects show off. All fine.

But the neglected child desperately needs to be good, *and to be seen to be good*. This can become a serious neurotic illness, as it gets in the way of ordinary impulsive human kindness, and interrupts the digestion of remorse as we learn to love. There is an immature need to be the good child to the good parent. But it goes against learning how to love.

The Chicago analyst, Kohut, used the colder Freudian word "narcissism" to create a whole theory: if your mother respects and praises you enough when you are little, thus providing you with your necessary "narcissistic supplies", then you build normal self-esteem. If she sells you short, the starvation can make you a malignant narcissist, like so many political leaders. Without exception, tyrants throughout history have been ready to sacrifice others, in order to appear more important and beloved themselves. It is interesting to see how such people react when confronted with the bad things they have done to others. They can re-arrange the facts to support their view, as though evidence does not matter.

Remember our exploration in the chapters above about the deeper need for life validation: the dark faith that I and my life *are* worth living above others, that God speaks especially to me, and that my value is a transcendent absolute (or, the psychiatrist might say, psychotic) truth. This was not helped, in Hitler's case, when a psychiatrist, in treating his hysterical blindness after a gas episode in 1914, told Hitler that he was a supernormal being, and he never forgot it. (Yet, I suspect that his suicide also expressed the self-hatred that was still bubbling away in the deeper levels of his psyche.)

The megalomaniac passions of the neglected child speak to us with great power and fascination. However well treated we were as children, it was never perfect, and history shows us that it is possible to ally ourselves with the superior demon's utter ruthlessness, and make a pact with any devil in the pursuit of "justice". The dictator can get votes from society since he expresses the unloved child in every one of us, and in that, he is irresistible. So, half-dazzled, we follow the needs of our own and others' neglected child selves, unconscious to the mayhem that may follow.

Seventh insight: love is insatiably greedy as well as generous, and shakes the roots of our personalities without our knowing it

In her book *The Past is Myself* (1968), Christina Bielenberg described a night train journey in which a fellow passenger confessed to her how he had shot dead a little Jewish boy even though the boy had held his hands up to him and called him "Uncle". The man asked her if he could ever be forgiven. No, she replied. (But later, she awoke with her head on his sleeping shoulder.)

How naïve and uncomplicated dynamic psychotherapy was when such stories were just things to read in a book in the mid-twentieth century. But if that man were to come to a therapist now, asking for help, then we would have to take him on, and try to find a path from his remorse to some sort of reconciliation. Nowadays, we are more accustomed to people finding self-forgiveness impossible, and coming to us with guilt they cannot shake off.

In the heart of the neglected child, love is greedy and vengeful in its demands for compensation. This is not usually shared with others as a conscious articulated reproach, either as a child, or still later as an adult. Yet, reparation may be taken with any kind of destructive behaviour, and against anybody at all. The instincts have a depth of determination that should scare us.

In this century, the neglected child is not one charismatic lad bullied by father and spoiled by mother. Our gated communities in all their different and complex forms are creating such neglected children every day, neglected and traumatised not only by their parents, but also by the immediate social environment. Each of them has the potential to discover their own psychotic validation and righteousness that will stop at nothing.

Note from the author's wife

The manuscript ends here. Three days after writing the above, Derry Macdiarmid died of cancer on 22 September 2006. He had survived six years with the diagnosis. One year beforehand, he had begun to tell his patients and friends. The day before he died, he wrote the following final sentences.

I have done my best to scare you with the appalling dangers presented by that great evolutionary enterprise of discovering or inventing love, while at the same time, I have hoped to lure you into making your dream life and the life of your imagination, at least as important, if not more important, than your rational life. So, off you go now into the world of dream and imagination and emotion.

Start your dream book tomorrow morning, and I give you the classic good wishes—get lost, and may you soon find yourself trespassing beyond the limits of the known world of conventional, half-frightened, love.

REFERENCES

Abel, E. (1992). *Virginia Woolf and the Fictions of Psychoanalysis*. Chicago, IL: Chicago University Press.

Aczel, A. D. (2005). *Descartes' Secret Notebook: A True Tale of Mathematics, Mysticism, and the Quest to Understand the Universe*. New York: Broadway.

Adler, A. (1927). *Understanding Human Nature*. New York: Greenberg.

Adler, A. (1931). *What Life Should Mean to You*. Boston: Little, Brown.

Adler, A. 1939[1933]. *Social Interest: A Challenge to Mankind*. New York: Putnam.

Adler, A. (1956). *The Individual Psychology of Alfred Adler: A Systematic Presentation in Selections from his Writings*. New York: Basic Books.

Adler, A. (2005). *The Collected Clinical Works of Alfred Adler. Case Readings and Demonstrations*. Bellingham, WA: Classical Adlerian Translation Project.

Ahmed, A. S., & Donnan, H. (Eds.) (1994). *Islam, Globalisation and Postmodernity*. New York: Routledge.

American Psychiatric Association (1987). *Diagnostic and Statistical Manual of Mental Disorders III-RWA*. Washington, DC: American Psychiatric Association.

Amiel, H.-F. (1885). *Amiel's Journal: The Journal Intime of Henri-Frédéric Amiel*, M. A. Ward (Trans.). London: Macmillan.

Badinter, E. (1981). *The Myth of Motherhood: An Historical View of the Maternal Instinct.* London: Souvenir Press.

Bair, D. (2004). *Jung: A Biography.* London: Little Brown.

Balint, M. (1959). *Thrills and Regressions.* London: Hogarth.

Balint, M. (1979). *The Basic Fault: Therapeutic Aspects of Aggression.* New York: Brunner-Mazel.

Balint, M. (1992). *The Basic Fault: Therapeutic Aspects of Aggression.* Evanston, IL: Northwestern University Press.

Barry, M. (2005). *Youth Policy and Social Inclusion: Critical Debates with Young People.* London: Routledge.

Bateson, G. (2000). *Steps to an Ecology of Mind.* Chicago, IL: University of Chicago Press.

Beckwith, C. A. (1922). *The Idea of God: Historical, Critical, Constructive.* London: Macmillan.

Berg, C. (1947). *Deep Analysis: The Clinical Study of an Individual Case.* New York: Norton.

Bielenberg, C. (1968). *The Past Is Myself.* London: Chatto & Windus.

Bishop, P. (2002). *Jung's Answer to Job: A Commentary.* Hove: Brunner-Routledge.

Blech, B. (2004). *The Complete Idiot's Guide to Jewish History and Culture.* New York: Alpha Books.

Bloom, H. (Ed.) (2008). *The Complete Poetry and Prose of William Blake.* Berkeley, CA: University of California Press.

Boardman, B. (Ed.) (2001). *The Poems of Francis Thompson.* London: Continuum.

Bollas, C. (1989). *The Shadow of the Object: Psychoanalysis of the Unthought Known.* New York: Columbia University Press.

Boss, M. (1958). *The Analysis of Dreams.* New York: Philosophical Library.

Boss, M. (1977). *"I Dreamt Last Night . . .": A New Approach to the Revelations of Dreaming—and its Uses in Psychotherapy.* New York: Gardner Press.

Bottome, P. (1957). *Alfred Adler: A Portrait from Life.* New York: Vanguard.

Bowlby, J. (1951). *Maternal Care and Mental Health.* Geneva: World Health Organization.

Browne, T. (1909). *Religio Medici and Other Writings.* New York: Dutton.

Browne, T. (2006). *Religio Medici, Hydriotaphia: And the Letter to a Friend.* Fairford, Glos: Echo Library.

Burns, R. (1896). *Burns Centenary 21st July 1896: Great Demonstration at Dumfries.* New York: Longmans Green.

Carnell, E. J. (1965). *The Burden of Søren Kierkegaard.* Grand Rapids, MI: Eerdmans.

Carroll, L. (1993). *Alice's Adventures in Wonderland*. London: Dover.

Carter, R. B. (1853). *On the Pathology and Treatment of Hysteria*. London: John Churchill.

Chamberlain, J., & Ree, J. (2001). *The Kierkegaard Reader*. Oxford: Wiley-Blackwell

Davies, H. (1992). The Hunter Davies interview: Sir Nicholas, too sexy for his trews? London: *The Independent*, 6 October.

Davis, M. (1977). *William Blake: A New Kind of Man*. Berkeley, CA: University of California Press.

Doane, J., & Hodges, D. (1993). *From Klein to Kristeva: Psychoanalytic Feminism and the Search for the Good Enough Mother*. Ann Arbor, MI: University of Michigan Press.

Dobbs, T. (2007). *Faith, Theology, and Psychoanalysis: The Life and Thought of Harry S. Guntrip. Princeton Theological Monograph Series, Vol. 72*. Eugene, OR: Pickwick.

Dunne, C. (2002). *Carl Jung: Wounded Healer of the Soul: An Illustrated Biography*. London: Continuum.

Edelstein, M. (1981). *Trauma, Trance, and Transformation: A Clinical Guide to Hypnotherapy*. London: Brunner-Mazel.

Ellenberger, H. F. (1970). *The Discovery of the Unconscious: The History and Evolution of Dynamic Psychiatry*. New York: Basic Books.

Epictetus (135 AD). *The Enchiridion*. In: *Handbook of Epictetus*, N. P. White (Trans.). Indianapolis, IN: Hackett.

Erikson, E. H. (1959). *Identity and the Life Cycle: Selected Papers, Volume 1, Issue 1*. Madison, CT: International Universities Press.

Eysenck, M. (2004). *Psychology: An International Perspective*. London: Taylor & Francis.

Fairbairn, W. (1952). *Psychoanalytic Studies of the Personality*. London: Routledge.

Fast, I. (1974). *Multiple Identities in Borderline Personality Organisation. British Journal of Medical Psychology, Volumes 46–47*: 291–300. Cambridge: Cambridge University Press.

Ferenczi, S. (1995). *The Clinical Diary of Sándor Ferenczi*, J. Dupont (Ed.), M. Balint & N. Z. Jackson (Trans.). Cambridge, MA: Harvard University Press.

Fisher, C., Gross, J., & Zuch, J. (1965). Cycle of penile erection synchronous with dreaming (REM) sleep. *Archives of General Psychiatry, 12*: 29–45.

Fordham, M. (1995). *Analyst–Patient Interaction: Collected Papers on Technique*. London: Routledge.

Freeman, J. (1959). *Face to Face*. BBC interview with C. G. Jung.

Freud, A. (1937). *The Ego and the Mechanisms of Defence*. London: Hogarth Press.

Freud, E. L. (Ed.) (1961). *Letters of Sigmund Freud 1873–1939*, T. Stern & A. Stern (Trans.). London: Hogarth Press.

Freud, S. (1890a). Psychical (or mental) treatment. *S.E.*, 7: 283–302. London: Hogarth.

Freud, S. (1892–1893). A case of successful treatment by hypnotism. *S.E.*, 1: 115–130. London: Hogarth.

Freud, S. (1893a). On the physical mechanism of hysterical phenomena: preliminary communication. *S.E.*, 2: 3–17. London: Hogarth.

Freud, S. (1895d). *Studies in Hysteria. S.E.*, 2. London: Hogarth.

Freud, S. (1900a). *The Interpretation of Dreams. S.E.*, 4–5. London: Hogarth.

Freud, S. (1905c). *Jokes and their Relation to the Unconscious. S.E.*, 8. Hogarth.

Freud, S. (1905d). *Three Essays on the Theory of Sexuality. S.E.*, 7: 130–243. Hogarth.

Freud, S. (1907a). Delusions and dreams in Jensen's *Gradiva. S.E.*, 9: 7–95. London: Hogarth.

Freud, S. (1909d). *Notes Upon a Case of Obsessional Neurosis. S.E.*, 10:155–318. London: Hogarth.

Freud, S. (1914d). On the history of the psycho-analytic movement. *S.E.*, 14: 7–66. London: Hogarth.

Freud, S. (1917b). A childhood recollection from *Dichtung und Wahrheit. S.E.*, 17: 147–156. London: Hogarth.

Freud, S. (1917e). Mourning and melancholia. *S.E.*, 14: 237–258. London: Hogarth.

Freud, S. (1930a). *Civilization and Its Discontents. S.E.*, 21: 59–145. London: Hogarth.

Freud, S. (1957). *The Origins of Psychoanalysis: Letters, Drafts and Notes to Wilhelm Fliess, 1887–1902*. New York: Doubleday.

Frieden, K. (1990). *Freud's Dream of Interpretation*. New York: State University of New York Press.

Friedman, D. M. (2001). *A Mind of its Own: A Cultural History of the Penis*. New York: Free Press.

Froebel, F. (1826). *The Education of Man*, W. H. Hailman (Trans.). New York: Appleton.

Gottesmann, C. (2005). *The Golden Age of Rapid Eye Movement Sleep Discoveries, 1965–1966*. New York: Nova.

Grayling, A. C. (2006). *Descartes: The Life of René Descartes and Its Place in His Times*. New York: Pocket Books.

Grayson, H. (1979). *Short-term Approaches to Psychotherapy*. New York: Human Science Press.

Greene, G. (1994). *A World of My Own: My Dream Diary*. New York: Viking.

Gresser, M. (1994). *Dual Allegiance: Freud as a Modern Jew*. New York: State University of New York Press.

Grinder, J., DeLozier, J., & Bandler, R. (1977). *Patterns of the Hypnotic Techniques of Milton H. Erickson, M.D.* Capitola, CA: Meta.

Groddeck, G. (1923). *Das Buch vom Es (The Book of the It)*. New York: International University Press.

Grosskurth, P. (1986). *Melanie Klein: Her World and Her Work*. New York: Knopf.

Guntrip, H. (2005). My experience of analysis with Fairbairn and Winnicott: how complete a result does psychoanalytic therapy achieve? In: J. Geller, J. Norcross, & D. Orlinski (Eds.), *The Psychotherapist's Own Psychotherapy: Patient and Clinician Perspectives* (pp. 63–80). Oxford: Oxford University Press.

Haley, J. (1973). *Uncommon Therapy: The Psychiatric Techniques of Milton H Erickson M.D.* New York: Norton.

Harriman, P. L. (1946). *Encyclopaedia of Psychology*. New York: Philosophical Library.

Hayman, R. (2002). *A Life of Jung*. New York: Norton.

Helms, D. B., & Turner, J. S. (1986). *Exploring Child Behavior*. Belmont, CA: Brooks-Cole.

Herodotus (2004). *The Histories*, G. C. Macaulay (Trans.) D. Latiner (Ed.). New York: Barnes & Noble Classics.

Hobson, J. A., (2004). *Dreaming: An Introduction to the Science of Sleep*. Oxford: Oxford University Press.

Horney, K. (1945). *Our Inner Conflicts*. New York: Norton.

Horney, K. (1950). *Neurosis and Human Growth: The Struggle Toward Self-Realization*. New York: Norton.

Horney, K. (1963). *The Collected Works of Karen Horney, Volume 1*. New York: Norton.

Horney, K. (1980). *The Adolescent Diaries of Karen Horney*. New York: Basic Books.

Horney, K. (1994). *Self-Analysis*. New York: Norton.

Horney, K. (1999). *The Neurotic Personality of Our Time*. London: Routledge.

Hudson, L. (1985). *Night Life: The Interpretation of Dreams*. London: Weidenfeld & Nicolson.

Jacobs, M. (1995). *D. W. Winnicott*. London: Sage

Jones, E. (1957). *Sigmund Freud: Life and Work. Volume 3*. New York: Basic Books.

Jones, E. M. (1993). *Degenerate Moderns: Modernity as Rationalised Sexual Misbehaviour*. San Francisco, CA: Ignatius Press.

Jouvet, M. (1963). A study of the neurophysiological mechanisms of dreaming. *Electroencephalography and Clinical Neurophysiology*, 24(Supp.): 133–157.

Jung, C. G. (1912). *Psychology of the Unconscious: A Study of the Transformation and Symbolisms of the Libido. A Contribution to the History of the Evolution of Thought*. New York: Moffat Yard, 1916 [reprinted New York: Dodd Mead, 1947]

Jung, C. G. (1951). *Aion: Researches into the Phenomenology of the Self*. Princton, NJ: Princeton University Press.

Jung, C. G. (1956). *Mysterium Coniunctionis: An Enquiry into the Separation & Synthesis of Psychiatric Opposites in Alchemy*. Zurich: Rascher.

Jung, C. G. (1958). *Answer to Job, C.W., 11*. Princeton, NJ: Princeton University Press.

Jung, C. G. (1965). *Memories, Dreams, Reflections*. New York: Vintage.

Jung, C. G. (1972). The structure and dynamics of the psyche, *C.W., 8*. London: Routledge & Kegan Paul.

Jung, C. G. (1977). The symbolic life, *C.W., 18*. London: Routledge & Kegan Paul.

Jung, C. G. (1988). "Nietzsche's Zarathustra": notes of the seminar given in 1934–1939, *C.W., 2*. Princeton, NJ: Princeton University Press.

Kalsched, D. (1996). *The Inner World of Trauma*. London: Routledge.

Kamen, A. (2005). *George W. Bush and the G-Word*. WA: *The Washington Post*, 14 October.

Kierkegaard, S. (1946). *Fear and Trembling: A Dialectical Lyric*. Oxford: Oxford University Press.

Kierkegaard, S. (1968). *The Attack on Christendom*. Princeton, NJ: Princeton University Press.

Kierkegaard, S. (2008). *Sickness Unto Death*. Radford, VA: Wilder.

Klein, M. (2003). *New Directions in Psycho-Analysis: The Significance of Infant Conflict in the Pattern of Adult Behaviour. Vol. 7*. London: Routledge.

Klein, M., & Riviere, J. (Eds.) (1964). *Love, Hate and Reparation*. New York: Norton.

Kohon, G. (1999). *No Lost Certainties to be Recovered: Sexuality, Creativity, Knowledge*. London: Karnac.

Lavie, P. (1998). *The Enchanted World of Sleep*. New Haven, CT: Yale University Press.

Layard, J. (1942). *Stone Men of Malekula*. London: Chatto & Windus.

Layard, J. (1945). *The Incest Taboo and the Virgin Archetype*. Zurich: Rhein-Verlag.

Layard, J. (1988). *The Lady of the Hare*. Boston, MA: Shambhala.

Lorenz, K. (2002). *On Aggression*. London: Routledge.

Lowrie, W. (1961). *A Short Life of Kierkegaard*. New York: Doubleday.

Lucas, G. (1977). *Star Wars*. Lucas Films.

Mahler, M., Pine, F., & Bergman, A. (1975). *The Psychological Birth of the Human Infant: Symbiosis and Individuation*. New York: Basic Books.

Mairet, P. (1999). *Alfred Adler: Problems of Neurosis: A Book of Case Histories*. London: Routledge.

Marks, I. M. (1981). *Cure and Care of Neuroses: Theory and Practice of Behavioural Psychotherapy*. New York: Wiley.

McGlashan, A. (1966). *The Savage and Beautiful Country*. London: Chatto and Windus.

McGuire, W. (Ed.) (1974). *The Freud–Jung Letters: The Correspondence Between Sigmund Freud and C. G. Jung*. Princeton, NJ: Princeton University Press.

Mead, M. (1928). *Coming of Age in Samoa: A Psychological Study of Primitive Youth for Western Civilisation*. New York: William Morrow.

Miller, H. (1960). *The Wisdom of the Heart*. New York: New Directions.

Miller, J. (2004). *The Transcendent Function: Jung's Model of Psychological Growth Through Dialogue With the Unconscious*. New York: State University of New York Press.

Minuchin, S. (1974). *Families and Family Therapy*. Cambridge, MA: Harvard University Press.

Minuchin, S., Rosman, B., & Baker, L. (1978). *Psychosomatic Families: Anorexia Nervosa in Context*. Cambridge, MA: Harvard University Press.

Morison, J. (1870). *Commentary on the Gospel According to Matthew*. London: Hamilton Adams.

Morton, A. (1997). *Diana: Her True Story – In Her Own Words*. London: Simon & Schuster.

Mossner, E. C. (1984). *A Treatise of Human Nature*. London: Penguin Classics.

Myers, J. E. B. (1998). *Legal Issues in Child Abuse and Neglect Practice*. Thousand Oaks, CA: Sage.

Nietzsche, F. (1908). *Ecce Homo, "Why I am a Destiny."* archive.org/The Complete Works of Friedrich Nietzsche.

Nietzsche, F. (1951). *My Sister and I*. New York: Boar's Head.

Nietzsche, F. (1966). *Beyond Good and Evil*. New York: Vintage.

Nietzsche, F. (1990). *My Sister and I*, O. Levy (Trans.). Los Angeles, CA: AMOK.

Nietzsche, F. (2001). *The Gay Science*. Cambridge: Cambridge University Press.

Ogawa, T. (Ed.) (1982). *History of Psychiatry: Mental Illness and its Treatments. Proceedings of the 4th International Symposium on the Comparative History of Medicine*. Tokyo: Saikon.

Parrinder, E. (1977). *Comparative Religion*. London: Sheldon Press.

Paskauskas, A. (Ed.) (1993). *The Complete Correspondence of Sigmund Freud and Ernest Jones 1908–1939*. Cambridge, MA: Harvard University Press.

Pereira, F., & Scharff, D. (2002). *Fairbairn and Relational Theory*. London: Karnac.

Philips, A. (1989). *Winnicott*. Cambridge, MA: Harvard University Press.

Prince, M (1975). *Psychotherapy and Multiple Personality: Selected Essays*. Cambridge, MA: Harvard University Press.

Quinn, S. (1987). *A Mind of Her Own: The Life of Karen Horney*. Ontario, Canada: Summit.

Quinn, S. (1988). *A Mind of Her Own*. New York: Addison-Wesley.

Rodis-Lewis, G. (1999). *Descartes: His Life and Thought*. New York: Cornell University Press.

Rohde, P. (1963). *Søren Kierkegaard: An Introduction to His Life and Philosophy*. NSW, Australia: Allen & Unwin.

Rohde, P. (1990). *The Diary of Søren Kierkegaard*. New York: Citadel Press.

Ruskin, J. (1930). *Lectures on Work, Traffic and War. The Crown of Wild Olive [and] the Cestus of Aglaia*. forgottenbooks.org

Sand, G. (1837). *Mauprat*. Paris: Bonnaire.

Scharff, D. E. (1995). *From Instinct to Self: Selected Papers of W. R. D. Fairbairn, Volume 1*. Englewood Cliffs, NJ: Jason Aronson.

Segal, J. (1992). *Melanie Klein*. London: Sage.

Shakespeare, W. (1623a). *The Winter's Tale*. London: First Folio.

Shakespeare, W. (1623b). *Coriolanus*. London: First Folio.

Shakespeare, W. (2007). *Complete Works of William Shakespeare*. London: Wordsworth Editions.

Shwartz, J. (2003). *Cassandra's Daughter: A History of Psychoanalysis*. London: Karnac.

Siegelman, E. Y. (1993). *Metaphor and Meaning in Psychotherapy*. New York: Guilford Press.

Skeat, W. (2004). *Aelfric's Lives of Saints, Part I*. MT: Kessinger.

Solomon, R. C. (1995). *A Passion for Justice. Emotions and the Origins of the Social Contract*. MD: Rowman & Littlefield.

Spitz, R. (1965). *The First Year of Life: A Psychoanalytic Study of Normal and Deviant Development of Object Relations*. New York: International University Press.

Steele, R., & Swinney, S. (1982). *Freud and Jung: Conflicts of Interpretation*. London: Routledge.

Strachey, J. (1985). *Bloomsbury/Freud: The Letters of James and Alix Strachey, 1924–1925*. New York: Basic Books.

Sutherland, J. D. (1971). Obituaries: Michael Balint (1896–1970). *International Journal of Psychoanalysis, 52*: 331–333.

Swami Paramananda (Ed.). (1919). *The Upanishads (Vol. 1): Isa-Upanishad, Katha-Upanishad, Kena-Upanishad, Mundaka Upanishad*. London: Vedanta Centre.

Thigpen, C., & Cleckley, H. (1957). *The Three Faces of Eve*. New York: McGraw-Hill.

Thoreau, H. D., & MacIver, R. (Eds.) (2006). *Thoreau and the Art of Life: Precepts and Principles*. North Ferrisburgh, VT: Heron Dance Press.

Tolstoy, L. (1869). *War and Peace*. New York: Modern Library.

Turner, V. (1967). *The Forest of Symbols: Aspects of Ndembu Ritual*. New York: Cornell University Press.

Vanderlinden, J., & Vandereycken, W. (1997). *Trauma, Dissociation, and Impulse Dyscontrol in Eating Disorders*. New York: Brunner-Mazel

Webster, R. (1995). *Why Freud was Wrong: Sin, Science and Psychoanalysis*. New York: Basic Books.

Weiss, L. (1986). *Dream Analysis in Psychotherapy*. Oxford: Pergamon Press.

Wickes, F. G. (1988). *The Inner World of Childhood. A Study in Analytical Psychology*. Salem, MA: Sigo Press.

Winnicott, D. W. (1947). Hate in the counter-transference. *International Journal of Psychoanalysis, 30*: 69–74.

Winnicott, D. W. (1964). *The Child, the Family and the Outside World*. London: Penguin.

Winnicott, D. W. (1975). *Through Paediatrics to Psychoanalysis*. New York: Basic Books.

Winnicott, D. W. (1984). *Deprivation and Delinquency*. London: Tavistock.

Winnicott, D. W. (1986). *Home Is Where We Start From: Essays by a Psychoanalyst*. New York: Norton.

Winnicott, D. W. (1987). *The Spontaneous Gesture: Selected Letters of D. W. Winnicott*, F. Rodman (Ed.). London: Karnac.

Winnicott, D. W. (1990). *The Maturational Process and the Facilitating Environment*. London: Karnac.

Winnicott, D. W. (1992). Through Paediatrics to Psychoanalysis: Collected Papers. London: Karnac.

Wolman, B. B. (1986). *Handbook of Parapsychology*. NC: McFarland.

Wright, N. (1995). *Mrs Klein*. London: Nick Hearn Books.

INDEX